Annual Editions: Child Growth and Development, 23/e

Chris J. Boyatzis

Ellen N. Junn

create.mheducation.com

ISBN-13: 9781259910906

ISBN-10: 1259910903

Contents

Detailed Table of Contents

Preface

We are delighted to welcome you to this edition of *Annual Editions: Child Growth and Development*. The amazing sequence of events of prenatal development that lead to the birth of a baby is an awe-inspiring process. Perhaps, more intriguing is the question of what the future may hold for this newly arrived baby. For instance, will this child become a doctor, a lawyer, an artist, a beggar, or a thief? Although philosophers and prominent thinkers such as Charles Darwin and Sigmund Freud have long speculated about the importance of infancy on subsequent development, not until the 1960s did the scientific study of infants and young children flourish.

Since then, research and theory in infancy and child development have exploded. Past accounts of infants and young children as passive, homogeneous organisms have been replaced with investigations aimed at studying infants and young children as active individuals with many inborn competencies who are capable of shaping their own environment, as well as by considering the larger context surrounding the child. In short, children are not "blank slates," and development does not take place in a vacuum; children arrive with many skills and grow up in a complex web of familial, social, historical, political, economic, and cultural spheres. Furthermore, new, cutting-edge and ingenious research methodologies are now making it possible to study intricate brain development and other complex behavioral and social changes from birth throughout childhood, vastly expanding the field's data and theories about child development.

As was the case for previous editions, we hope to achieve at least four major goals with this volume. First, we hope to present you with the latest research and thinking to help you better appreciate the complex interactions that characterize human development in infancy and childhood. Second, in light of the feedback we received on previous editions, we have placed greater emphasis on important contemporary issues and challenges, exploring topics such as understanding development in the context of current societal and cultural influences. Third, attention is given to articles that also discuss effective, practical applications. Finally, we hope that this anthology will serve as a catalyst to help students become more effective future professionals and parents.

To achieve these objectives, we carefully selected articles from a variety of sources, including scholarly research journals and texts as well as semiprofessional journals and popular publications. Every selection was scrutinized for readability, interest level, relevance, and currency. In addition, we listened to the valuable input and advice from members of our board, consisting of faculty from a range of institutions of higher education, including community and liberal arts colleges as well as research and teaching universities. We are most grateful to the advisory board as well as to the excellent editorial staff of McGraw-Hill Create®/Contemporary Learning Series.

Annual Editions: Child Growth and Development is organized into four major units: Prenatal Development and Child Cognition, Language, Learning and Education; Social and Emotional Development; Parenting and Family Issues; and Cultural and Societal Issues.

In addition, we provide student learning outcomes, critical thinking questions, and relevant web links for each article so that instructors will have a variety of important resources and options available for students.

Instructors for large lecture courses may wish to adopt this anthology as a supplement to a basic text, while instructors for smaller sections might also find the readings effective for promoting student presentations or for stimulating engaging discussions and applications. Whatever format is utilized, it is our hope that the instructor and the students will find the readings interesting, illuminating, and provocative.

As the title indicates, *Annual Editions: Child Growth and Development* is by definition a volume that undergoes continual review and revision. Thus, we welcome and encourage your comments and suggestions for future editions of this volume.

Editors

Chris J. Boyatzis is a professor of psychology at Bucknell University, where he received the Lindback Award for distinguished teaching, and serves as a director of the Bucknell in Denmark summer program. He received his BA with distinction in psychology from Boston University and his MA and PhD in developmental psychology from Brandeis University. His primary research interests are religious and spiritual development from childhood into early adulthood and cultural differences in parenting. He was formerly president of Division 36 (Society for the Psychology of Religion and Spirituality) of the American Psychological Association, is an associate editor of Psychology of Religion and Spirituality, and serves on the editorial board of several other journals.

Ellen N. Junn

Ellen Junn is the 11th president of California State University, Stanislaus, with over 10,000 students located in Turlock, CA. She received her BS with distinction in psychology and with high honors from the University of Michigan and her MA and PhD in cognitive and developmental psychology from Princeton University. Dr. Junn's areas of research include student success, educational equity, college teaching effectiveness, faculty development, public policy as it affects children and families, and earthquake safety for preschools. She has expertise in early childhood education, having been appointed by California Governor Pete Wilson to serve on the Superintendent of Instruction, Delaine Eastin's Universal Preschool Task Force in 1998. In addition, she served as a Past President for the California Association for the Education of Young Children (CAEYC) and was a Governing Board member of the National Association for the Education of Young Children (NAEYC), a non-profit professional organization that grants accreditation to preschools and early childhood programs in the United States and internationally.

Editors/Academic Advisory Board

Members of the Academic Advisory Board are instrumental in the final selection of articles for each edition of Annual Editions. Their review of articles for content, level, and appropriateness provides critical direction to the editors and staff. We think that you will find their careful consideration well reflected in this volume.

Ethan Adler
University of Rhode Island

William Aronson
Florida International University

Melissa Barnett
University of Arizona

Leilani M. Brown
University of Hawaii – Manoa

Susan Carrigan
Murray State College

Kelly Cartwright
Christopher Newport University

Joyce Chang
University of Central Missouri

Kristi Cordell-McNutty
Angelo State University

Iris Dimond
Cosumnes River College

Kathleen E. Fite
Texas State University - San Marcos

Winona Fleenor
Virginia Highlands Community College

Elaine Foster
Grambling State University

Nathalie Franco
Broward College Central

James Guinee
Lake Superior State University

Deborah Harris-Sims
University of Phoenix and Strayer University

Carlene Henderson
Sam Houston State University

Ronald Hixson
Southwest Texas Junior College

Debra Hollister
Valencia Community College East

Marla Johnston
Farmingdale State College

Marguerite Kermis
Canisius College

John Klein
Castleton University

Marina Klimenko
University of Florida

Jean Kubeck Hillstrom
New York City College of Technology, CUNY

Carol LaLiberte
Westfield State University

Joseph Lao
Teachers College Columbia University

Bonnie Lawler
Florida Southwestern State College

Dennis A. Lichty
Wayne State College

Geri Lotze
Virginia Commonwealth University

Nicole Martin
Kennesaw State University

R. Mathur
San Jose State University

Nancy McCarley
Armstrong Atlantic State University

John W. McNeeley
Daytona State College

Richard Metzger
Stevenson University

William A. Mosier
Wright State University

Dawn Munson
Elgin Community College

Lisa Newell
Indiana University Pennsylvania Indiana

Judith Newman
Penn State Abington

Don Norton
Cuesta College

Terri Pardee
Spring Arbor University

Gary Popoli
Stevenson University

Michael Poulakis
University of Indianapolis

Frankie Rabon
Grambling State University

Mary Eva Repass
University of Virginia

Claire N. Rubman
Suffolk County Community College

Sara Rutledge
Mount Aloysius College

Stephen T. Schroth
Knox College

H. Russell Searight
Lake Superior State University

Kathleen Sheridan
National Louis University Chicago

Linda A. Sidoti
The College of Saint Rose

Theresa Simantirakis
Wright College

Rosalind Smith
Lamar Community College

Mary Helen Spear
Prince George's Community College

Robert Stennett
University of North Georgia, Gainesville

Angela Sullivan
Concordia College

Sapna Thapa
University of Wisconsin – Stout

Sandra M. Todaro
Bossier Parish Community College

Paula Tripp
Oklahoma State University, Stillwater

Shawn Watters
University of Akron Wayne College

Laura Wilhelm
Oklahoma City University

Loraine Woods
Mississippi Valley State University

Elaine Zweig
Collin College

Prenatal Development, Birth, and Child Cognition, Language, Learning, and Education

UNIT

Prepared by: Chris J. Boyatzis, *Bucknell University* and
Ellen N. Junn, *California State University, Stanislaus*

Prenatal Development, Birth, and Child Cognition, Language, Learning, and Education

We have come a long way from the earliest times in the late 17th century when John Locke described the minds of infants as "tabula rasa," or even from the days when William James in 1890, coined the phrase, "booming, buzzing confusion" to characterize the experience of infants. Today, infants and young children are no longer viewed by researchers as blank slates, passively waiting to be filled up with knowledge. Current experts in child development and cognitive science, now armed with ample research data, have radically reformulated these assumptions about children's cognitive abilities to portray infants and young children as coming into the world with rudimentary, yet actively developing abilities that also are intimately and profoundly affected by their environment.

In this first subsection, the articles selected were designed to highlight this new knowledge. For example, researchers today continue to discover the complex interplay between brain maturational development and external or environmental experience. For example, new alarming data points to the potential long-term damaging effects of harmful everyday chemical toxins on early brain and physical development whether in utero or during infancy and early childhood. Similarly, since infants are born very dependent on intensive caretaking by parents and other caregivers, it should come as no surprise that their earliest, most formative relationships with these first caregivers

take on primary and crucial significance in fostering a solid foundation from which to build strong cognitive and social–emotional abilities for infants and young children in the areas of language development and reading, cognitive, conceptual learning, logical reasoning, and problem-solving skills. The new research and theory elucidates how these developing cognitive, learning skills, and preferences can be dramatically influenced by parents, teachers, and schooling. Moreover, researchers are examining the role of schooling environments (formal and home schooling), and the importance of different kinds of play, including abundant time for unfettered or free, as well as guided play activities, as a critical vehicle for promoting active learning, creativity, and brain development in children.

Indeed, today perhaps more than ever in the last few decades, public and parents' thirst for not only knowing about these foundational cognitive skills, but more importantly, how they can, as parents, teachers, and educators, further promote and nurture these cognitive skills continues to gain much interest from the public.

We hope that readers will enjoy the variety of articles, research, approaches, and real-life applications in thinking about how to optimize the development of infants and young children presented in this unit.

Article

Prepared by: Chris J. Boyatzis, *Bucknell University* and
Ellen N. Junn, *California State University, Stanislaus*

Chemical Threats

Researchers are discovering potential links between chemicals in common household items and damage to developing brains.

STACY LU

Learning Outcomes

After reading this article, you will be able to:

- Identify some common environmental and household toxins that may cause damage to children's brains, especially if exposed to these chemicals while children's brains are still developing—particularly while in utero or during early childhood.

- Recognize that the impact of toxic chemical exposure to children impacts boys versus girls differently, often producing more harmful impacts to boys rather than girls.

- Understand that testing and governmental regulations for many of these endocrine-disrupting chemicals are not common and often quite difficult to regulate or prohibit.

We know that lead and alcohol can harm children's brains, but a growing amount of research suggests that chemicals known as endocrine disruptors—found in everyday household products including pesticides, plastics and fire repellants—may also contribute to a range of behavioral and learning problems, including autism and attention-deficit hyperactivity disorder (ADHD). Endocrine disruptors can affect the way estrogen, androgen and thyroid hormones are produced, transmitted and metabolized, affecting developing brains as well as reproductive health.

Common in the environment, in wildlife and in almost every human, they can be transmitted to fetuses in utero, and are often present in greater concentrations in infants and young children, just when their developing brains may be most vulnerable.

Hundreds of studies have explored the mechanisms of how these chemicals affect animals' hormones, and more recent human studies suggest effects on children's learning and behavior. They may be slight in an individual, a difference of an IQ point or two or a "quirk that veers children off their normal path of development," says Kimberly Yolton, PhD, a developmental psychologist and researcher at Cincinnati Children's Hospital. "In the environmental toxins I'm studying, the changes are very subtle and difficult to detect, but they're there."

In a 2012 report, the United Nations Environment Programme and World Health Organization (WHO) said endocrine disruptors pose "significant health implications" and called for more research on them. In 2014, an Endocrine Society panel concluded that endocrine disruptors likely contributed to neurobehavioral deficits and disability, including autistic disorders. The panel estimated that the total costs to the EU are some 150 billion euros (U.S. $170 billion) per year in treatment and lost productivity (*Journal of Clinical Endocrinology and Metabolism*, 2015). In addition, many researchers suspect that the cumulative effect of endocrine disrupting chemicals is contributing to the rise of neurodevelopmental disorders in children over the past two decades.

"The concentrations of hormones regulating [neurodevelopment] are low in the body, so it doesn't take much to disrupt the endocrine system," says psychologist David Bellinger, PhD, senior researcher at Boston Children's Hospital and a professor of environmental health at the Harvard School of Public Health who has studied the issue. "And that's not going to [affect] just one cognitive outcome, it's going to hit many sex and social behaviors."

Everyday Household Toxins

What worries some scientists is that endocrine disrupting chemicals are virtually inescapable and appear to be harmful even in low quantities. For example, some pesticides with known toxicity have been associated with developmental delays and autism in children exposed to high levels of the chemicals, such as children in agricultural communities, according to a number of studies from researchers at the University of California, Davis (*Environmental Health Perspectives*, 2014).

Yet even common household chemicals may present a risk. In a national sample of 687 children ages 8 to 15, boys with detectable levels of pyrethroid pesticides—the most commonly used insecticide in homes—in their urine were more than twice as likely to have hyperactive and impulsive symptoms compared with boys who had levels below detection, according to a study by Melissa Wagner-Schuman, MD, of Cincinnati Children's Hospital, and colleagues, including Yolton (*Environmental Health*, 2015). The association was not seen in girls. Because these chemicals appear to have effects on sex hormones in animal models, outcomes that differ by gender are common in endocrine disruption research, Yolton says. As a potential mechanism, the researchers pointed out that mice exposed to pyrethroids show effects on the brain's dopamine transporter levels, especially in male mice. Previous studies have suggested that pyrethroids disrupt dopamine levels in humans, a condition associated with ADHD.

Other endocrine disruptors may be even more prevalent than those in pesticides. Phthalates, for example, are added to plastics to make them flexible and are known to leach into the environment. In experimental studies, these chemicals have been shown to alter levels of some thyroid hormones, according to a 2014 review in *NeuroToxicology* by Amir Miodovnik, MD, a developmental pediatrician and researcher at Boston Children's Hospital, along with Bellinger and other colleagues. Thyroid hormones are important to brain cell growth, neuronal migration and differentiation, as well as in the formation of synapses. Human studies suggest that early exposure to phthalates may be associated with a variety of childhood outcomes, including disruptive behavior, reduced masculine play in boys, and social and learning problems. In 2008, Congress banned some phthalates from "accessible parts" in children's toys and child-care products, but phthalates are still used in vinyl, plastic wrap and food containers, and in scented products, such as dryer sheets and air fresheners. They're also elements of fragrances used in scented soaps, lotions and shampoos, one reason that women of reproductive age may have higher levels of the chemical in their bodies than men.

Pam Factor-Litvak, PhD, and colleagues from the Columbia University Mailman School of Public Health found that children exposed during pregnancy to elevated phthalate levels had IQ scores more than six points lower, on average, than children exposed at lower levels (*PLOS ONE*, 2014). A study by Roni Kobrosly, PhD, of Mount Sinai Hospital, and colleagues looked at phthalate levels of 153 pregnant women. The researchers

found that higher levels of some phthalates in the pregnant women were associated with conduct and attention problems in their male children (*Environmental Health Perspectives*, 2014).

Phthalate exposure may also affect social communication, "one of the core symptoms of autism," says Miodovnik. He and colleagues analyzed phthalate concentrations obtained from 404 inner-city pregnant women whose children were later evaluated for social impairments at ages 7 to 9. The children of mothers with higher concentrations of phthalates had poorer scores on measures of social cognition, social communication and social awareness (*NeuroToxicology*, 2011).

Another ubiquitous chemical is bisphenol A (BPA), which is used to make polycarbonate plastics. It's in some food containers, including the lining of many soda and soup cans, as well as thermal receipt paper commonly used in cash registers. BPA can also migrate into the mouth from compounds used in dental sealants and fillings. It's been found in the urine of more than 90 percent of a nationally representative population. Research shows it might act like estrogen in the body and potentially alter estrogen, androgen and thyroid transmission signals, according to Thaddeus Schug, PhD, a researcher at the National Institute of Environmental Health Sciences, and colleagues (*Endocrinology*, 2015). Studies in animals and humans suggest it affects reproductive and social behaviors. Neuroscientist Sarah Evans, PhD, of Mount Sinai Hospital, and colleagues, conducted a study of 125 women with detectable BPA in their urine at 27 weeks of pregnancy. The researchers found a significant association between levels of BPA and rule-breaking, depression and conduct problems in boys age 6 to 10, but not in girls (*NeuroToxicology*, 2014).

Critical Windows of Exposure

Timing appears to matter as well as gender; a number of studies show that prenatal exposure to toxins is more likely to be associated with IQ drops and behavior issues in boys than in girls. A team of researchers at Columbia University Mailman School of Public Health measured pre- and post-natal BPA exposure and behavioral measures in children at ages 3 to 5 and again at ages 7 to 9 (*Environmental Research*, 2015). Boys exposed to higher levels of BPA showed more behavioral problems at both time points, including aggression and rule-breaking, as well as sleep problems, though girls had no similar detectable issues. With exposure in early childhood, though, the chemical appeared to affect girls more than boys.

"Boys and girls develop very differently, and so when there is disruption of the endocrine system, it's going to affect them differently," Yolton says.

Those effects are even more striking when it comes to reproductive health. Evidence in animal studies suggests that very high levels of endocrine disruptors may lead to congenital anomalies in males and early puberty in females, according to a 2012 report by the WHO. Phthalates specifically are associated with uterine abnormalities and with reduced testicle weight and sperm production, and flame retardants with cryptorchidism, or undescended testes.

Humans can excrete BPA, but another class of chemicals used as flame retardants in mattresses, furniture foam and carpet backing tends to linger, particularly in fatty tissue. Manufacturers began to phase out one of these chemical classes, polybrominated diphenyl ethers (PBDEs), in 2004 after scientists found it accumulated in our bodies, in breast milk and in the larger environment. Particles of these chemicals migrate from products and settle into dust, so crawling children who often put fingers and items into their mouths are more likely to come into contact with them, leading to body levels some three to nine times that for adults.

PBDEs are chemically similar to thyroid hormones, which explains why they may tamper with brain development. In a study by epidemiologist Aimin Chen, MD, of the University of Cincinnati College of Medicine, and colleagues, higher prenatal exposure to PBDEs was correlated with lower IQs of up to five points and higher hyperactivity in 5-year-old children, though researchers saw no effects at earlier ages (*Environmental Health Perspectives*, 2014). A 2013 study in the same journal by epidemiologist Brenda Eskenazi, PhD, and colleagues from the University of California, Berkeley, found that children whose mothers had the highest urine levels of PBDEs were more likely to have impaired attention at age 5, decreases in verbal and total IQ scores at age 7, and poorer fine motor coordination during both time frames.

The chemicals have also been implicated in autism. Led by Janine LaSalle, PhD, a biologist at the University of California, Davis, researchers studied female mice with a genetic mutation associated with autism, and exposed some of them to PBDEs. Their female offspring showed impaired learning, memory and social skills (*Human Molecular Genetics*, 2012).

Safe Until Proven Toxic

Though there are hundreds of animal studies involving endocrine disruptors, studying the potential effects of endocrine disruptors in humans is daunting. First, proving causation is extremely difficult, involving an "incalculable number of parameters," says Susan Koger, PhD, professor of psychology at Willamette University and co-author of the forthcoming book "Psychology for Sustainability" (Scott, Amel, Koger, & Manning, 2016).

"Endocrine disruptors are manipulating our biochemical milieu and interacting with our own hormonal system, and it's very difficult to determine their specific impacts because there are so many variables," Koger says.

Because of the different ways they signal cell receptors, some chemicals, including BPA, may have what's called a nonmonotonic dose response curve, with a small exposure sometimes being more harmful than a larger one. Plus, there are many ways humans take them in: via food, including breast milk, through the skin or by breathing them. Exposures, even to the same toxin, may affect one developmental stage but not another, or their effects may vary according to genetic makeup. And finally, effects may not show up until years—or generations—later.

"The dream study involves measuring reliable biomarker levels, including chemical mixtures, in a large cohort of women starting prenatally and covering multiple time points throughout pregnancy and beyond," Miodovnik says. "In addition, health outcomes in the offspring would be assessed using the same, well-validated instruments. Finally, the analysis would control for other confounding risk factors, including the home environment, secondhand tobacco smoke, and family history of psychopathology."

The chemicals may also interact with each other in ways that we don't understand, as Yolton pointed out in a 2014 review in *Neurotoxicology and Teratology*.

"When we study these combinations by putting multiple exposures into our statistical models, we find different results than when we examine one toxicant at a time," she says. "For example, exposure to lead is clearly harmful, but we're also seeing more dramatic associations when we add flame retardants and other chemicals," adding that research with sufficient sample sizes and lab testing to measure combinations in humans would cost "gobs of money."

Poverty may be another contributing factor, and not only because poor children are more likely to live in areas where they're exposed to pollution or industrial byproducts. Frederica Perera, PhD, at Columbia's Mailman School, and colleagues found that even with equal exposure to air pollution, children in families facing greater material hardship had poorer working memory scores (*Neurotoxicology and Teratology*, 2015). Previous studies showed isolated animals exposed to lead had poorer cognitive function than animals in enriched environments.

"There are lots of data now showing that prenatal stress can change the patterns of DNA methylation, and that appears to be transmissible between generations," says psychologist Bernard Weiss, PhD, professor emeritus at the University of Rochester Medical Center, who has researched toxicants for decades. "So here you have an effect of a stressful socioeconomic environment on brain function, plus exposure to toxic substances. That's a lethal combination." Lifestyle may promote resiliency, too. Yolton studied neonatal exposure to phthalates and behavioral outcomes in 5-week-old babies. The babies born to mothers with higher levels of one kind of phthalate in their urine actually showed developmental benefits; they were more easygoing and had better self-regulation and movement abilities (*Neurotoxicology and Teratology*, 2011). However, the mothers were generally more affluent and had healthier lifestyles, which Yolton says may have outweighed harmful chemical influences.

In another study in *Environmental Health* (2013), she found that pregnant women with higher levels of pesticides in their bodies also ate more fruits and vegetables. They also had higher education and income. The babies showed no harmful effects from the pesticides. In fact, they were more active and showed better attention skills than infants of women with lower levels—but that may be because of more beneficial environments and their mothers' healthier diets, Yolton says.

"These things are everywhere, but at some level, maybe some of these chemicals are OK and we can keep using them. But the ones that are unsafe, we need to get off the market," she says. Yet there are relatively few studies showing a lack of effect of endocrine disruptors—a negative outcome "isn't as flashy or exciting," she says—which makes it even harder for officials and the public to assess and prevent truly harmful exposures.

The field also needs more developmental psychologists working with environmental epidemiologists, experts say.

"Researchers will call me and say, 'Which instrument should I use to measure this outcome?'" Yolton says. "Having more psychologists in this field is critical because these environmental toxicants are primarily acting on the central nervous system, and who studies the development of the brain over time? We do."

The Regulatory Environment

Current regulations in the United States don't encourage testing of endocrine-disrupting chemicals. Through the Toxic Substances Control Act of 1976, the U.S. Environmental Protection Agency (EPA) may require chemical manufacturers to provide evidence that a new product is safe only if the EPA can prove it poses an "unreasonable" risk to humans that far outweighs cost considerations. However, the EPA has only 90 days to request testing and has only done so for some 200 chemicals. Meanwhile, manufacturers often dispute what findings there are, contributing to delays, researchers say. As a result, of the roughly 83,000 chemicals in use, only five have been broadly regulated with limits on their production and use. Even asbestos use is still legal. In contrast, under what's called the "precautionary principle," the European Union requires manufacturers to test their own products for safety before they can go to market.

The Government Accountability Office deemed the EPA's review and control process for toxic chemicals "high risk" in 2009, due to its failure to limit people's exposure to risky substances. "It's like Sisyphus—as soon as you roll the boulder up the mountain, it starts to roll down as chemical manufacturers counter your studies with their own data. They may say, 'Well, you haven't replicated the study results yet,' or, 'You can't rely on epidemiological studies to show that the chemical causes harm,'" Miodovnik says. "But the truth is, epidemiological studies in humans are not designed to establish the mechanism or the level at which these chemicals cause toxicity."

Yet if scientists do find evidence of harm for one chemical, its replacement may be from the same class, and potentially with the same or worse risks—what scientists call a "regrettable substitution." For example, many manufacturers have replaced BPA with BPS, a similar chemical, and early testing shows that BPS may also have endocrine activity. Companies are replacing PBDEs with chemical compounds in the same class, halogenated flame retardants. The American Academy of Pediatrics, along with a number of other organizations, petitioned the Consumer Product Safety Commission in March to ban that entire class of chemicals in four types of consumer products, claiming they presented the same range of exposure and health risks.

Many agree the system needs overhauling. At Monitor press time, the Senate was debating a new bill introduced by Sens. Tom Udall (D-N.M.) and David Vitter (R-La.) that would require testing of all chemicals on or coming to market, among other reforms. Many previous bills have failed, however, as environmental groups and Democrats argued they didn't go far enough, and the Udall-Vitter bill may share the same fate. The EPA, along with the National Institutes of Health (NIH) and the Food and Drug Administration, is developing a strategy it calls Toxicology Testing in the 21st Century, or Tox21, that uses robots, in vitro testing and computational models to assess risk and set review priorities. The system can test thousands of chemicals at once, potentially bypassing lengthy animal studies, says Linda Birnbaum, PhD, director of the NIH's National Toxicology Program and the National Institute of Environmental Health Sciences. "We're trying to move toxicology into a more predictive science where we take a systems biology approach," she says, adding that of chemicals tested so far, "We're definitely seeing some things giving us signatures of biological activity." In the meantime, researchers in the field worry about a process that leads to too little prevention, too late.

"It usually does take us a while to sort out these things," Bellinger says. "It took about 20 years before we started to see a strong signal from lead. The animal toxicological evidence is very persuasive [for endocrine disruptors]; it would be nice to go from animal studies to regulation and not wait for human studies. It makes sense to shift the onus to industry to show these products are safe before they're introduced to market so we can stop using our children as guinea pigs."

Further Reading

Bellinger, D. C. (2013). Prenatal exposures to environmental chemicals and children's neurodevelopment: An update. *Safety and Health at Work, 4*(1), 1–11. doi:10.5491/SHAW.2013.4.1.1

Grandjean, P., & Landrigan, P. J. (2014). Neurobehavioural effects of developmental toxicity. *The Lancet Neurology, 13*(3), 330–338. doi:10.1016/S1474–4422(13)70278–3

Lanphear, B. (2015). The impact of toxins on the developing brain. *Annual Review of Public Health, 36*, 211–230. doi: 10.1146/annurev-publhealth-031912–114413

Schug, T., Blawas, A., Gray, K., Heindel, J., & Lawler, C. (n.d.). Elucidating the links between endocrine disruptors and neurodevelopment. *Endocrinology*, 1941–1951. doi: http://dx.doi.org/10.1210/en.2014-1734

Weiss, B. (2011). Endocrine disruptors as a threat to neurological function. *Journal of the Neurological Sciences, 305*(1–2), 11–21. doi:10.1016/j.jns.2011.03.014

United States Environmental Protection Agency. (2013). *America's Children and the Environment* (3rd. Ed.). (Report No. 1909T/1107T) Retrieved from www.epa.gov/ace/pdfs/ACE3_2013.pdf

Critical Thinking

1. If you are a prospective parent, what precautions would you take to avoid or reduce your contact or your child's contact with endocrine-disrupting chemicals while pregnant or raising an infant or toddler?

2. If you wanted to work to pass more laws to test and safeguard children from these toxic chemicals, what barriers might you face, and how might you approach legislators and the public?

3. Why do you think these harmful chemicals produce greater risk to boys versus girls?

Internet References

Common Household Chemicals and the Allergy Risks in Pre-School Age Children
https://journals.plos.org/plosone/article?id=10.1371/journal.pone.0013423

Effect of Endocrine Disruptor Pesticides: A Review
https://www.mdpi.com/1660-4601/8/6/2265

Endocrine Disruptors and Autism Spectrum Disorder in Pregnancy: A Review and Evaluation of the Quality of the Epidemiological Evidence
https://www.mdpi.com/2227-9067/5/12/157/htm

Endocrine disruptors and childhood social impairment
https://www.sciencedirect.com/science/article/pii/S0161813X10002354

Prenatal Exposure to Endocrine-Disrupting Chemicals in Relation to Autism Spectrum Disorder and Intellectual Disability
https://www.ncbi.nlm.nih.gov/pubmed/30789431

Article

Prepared by: Chris J. Boyatzis, *Bucknell University* and
Ellen N. Junn, *California State University, Stanislaus*

"Possibly the Worst Approach"

In an effort to protect kids from food allergies, American parents have been doing the opposite.

MELINDA WENNER MOYER

Learning Outcomes

After reading this article, you will be able to:

- Describe evidence of the benefits of exposing babies to different foods, including some that may cause allergic reactions.

- Explain when babies should be exposed to solid foods, including foods that might cause allergies.

- Use evidence from allergies in different countries to evaluate the basic hypothesis that exposure to foods can lower babies' sensitivity to them.

The news last month of a clinical trial showing that infants at a high risk for peanut allergies were much less likely to actually develop these allergies if they were fed regular peanut snacks made me want to reach for a spoonful of peanut butter to shove down my 7-month-old's throat. But then visions of hives and red puffy welts danced in my head and I reconsidered. Like many parents, I have long been under the impression that the best way to prevent food allergies in kids is to *delay* giving them allergenic foods such as peanuts and eggs until they're older. So before presenting my daughter with a bowl full of Jif based on a single finding, I decided to dig into the research.

If your kid seems a little sensitive to a particular food, the worst thing to do may be to stop giving her that food.

The simplest way to sum up my conclusion is to say that my daughter tried her first bite of peanut butter last week. She made

a stink face but was otherwise fine. As it turns out, the outcome of the recent trial, which was covered by many news organizations as if it shattered current established dogma, was actually not terribly surprising if you've been following current advice and research on food allergies. It's been clear for a while that waiting a year or longer to feed your child peanut butter and eggs is useless at best. Some research even suggests that the earlier you introduce these foods the better—4 months, in other words, may be better than 6 months, even though the American Academy of Pediatrics' official recommendation is to wait until 6 months to give babies any solid food. Even crazier: If your kid seems a little sensitive to a particular food—perhaps dairy gives her a minor rash around the mouth or loose stools—the worst thing to do may be to stop giving her that food.

First, let me quash the widely held notion that delaying the introduction of allergenic foods to babies is a good idea. That approach was based in part on the flawed notion that it's smart to let an infant's gastrointestinal and immune systems "mature" for a while so they can better handle allergenic foods, and some studies from the 1990s did support it. But then contradictory studies began flooding in, and scientists now believe that exposing the gastrointestinal system to an allergen early in life is unlikely to cause an allergy. It probably does the opposite. (More on that later.)

In light of the changing tide, back in 2008, the American Academy of Pediatrics published new recommendations that reversed its old dogma. "Although solid foods should not be introduced before 4 to 6 months of age," it wrote, "there is no current convincing evidence that delaying their introduction beyond this period has a significant protective effect." Unfortunately, a lot of pediatricians haven't gotten the memo and are still giving parents outdated advice, which may explain why everyone was so shocked by last month's trial results. Also, in 2012, the AAP confused things further when it started telling parents to wait until 6 months to feed babies *any* solid food, a recommendation that was designed to encourage mothers to breastfeed for longer.

Here's the thing, though: When it comes to preventing food allergies, research is starting to suggest that it may be better to give babies allergenic foods closer to 4 months than 6 months. You should never give babies *under* the age of 4 months solid food, and you also shouldn't force solid food on a baby who isn't showing signs of being ready. But once your infant does seem ready, you can go for it—give her eggs, peanut butter, strawberries, the works (though be sure to read the caveats below). One recent Finnish study found that babies introduced to solid foods such as oats, potatoes, and meat before the age of 6 months were less likely to develop food allergies. Another study by some of the same authors found that babies—particularly those with a family history of allergies—who were fed a larger variety of solid foods at 4 months developed fewer skin allergies than those fed a smaller variety at 4 months. Another study reported that babies who were fed cereal grains before they hit the 6-month mark were less likely to develop wheat allergies than babies who were first fed grains after 6 months. And a rather shocking and controversial 2010 study reported that newborns who were given cow's milk formula within two weeks of birth had 19 times lower odds of developing a cow's milk allergy compared with newborns who were not. "Solid food introduction from 4 months of age, including a wide range of healthy foods and potential food allergens such as eggs, peanuts, and fish, is our current best advice," says Debbie Palmer, head of the Childhood Allergy and Immunology Research team at the University of Western Australia, who has published extensively on the topic.

The American Academy of Allergy, Asthma & Immunology recently published detailed recommendations on this front, and its advice is basically this: Breastfeed your baby exclusively for the first 4 months of life; if you can't, and your baby has a family risk of allergy, consider using a hydrolyzed formula. Then, regardless of whether your baby has a family risk of allergy or not, feed your 4-to-6-month-old "complementary" foods first, one at a time, waiting a few days in between, while continuing to breastfeed or feed formula. These include rice and oat cereals, vegetables, fruits (including berries—they're fine), and certain meats. If your baby has tried and done well with a few of these, start giving her tastes of allergenic foods such as peanut products and eggs. (But before you start giving your baby Cracker Jacks, there are a few important caveats: Never feed babies whole peanuts, because they can choke on them. If your baby has a sibling with a food allergy, you may want to consult an allergist before giving her those same allergenic foods. And babies still shouldn't be given cow's milk as their main drink before their first birthday because it's too low in iron and may lead to anemia.)

So how does this approach work? After all, you have to be exposed to something repeatedly in order to become "sensitized" to it and develop an allergy. That's part of the established allergic cascade. So why would eating something repeatedly prevent allergies? As it turns out, *how* a person is exposed to an allergen really matters. Most scientists now believe, based on what is called the dual-allergen-exposure hypothesis, that a person becomes allergic to, say, peanuts by being exposed to peanut proteins through the skin. (If you have peanut eaters in your home, peanut proteins are probably all over your house, no matter how frequently you vacuum.) Eating peanuts, on the other hand, helps to promote tolerance to them, thereby decreasing allergy risk. The epidemiology of peanut allergies supports this idea. In countries where peanuts are not regularly consumed, such as in parts of Europe, peanut allergies are rare, because babies are less likely to become sensitized to peanut proteins through the skin. In the Middle East and Africa, where peanuts are regularly consumed by everyone but babies also eat peanuts at a young age, rates of peanut allergy are also low, because babies become sensitized to peanuts but also tolerant of them. It's really only in the countries where peanuts are a food staple and yet babies don't regularly eat them—such as in the U.S. and in Canada and in the U.K.—that peanut allergies are so common, because infants become sensitized but not tolerant. In other words, here in America, the old recommendation to "delay the oral introduction of peanuts and eggs was quite possibly the worst approach," Palmer says. Oops!

This theory suggests something else interesting too: People who are allergic to a food might become less allergic the more they eat it. And actually, this is one of the findings from last month's trial. At the beginning of the trial, researchers gave peanut allergy skin prick tests to all the enrolled infants. Even if the infants tested positive—indicating that they were probably allergic to peanuts—the researchers advised the parents to give their babies small amounts of peanut snacks regularly, as long as they did not have dangerous reactions to it in an initial food challenge, until their kids reached their fifth birthday. The researchers told a second group of parents whose babies had tested positive on these skin prick tests to avoid peanuts until age 5. Then, years later, the researchers gave allergy tests to all the 5-year-olds and found that those who had regularly consumed the peanuts were one-third as likely to be allergic to peanuts compared with the kids who had been told to avoid them.

These findings suggest that if your children have a mild reaction to a food—maybe it makes them break out in a mild rash or causes digestive troubles—then "they would be best to continue to include having small amounts on a regular basis," Palmer says. (Of course, you should consult an allergist too.) A number of other small studies support this idea, known as "immunotherapy," for overcoming various types of food allergies, but it's still unclear how long the effects last—it may be that people have to keep consuming the allergen regularly to avoid becoming allergic again—and exposing allergic individuals to their offending allergens can, of course, be risky. By the way, if you do suspect your kid has a food allergy, go get him tested—one study found that only 14 percent of parentally diagnosed food allergies are actual food allergies. Plus, those that do exist often resolve themselves over time, so consider getting your child retested once a year. There's certainly no reason to keep peanut butter out of the house if you don't have to.

Critical Thinking

1. Why have children's food allergies become more common?
2. Based on evidence in the article, are mothers good judges of their children's food allergies? What might cause mothers to "over-diagnose" their children's allergies?

3. If you were to design a new "baby food" campaign to distribute to new parents, what would it look like? How would your recommendations reflect the information presented in this article?

Internet References

KidsHealth.org
http://kidshealth.org/parent/general/body_basics/immune.html
NBC News
http://www.nbcnews.com/id/48489391/ns/health-childrens_health/t/ask-dr-ty-will-early-exposure-colds-boost-immunity/
Parents.com
http://www.parents.com/health/cold-flu/cold/boost-childs-immunity/
WebMD.com
http://www.webmd.com/parenting/features/immune-system

Kindergartners Get Little Time to Play. Why Does It Matter? by Christopher Brown

12

Article

Prepared by: Chris J. Boyatzis, *Bucknell University* and
Ellen N. Junn, *California State University, Stanislaus*

Kindergartners Get Little Time to Play. Why Does It Matter?

CHRISTOPHER BROWN

Learning Outcomes

After reading this article, you will be able to:

- Describe the social, emotional, and academic benefits of play for children.

- Advocate for a more balanced approach to instruction.

- Define the importance of social interaction with peers during play.

B eing a kindergartner today is very different from being a kindergartner 20 years ago. In fact it is more like first grade.

Researchers have demonstrated that five-year-olds are spending more time engaged in teacher-led academic learning activities than play-based learning opportunities that facilitate child-initiated investigations and foster social development among peers.

As a former kindergarten teacher, a father of three girls who've recently gone through kindergarten, and as researcher and teacher-educator in early childhood education, I have had kindergarten as a part of my adult life for almost 20 years.

As a parent, I have seen how student-led projects, sensory tables (that include sand or water) and dramatic play areas have been replaced with teacher-led instructional time, writing centers and sight words lists that children need to memorize. And as a researcher, I found, along with my colleague Yi Chin Lan, that early childhood teachers expect children to have academic knowledge, social skills, and the ability to control themselves when they enter kindergarten.

So, why does this matter?

All Work, and Almost No Play

First, let's look at what kindergarten looks like today.

As part of my ongoing research, I have been conducting interviews with a range of kindergarten stakeholders—children, teachers, and parents—about what they think kindergarten is and what it should be. During the interviews, I share a 23-min film that I made last spring about a typical day in a public school kindergarten classroom.

The classroom I filmed had 22 kindergartners and one teacher. They were together for almost the entire school day. During that time, they engaged in about 15 different academic activities, which included decoding word drills, practicing sight words, reading to themselves and then to a buddy, counting up to 100 by 1's, 5's, and 10's, practicing simple addition, counting money, completing science activities about living things and writing in journals on multiple occasions. Recess did not occur until last hour of the day, and that too for about 15 min.

For children between the ages of five and six, this is tremendous amount of work. Teachers too are under pressure to cover the material.

When I asked the teacher, who I interviewed for the short film, why she covered so much material in a few hours, she stated,

> There's pressure on me and the kids to perform at a higher level academically.

So even though the teacher admitted that the workload on kindergartners was an awful lot, she also said she was unable to do anything about changing it.

She was required to assess her students continuously, not only for her own instruction but also for multiple assessments such as quarterly report cards, school-based reading assessments, district-based literacy and math assessments, as well as state-mandated literacy assessments.

In turn, when I asked the kindergartners what they were learning, their replies reflected two things: one, they were learning to follow rules; two, learning was for the sake of getting to the next grade and eventually to find a job. Almost all of them said to me that they wanted more time to play. One boy said:

> I wish we had more recess.

These findings mirror the findings of researchers Daphna Bassok, Scott Latham, and Anna Rorem that kindergarten now focuses on literacy and math instruction. They also echo the statements of other kindergarten teachers that kids are being prepared for high-stakes tests as early as kindergarten.

Here's How Play Helps Children

Research has consistently shown classrooms that offer children the opportunities to engage in play-based and child-centered learning activities help children grow academically, socially, and emotionally. Furthermore, recess in particular helps children restore their attention for learning in the classroom.

Focus on rules can diminish children's willingness to take academic risks and curiosity as well as impede their self-confidence and motivation as learners—all of which can negatively impact their performance in school and in later life.

Giving children a chance to play and engage in hands-on learning activities helps them internalize new information as well as compare and contrast what they're learning with what they already know. It also provides them with the chance to interact with their peers in a more natural setting and to solve problems on their own. Lastly, it allows kindergartners to make sense of their emotional experiences in and out of school.

So children asking for more time to play are not trying to get out of work. They know they have to work in school. Rather, they're asking for a chance to recharge as well as be themselves.

As another kindergarten boy in my study told me,

> We learn about stuff we need to learn, because if we don't learn stuff, then we don't know anything.

Learning by Exploring

So what can we do to help kindergartners?

I am not advocating for the elimination of academics in kindergarten. All of the stakeholders I've talked with up to this point, even the children, know and recognize that kindergartners need to learn academic skills so that they can succeed in school.

However, it is the free exploration that is missing. As a kindergarten teacher I filmed noted:

> Free and exploratory learning has been replaced with sit, focus, learn, get it done, and maybe you can have time to play later.

Policy makers, schools systems, and schools need to recognize that the standards and tests they mandate have altered the kindergarten classroom in significant ways. Families need to be more proactive as well. They can help their children's teachers by being their advocates for a more balanced approach to instruction.

Kindergartners deserve learning experiences in school that nurtures their development as well as their desire to learn and interact with others. Doing so will assist them in seeing school as a place that will help them and their friends be better people.

Critical Thinking

1. Talk to a parent of a child in kindergarten and ask about the play experiences their child has on a daily basis. Describe your conversation.

2. How does the parent's description of their child's daily play experiences compare to what you read in this article?

Internet References

It's Playtime—National Association of Elementary School Principals
https://www.naesp.org/principal-septemberoctober-2013-early-learning/it-s-playtime

Keeping Play in Kindergarten—New America
https://www.newamerica.org/education-policy/edcentral/kinderplay/

Play and Children's Learning—National Association for the Education of Young Children
http://www.naeyc.org/play

What Happened to Kindergarten?—Scholastic Teacher
https://www.scholastic.com/teachers/articles/teaching-content/what-happened-kindergarten/

CHRISTOPHER BROWN is an associate professor of Curriculum and Instruction in Early Childhood Education, University of Texas at Austin.

Brown, Christopher, "Kindergartners Get Little Time to Play: Why Does it Matter?" *The Conversation*, April 27, 2016.

Prepared by: Chris J. Boyatzis, *Bucknell University* and
Ellen N. Junn, *California State University, Stanislaus*

Article

How Ending Behavior Rewards Helped One School Focus on Student Motivation and Character

LINDA FLANAGAN

Learning Outcomes

After reading this article, you will be able to:

- Discuss the effects of rewards on children's behavior.

- Understand student motivation and altruism.

Handing out colored bracelets and upbeat stickers when students behave well seems like an effective strategy for encouraging civility. Little prizes and public praise would seem to encourage honesty, generosity and other marks of good character, and for years schools have relied on such rewards to elicit the behavior they desire in their students.

At Lincoln-Hubbard School in Summit, New Jersey, for example, teachers used to hand out stickers to elementary school children with the words "I was caught doing something right" when a child behaved properly. At Glenwood Elementary School in Short Hills, New Jersey, some second-graders who conducted themselves well were rewarded with beans that they could trade in for toys at the end of the week. "You would get them for a bunch of different things, like helping the teacher," said Brian Smith, when recalling the class reward system. "It made the problematic kids not want to be as problematic."

Rewards can be seductive, according to Marvin Berkowitz, a professor of education at University of Missouri-St. Louis and author of *You Can't Teach Through a Rat*. They're easy, they seem to work—particularly with the hard-to-reach kids—and many teachers are taught according to the behaviorist model, which posits that people repeat conduct that's reinforced and avoid what's punished. "We are breeding a new generation of kids who are well trained to be reward and recognition torpedoes," Berkowitz writes.

But a substantial body of social science research going back decades has concluded that giving rewards for certain types of behavior is not only futile but harmful. In his book *Drive: The Surprising Truth About What Motivates Us*, Daniel Pink identifies seven drawbacks to extrinsic rewards: they cripple intrinsic motivation, limit performance, squash creativity, stifle good conduct, promote cheating, can become habit-forming, and spur a short-term mindset. Giving prizes for routine and mindless tasks can be moderately effective, Pink writes. But offering rewards for those tasks that are "inherently interesting, creative, or noble...is a very dangerous game." When it comes to promoting good behavior, extrinsic rewards are "the *worst* ineffective character education practice used by educators," Berkowitz writes.

Private words of encouragement replaced the monthly awards assemblies.

A handful of schools are heeding the research and beginning to back away from the practice. In Florissant, Missouri, students at Northview High School no longer receive rubber bracelets when they do something right. Monthly awards assemblies celebrating the student who demonstrated superior character in the area of responsibility, say, have vanished. Under the direction of Stephanie Valleroy, the now-retired principal of Northview, the school moved decidedly away from prizes and public affirmation of good behavior.

Valleroy decided to change the school's culture in 2007, after she and other educators on her staff attended conferences on character education, including events hosted by Leadership Academy in Character Education at the University of Missouri-St. Louis. Inspired by what she'd learned, especially about the corrosive effect of rewards, she returned to Northview and launched a character education committee and school leadership team. Valleroy knew she needed staff buy-in, and over a period of years sent educators to conferences on character. Together, they revamped lesson plans to incorporate character development into all aspects of the curriculum, and shared the new plans on the school intranet. She also worked with the staff to craft a new mission statement for the school that put character at the center.

Some teachers struggled at first with the removal of extrinsic rewards. "'What do you mean we're not giving out Northview bracelets?'" Valleroy recalled some teachers asking. She told them: "We're just not." Parents embraced it right away; Valleroy had been at Northview for more than 20 years when she made the change, and parents trusted her.

Instead of handing out prizes, teachers tried to reach children by talking about what's inside them. "We consistently talked to them about what were their motivations from the heart," Valleroy said. Rather than say "don't do this," teachers would remind students of the school's mission and rules, which focused on respect, responsibility and work ethic. Teachers often asked students, "What's your responsibility in this?" The school also folded service into the curriculum, which required children to take on a project that aided the school, community, country or world. Private words of encouragement replaced the monthly awards assemblies. "I would pull kids aside and say 'I know you did a really good job in X,' but not in public," Valleroy said. "It was just a comment, not an ordeal," she added.

Not only did the children shrug when the rewards disappeared, Valleroy said, they also welcomed the character-infused approach to learning. Teachers overheard students talking about being responsible and respectful. Kids who ordinarily kept quiet in class volunteered frequently, and more stepped up to help their classmates. The service learning also had a dramatic impact, according to Valleroy: Students took pleasure in helping others, and recognized that they had abilities worth sharing. "Their academic skills and attention and willingness to participate in academics grew immensely," Valleroy said.

"Removing extrinsics was a huge part of its success," she added.

What's especially noteworthy about the school's embrace of prize-free character education is that Northview serves only children needing special education; all 180 students who attend require support that's not available in mainstream schools. Even more so than in regular classrooms, special education relies heavily on extrinsic rewards with its students. "The use of extrinsics is a common practice in special education and it was simply what we did," Valleroy said.

Curiously, the students who responded most positively to the shift were the ones with great emotional needs, often the toughest challenges for teachers and most likely to be controlled with rewards, according to Valleroy. These students wanted to help in other classrooms as a part of their service learning, and began to form natural relationships with the other kids along the way. Valleroy saw them step up to leadership roles, and many spoke at graduation about how far they'd come. "It was incredible to see that growth," Valleroy said.

After Valleroy retired, Brian O'Connor took over as principal and continued to emphasize character development and intrinsic motivation. The school population is familiar with adversity: most of the students at Northview High School qualify for free or reduced lunch and many live in foster care, according to Valleroy. In spite of those obstacles, she reports that 89 percent graduate, 87 percent report feeling safe at school, and attendance rates hover at 90 percent.

Mainstream schools could also do away with extrinsic rewards, Valleroy said. "It would be a paradigm shift," she said. "But it absolutely could be done."

Critical Thinking

1. What are some ways that rewarding children for good behavior might promote but also hinder good behavior?

2. Might there be individual differences between children in how rewards may affect them? What could some sources be of those individual differences?

Internet References

38 NGOs dedicated to improve education
https://www.raptim.org/38-ngos-dedicated-improve-education/

How to help your child get motivated in school
https://childmind.org/article/how-to-help-your-child-get-motivated-in-school/

Article

Prepared by: Chris J. Boyatzis, *Bucknell University* and
Ellen N. Junn, *California State University, Stanislaus*

Time to Play: Recognizing the Benefits of Recess

CATHERINE RAMSTETTER AND ROBERT MURRAY

Learning Outcomes

After reading this article, you will be able to:

- Identify the role of play in children's development.

- Discuss the importance of daily recess for all children.

- Explain how daily recess can improve academic performance.

One sunny day in May, Ms. Brown tells her first-grade class, "OK, boys and girls, it's time for recess." As the children leave the classroom in an organized fashion, three other first-grade classes join them out on the playground, an open field with one tree and a six-foot-tall monkey bar structure. Under the teachers' watchful eye, the children climb and play.

After 15 min, one of the teachers blows a whistle, and the children run back to the building, where another teacher leads them in. Aside from a few latecomers to the door, every child has entered the building in less than 30 s. Back in the classroom, Ms. Brown begins a song about not dawdling, and the children move to the carpet for a group story discussion.

Earlier that day, Ms. Brown wasn't so sure all of her students should go to recess. Connor had acted out one too many times, and she was thinking he didn't deserve to go out and play. But then, she remembered her training last spring and summer with LiiNK trainers (a project described later in this article), who urged her not to withhold recess as punishment.

So when recess arrived, Ms. Brown decided to allow Connor to go out; she even let him be the first student out the door. The break from his desk ends up helping him refocus. Upon returning to the classroom, Connor apologizes to Ms. Brown and promises to behave better. She believes it. The rest of the day is pleasant for her and Connor—indeed, for the whole class.

While denying recess to a misbehaving student is common for many teachers, Ms. Brown's response may not be. Her decision to allow Connor to attend recess and his subsequent apology show the power of unstructured play time for students during school.

What Is Recess?

The American Academy of Pediatrics (AAP), in its 2013 policy statement titled "The Crucial Role of Recess in School," describes recess as "a necessary break in the day for optimizing a child's social, emotional, physical, and cognitive development."[1] Recess ought to be safe and well supervised, yet teachers do not have to direct student activity. The frequency and duration of breaks should allow time for children to mentally decompress, and schools should allow students to experience recess periods daily.

As the AAP makes clear, outdoor play "can serve as a counterbalance to sedentary time and contribute to the recommended 60 min of moderate to vigorous activity per day."[2] An effective recess is one where children demonstrate their ability to stay within the boundaries of their play space, negotiate conflict with each other, and then return to academic learning. The peer interactions that take place during recess allow for communication, cooperation, and problem solving, complementing the classroom experience.[3] Unstructured play, with adult supervision, gives children the opportunity to develop important social and emotional skills, which is essential to a well-rounded education.

The AAP's policy statement on the role of recess in school cited four critical benefits of recess: (1) greater levels of physical activity and fitness, (2) improved attentiveness in class, (3) improved cognition and learning, and (4) practice of peer-to-peer social and emotional skills. The latter, often overlooked, is cited by child development experts as a fundamental skill set, laying the basis for social success in later life. As a result, the AAP concluded that "recess should be considered a child's personal time, and it should not be withheld for academic or punitive reasons."[4]

After all, "it is the supreme seriousness of play that gives it its educational importance," said Joseph Lee, the father of the playground movement. "Play seen from the inside, as the child sees it, is the most serious thing in life . . . Play builds the child . . . Play is thus the essential part of education."[5]

A Harvard-educated author and philanthropist, Lee advocated for playgrounds in city schools and parks in the late 19th and early 20th century. He was a leader in promoting school attendance and safe havens for play for all children, especially poor children in the urban core of Boston. In the 1890s, children were forbidden from playing games in the streets and there were no playgrounds in the poorest neighborhoods, where adolescent boys were routinely arrested for delinquency. Lee was from a wealthy Boston family, and, recalling the childhood he experienced—one filled with games, dancing, and play—he took it upon himself to find a solution. He gained permission to clear a vacant lot and provide materials and equipment he felt children would be likely to play with or on, such as dirt piles, large pipes, and sand. And, as he predicted, children came to play.

Over the next decades, Lee's initiative spread from Boston to Chicago and extended into municipal investment in parks and recreation centers for boys and girls. Lee's efforts also extended to public education. He was determined that poor children receive the same kind of educational opportunity in schools as their more affluent peers by being educated by teachers who were trained as teachers. He personally underwrote the creation of Harvard University's School of Education in 1920. It was during this period of growth in urban education and play space for children that recess—as a time during the school day for children to play in a designated space—came to be.[6]

Lee's vision of play in education still resonates today. Given that the new federal Every Student Succeeds Act (ESSA) removes the emphasis on high-stakes standardized testing in schools and includes nonacademic indicators as a component of a student's "well-rounded education,"[7] schools that have narrowly focused on scores to the detriment of students' well-being can now correct the imbalance. In doing so, they can ensure that recess, which plays a vital role in social and emotional development, maintains its rightful place in the school day.

The Current State of Recess

Beyond Lee's advocacy of playgrounds and recreation, it is difficult to document a precise history of recess. In fact, when the School Health Policies and Programs Study (SHPPS) was initiated in 1994 by the Centers for Disease Control and Prevention (CDC) with the purpose of providing "the first in-depth description of policies and programs related to multiple components of the school health program at the state, district, school, and classroom levels,"[8] recess was not included.

It wasn't until 1997 that the CDC defined recess as "regularly scheduled periods within the elementary school day for unstructured physical activity and play."[9] Recess was first included in the 2000 SHPPS, among various opportunities in schools for children to engage in physical activity. Prior to that, what we know about recess as an experience during the school day—an experience of childhood—is something that is informed by individual and collective memories.

Since then, in addition to SHPPS, other published research about recess practices and policies in the United States has included studies on a smaller scale, in a school or district. These explore various aspects of recess, under the assumption that recess is given for every child in that school or district.[10] Few studies, however, actually examine how recess varies within and across schools and districts (for instance, how teachers monitor and handle recess in the same school and grade).

Largely, the documentation of what happens in the daily, lived experience of recess in schools remains uneven and takes the form of blog posts, news stories, and other social media sharing. The limitations of understanding the delivery and experience of recess at individual schools aside, since the mid- to late-1990s, a growing body of evidence has emerged about the value of and practices and policies related to physical activity—of which recess is one part. Since its inception in 1994, SHPPS has been repeated in 2000, 2006, 2012, and 2014.

According to SHPPS data from 2014, "82.8 percent of elementary schools provided daily recess for students in all grades in the school."[11] (For a summary of current recess practices, see the table to the right.) Because this study surveys principals and "lead health education teachers," this statistic doesn't necessarily paint a complete picture of where, when, or how recess is provided,* and the documentation about current practices only includes data collected from those schools that reported having regularly scheduled recess. Even with these limitations, however, the 2014 SHPPS research is useful. It shows that, among elementary schools with regularly scheduled recess, the percentage of schools providing recess decreases from first to sixth grade. The average number of days with recess per week across all grades was 4.9, and the average time spent in recess was 26.9 minutes per day.

Decisions about timing, duration, location, and activities for recess are typically made at the school or grade level. While there is no recommended duration (minutes per day) or timing for

---

*To see the original questionnaires given to principals and teachers, visit www.cdc.gov/healthyyouth/data/profiles/questionnaires.htm.

Elementary School Recess by the Numbers

PRACTICE	ELEMENTARY SCHOOLS
Students participate in regularly scheduled recess during the school day in[1]	
Kindergarten	94.9%
First grade	95.0%
Second grade	94.7%
Third grade	94.3%
Fourth grade	93.3%
Fifth grade	90.6%
Sixth grade	34.9%
Average number of minutes students spend in recess each day[2]	26.9
Staff prohibited or actively discouraged from excluding students from all or part of recess as punishment for bad behavior or failure to complete classwork	54.4%
Recess structure	
Students engage in free play or physical activity	93.1%
Students are required or encouraged to use physical activity or fitness stations	2.8%
Other	4.0%
Recess is held outdoors, weather permitting	100%
When recess cannot be held outside	
Students participate in physical activity in the gymnasium, a multipurpose room, or the cafeteria	29.8%
Students participate in physical activity in regular classrooms	17.9%
Students watch a DVD/video[3]	5.8%
Students engage in other sedentary activities (e.g., board games)	39.5%
Other	7.0%

[1]Among elementary schools with students in that grade.
[2]Among schools in which students participate in regularly scheduled recess.
[3]Does not include physical activity DVDs/videos.

Source: School Health Policies And Practices Study, *Results From The School Health Policies and Practices Study* 2014 (Atlanta: Centers for Disease Control and Prevention, 2015), 50.

recess, one of the largest studies published on recess found that for 8- to 9-year-olds, at least one or more daily recess periods of at least 15 min was associated with better class behavior ratings from teachers than no daily recess or fewer minutes of recess.[12]

According to SHPPS data from 2000 to 2014, among schools that offer recess, the percentage of classes having regularly scheduled recess immediately after lunch decreased from 42.3 percent in 2000 to 26.2 percent in 2014. This may be a result of a decrease in recess opportunities, or it may reflect schools shifting recess times to before lunch, which has been shown to increase meal consumption and decrease food waste, while improving lunchroom behavior and increasing attention in the classroom following lunch.[13]

A comparison of results from the SHPPS surveys in 2006 and 2014 also indicates an alarming trend: in 2006, 96.8 percent of elementary schools provided recess for at least one grade in the school, compared with 82.8 percent in 2014. Using self-reported data from high-level administrators at the district level, these surveys show that even though more than 80 percent of districts claim to provide daily recess, a 2014 analysis conducted by the CDC and the Bridging the Gap research program revealed that 60 percent of districts had no policy regarding daily recess for elementary school students and that only 20 percent mandated daily recess.

Additionally, a 2006 analysis by the National Center for Education Statistics found noticeable disparities[14]:

- City schools reported the lowest average minutes per day of recess (24 min in first grade to 21 min in sixth grade).
- Rural schools reported the highest average minutes per day (31 min in first grade to 24 min in sixth grade).
- The lowest minutes per day of recess (21 min in first grade to 17 min in sixth grade) occurred in schools where 75 percent or more of the students were eligible for free or reduced-price lunch.

Decreased opportunities for recess have been associated with increased academic pressure. Recess has been the victim of the perceived need to spend more time preparing students for standardized testing and, generally, to meet increased demands for instructional time. Diminishing recess first began in the early 1990s, and it further declined with the enactment of No Child Left Behind in 2001, which emphasized English language arts and mathematics. To focus on these core areas, districts reduced time for recess, art, music, physical education, and even lunch.[15] In addition, recess often was and is withheld from students as punishment for disruptive behavior and/or to encourage task completion, even though research shows this practice "deprives students of health benefits important to their well-being."[16]

Interestingly, the emergence of a national health crisis in the United States—the rising rates of obesity in children—has sparked a reevaluation of recess. Recess was included, along with physical education and other opportunities for school-based physical activity, in the wellness policy requirement enacted in 2004 as part of the Child Nutrition and Special Supplemental Nutrition Program for Women, Infants, and Children Reauthorization Act.* (But, as we just noted, a recess-specific policy is lacking in 40 percent of school districts.) In 2014, this requirement was bolstered by an approved rule under the Healthy, Hunger-Free Kids Act of 2010,[17] which "expands the requirements to strengthen policies and increase transparency. The responsibility for developing, implementing, and evaluating a wellness policy is placed at the local level, so the unique needs of each school under the [district's] jurisdiction can be addressed."[18] By June 30, 2017, all schools/districts must have a wellness policy that meets all required components.

In conjunction with these federal initiatives, some state legislatures have explored recess as part of a broader school-based wellness or physical activity education bill. Accurately documenting what these legislative actions mean for recess is difficult, partially because recess could fall under a variety of

laws or policies, and also because the way the law or policy is written can vary. (For example, a mandate may require a set number of minutes per day for physical activity, with recess included, or it might require recess be specifically included in a district wellness policy.)

To supplement CDC and SHPPS information, the National Association of State Boards of Education's State School Health Policy Database is updated as states enact or revise laws and policies. Within states, districts can add to or build on any federal or state requirement.[†] A similar database does not exist for district-level school health policies, but as indicated by Bridging the Gap's research, such policies often do not include recess.

With the renewed emphasis on a "well-rounded education," thanks to ESSA, states and schools now have additional incentive to elevate policies and practices for regular recess as part of a robust package of "nonacademic" health and physical activity initiatives, which research has shown to positively affect academic progress.

ESSA requires states to select at least one nonacademic indicator that each school district will report. Funds for implementing the federal law will be allocated to the states to distribute, and they include funds for professional development and programs to support students' physical health as well as their mental and behavioral health. Recess offers a unique way to address both.

Integrating Recess into School Culture

In 2011, the Chicago Public Schools (CPS) announced it would reintroduce daily recess in the 2012 school year, making it "the first large urban district to once again require daily recess at the elementary and middle school levels."[19] This move was prompted by a groundswell of parents, community members, and concerned district employees, who led the push for recess reinstatement during their struggle to lengthen the school day. We could find no published accounts on the decision to eliminate recess in the first place; however, based on the timing (recess was discontinued in the early 1980s), we can surmise it was both a cost-cutting measure and a response to concerns that students spend as much time as possible on academics.

Thus, in the fall of 2012, when CPS extended the school day by at least 30 min across the district, recess once again became a daily occurrence at all elementary and middle schools. Exactly

---

*The wellness policy language only includes recess as one of the ways schools can address student physical activity. Schools are only required to have a policy that addresses nutrition services, nutrition education, physical education, and physical activity. The federal law does not prescribe the duration, timing, or type of activities. Some states have laws, some have recommendations that are codified, and some have nothing (which is the case for recess in most states).

†For a state-by-state listing of recess policies in schools, see www.nasbe.org/healthy_schools/hs/bytopics.php?topicid=3120.

how these minutes are used varies at each school, but reinstating recess did not take away instructional time. Once recess was reinstated, the CPS Office of Student Health and Wellness codified daily recess by making it a provision of the district's Local School Wellness Policy that was passed in 2012, which mandates that all CPS K-8 students receive a minimum of 20 min of recess each day.[20] The office provides ongoing support for teachers and administrative personnel to engage in daily recess and other wellness practices. Reinstating recess not only required dedicating the time for it but also required training and resources for schools and teachers to ensure it was safe and consistent across a large number of schools in a wide variety of neighborhoods.

More recently, in September 2015, the Seattle Public Schools and the local teachers union agreed to a guaranteed minimum of 30 min of daily recess for elementary school students, although teachers had originally asked for 45 min.[21]

Such changes in recess require schools to rearrange schedules. But even in districts where recess is required, how students experience it is sharply inequitable, as demonstrated at Detroit's Spain Elementary-Middle School, where "students are forced to walk the halls during recess, because the gym is shut down due to mold and the outdoor playground emits burning steam—even during Detroit snowstorms."[22‡] Children in poverty also have less access to free play, fewer minutes of physical activity during the day, and the fewest minutes of recess in school.[23]

Promising Programs

Ongoing research continues to expand our understanding of why recess and play are crucial. Some studies are exploring play spaces, specific activities, and the benefits of close supervision, while others are examining the benefits of accumulated physical activity and social interactions. While much is being learned from practices in other countries, three programs in the United States are particularly instructive: Peaceful Playgrounds, Playworks, and the Let''s Inspire Innovation 'N Kids (LiiNK) Project out of Texas Christian University.* Each offers a slightly different philosophy and approach, but the commonalities are that recess is well supervised and that every child experiences daily, safe play time during the school day. Each program is annually evaluated, and findings have demonstrated the benefits of recess as a component of a whole-child education.

Peaceful Playgrounds began in 1995 and is grounded in the following principles: teaching conflict resolution, establishing clear rules and expectations, providing low-cost equipment,

and designing a play space that invites exploration and interaction and minimizes potential for conflict. Peaceful Playgrounds offers training for school personnel in the wealth of games available to children and provides blueprints, playground stencils, and playground game guides. The program emphasizes free choice by students.

Playworks, which began in 1996 as Sports4Kids, focuses on using safe play and physical activity during recess and throughout the day to improve the climate at low-income schools. The program offers a variety of services that hinge on training or providing Playworks "coaches" to "enhance and transform recess and play into a positive experience that helps students and teachers get the most out of every learning opportunity." According to a survey of Playworks schools, staff report a decrease in bullying and disciplinary incidents, an increase in students' physical activity during recess, and an increase in students' abilities to focus on class activities.[24]

The *LiiNK Project*, a school curriculum modeled after one in Finland (whose academic performance consistently ranks in the top five countries in the world—well above the United States), was created three years ago to balance a focus on academics and the social and emotional health of children and teachers. Ms. Brown, the first-grade teacher mentioned earlier, teaches in a LiiNK school.

While LiiNK received national media attention in 2016 as strictly a recess program, it emphasizes more than just embedding additional recess into the school day. It also focuses on preparing teachers and administrators to redesign learning environments through recess, character education, and teacher training, in order to combat critical issues affecting the development of noncognitive skills, such as empathy in students.[25] Preliminary pilot data are compelling: in schools implementing the LiiNK curriculum, student achievement significantly improved, as did students' listening, decision-making, and problem-solving abilities.[26]

Other recess practices, both in the United States and in other countries, have demonstrated positive effects for students and teachers. As discussed previously, the move to conduct recess before lunch is associated with decreased food waste, increased consumption of fruits and vegetables, and better behavior in the lunchroom and upon returning to the classroom.

In studies with British children, providing large equipment and playground markings increased physical activity levels.[27] A study in Belgium found a similar effect on physical activity levels through providing smaller, less costly games and equipment.[28] Across the globe, simply providing these kinds of

---

‡For more on health and safety in schools, see "A Matter of Health and Safety" in the Winter 2016–2017 issue of American Educator, available at www.aft.org/ae/winter2016-2017/roseman.

*For more about the programs described here. See www.peacefulplaygrounds.com, www.playworks.org, and www.linkproject.tcu.edu.

portable play Equipment, such as balls and jump ropes, encourages children to be active during recess.[29]

Holding recess outside invites self-directed play where children choose what to do, from playing make-believe games, to reading or daydreaming, to socializing and engaging in physically active games; the experience is up to the child. Certainly, these activities can also occur in an indoor setting, but the opportunity for exploration is limited.[30] Interestingly, a large controlled study in China found that outdoor recess may help prevent or minimize nearsightedness in children.[31]

Meanwhile, children in Japan experience recess in 5- to 10-min bouts approximately every hour, based on the premise that a child's attention span wanes after 40–50 minutes of academic instruction.[32]

Given the evidence of the value of recess for children and teachers, what can educators, schools, and districts do to promote this critical aspect of the education of the whole child? Daily decisions about who gets recess and when and where it will happen are often made by teachers; thus, teachers are a crucial link for recess. Policies that support daily recess for all children are also essential, especially when it comes to the practice of withholding some or all of recess for disciplinary reasons.[33]

It is imperative to treat recess time as a child's personal time (similar to the way adults take breaks and choose how to spend them) and to make this explicit in policy and in practice. Recess time should not be usurped to fulfill a physical activity requirement. That is, if the school is required to offer opportunities outside of physical education classes, recess should only be included as an optional or supplemental opportunity. During recess, it should be as acceptable for children to engage in other types of play as it is for them to engage in physical activity. In addition to policy, teachers, administrators, and school staff would benefit from coursework during initial preparation, as well as from ongoing professional development, in recess management and in establishing and carrying out alternatives to discipline other than withholding recess.

Other ways to promote recess include:

- Advocating for district and school policies that require or recommend daily recess for every child.
- Disseminating information on the benefits of recess and the successful programs and practices described above.
- Including recess-type games and the practice of conflict resolution in physical education teacher training and in school physical education curricula.[†]

- Encouraging state and district boards of education to integrate the social and emotional benefits of recess in health education curricula.
- Collaborating with school wellness councils, school health and wellness teams, and parent–teacher groups to reinforce policies for recess, fund the purchase and maintenance of playground or recess equipment, and train playground monitors and teachers.

Daily recess for every child supports a school's mission of providing a high-quality, comprehensive, and meaningful education, so student grow and reach their full potential. Participating in recess offers children the necessary break to optimize their social, emotional, physical, and cognitive development. It not only helps them get important daily physical activity but also requires them to engage in rule-making, rule-following, and conflict resolution with peers. These are essential life skills that children can learn to master through the serious act of play.

Notes

1. American Academy of Pediatrics, "Policy Statement: The Crucial Role of Recess in School," Pediatrics 131, no. 1 (2013): 186.

2. American Academy of Pediatrics, "Policy Statement," 186.

3. American Academy of Pediatrics, "Policy Statement," 186.

4. American Academy of Pediatrics, "Policy Statement," 186.

5. Joseph Lee, *Play in Education* (New York: Macmillan, 1915), 3–7.

6. The history of Joseph Lee's life is informed by Donald Culross Peattie, *Lives of Destiny: As Told for the "Reader's Digest"* (Boston: Houghton Mifflin, 1954), 80–88.

7. Every Student Succeeds Act, Pub. L. No. 114–95, § 8002(21), 129 Stat 2099 (2015).

8. Lloyd J. Kolbe, Laura Kann, Janet L. Collins, Meg Leavy Small, Beth Collins Pateman, and Charles W. Warren, "The School Health Policies and Programs Study (SHPPS): Context, Methods, General Findings, and Future Efforts," *Journal of School Health* 65 (1995): 339.

9. *Promoting Better Health for Young People through Physical Activity and Sports* (Washington, DC: U.S. Department of Health and Human Services and U.S. Department of Education), app. 7, accessed January 19, 2017, www.thenewpe.com/advocacy/promotingPA.pdf.

10. A notable exception explored the effects of recess in one classroom in a school that had eliminated recess. See Olga S. Jarrett, Darlene M. Maxwell, Carrie Dickerson, Pamela Hoge, Gwen Davies, and Amy Yetley, "Impact of Recess

---

[†]Physical education is intended to impart not only sport-specific physical and competition skills but also lifelong physical health skills, like rule and goal setting, rule following, and general fine and gross motor skills. While separate from recess, physical education is one class that offers a place where children can learn recess-type games, or games that require imagination and physical movement, as well as appropriate ways to negotiate conflict with others.

on Classroom Behavior: Group Effects and Individual Differences," *Journal of Ecducational Research* 92 (1998): 121–126.

11. Centers for Disease Control and Prevention, "School Health Policies and Practices Study: 2014 Overview" (Atlanta: U.S. Department of Health and Human Services, 2015), 1.

12. Romina M. Barros, Ellen J. Silver, and Ruth E. K. Stein, "School Recess and Group Classroom Behavior," *Pediatrics* 123 (2009): 431–436.

13. Ethan A. Bergman, Nancy S. Buergel, Annaka Femrite, Timothy F. Englund, and Michael R. Braunstein, *Relationship of Meal and Recess Schedules to Plate Waste in Elementary Schools* (University, MS: National Food Service Management Institute, 2003); Montana Office of Public Instruction School Nutrition Programs, *Pilot Project Report: A Recess before Lunch Policy in Four Montana Schools, April 2002–May 2003* (Helena: Montana Office of Public Instruction, 2003); and Joseph Price and David Just, "Lunch, Recess and Nutrition: Responding to Time Incentives in the Cafeteria" (paper, Social Science Research Network, December 9, 2014), doi: 10.2139/ssrn.2536103.

14. Basmat Parsad and Laurie Lewis, *Calories In, Calories Out: Food and Exercise in Public Elementary Schools, 2005* (Washington, DC: National Center for Education Statistics, 2006), 62.

15. Jennifer McMurrer, *Instructional Time in Elementary Schools: A Closer Look at Changes for Specific Subjects*, From the Capital to the Classroom: Year 5 of the No Child Left Behind Act (Washington, DC: Center on Education Policy, 2008).

16. Centers for Disease Control and Prevention, "Guidelines for School and Community Programs to Promote Lifelong Physical Activity among Young People," *Morbidity and Mortality Weekly Report* 46, no. RR-6 (March 7, 1997): 12.

17. Healthy, Hunger-Free Kids Act of 2010, Pub. L. No. 111-296, § 204, 124 Stat. 3216 (2010).

18. "Local School Wellness Policy Implementation under the Healthy, Hunger-Free Kids Act of 2010: Summary of the Final Rule," U.S. Department of Agriculture, July 2016, accessed December 15, 2016, www.fns.usda.gov/sites/default/files/tn/LWPsummary_finalrule.pdf.

19. "CPS' Daily Recess Is More Than Just Play," Healthy Schools Campaign, February 17, 2015, www.healthyschools campaign.org/chicago-focus/cps-daily-recess-is-more-thanjust-play-5395.

20. "Local School Wellness Policy for Students," Chicago· Public Schools Policy Handbook, § 704.7, October 24, 2012, http://policy.cps.edu/download.aspx?ID=81.

21. Rachel Lerman, "Seattle District, Teachers Agree to Higher Pay for Subs, Longer Recess, but Strike Could Still Happen," *Seattle Times*, September 6, 2015.

22. Katie Felber, "Heartbreaking Video Depicts Harsh Reality of Detroit Public Schools," Good, January 19, 2016, www.good.is/videos/heartbreaking-video-detroit-public-schools.

23. Parsad and Lewis, *Calories In, Calories Out.*

24. "2016 Annual Survey Results—National," Playworks, accessed December 8, 2016, www.playworks.org/about/annual-survey/national.

25. Debbie Rhea, "Recess: The Forgotten Classroom," *Instructional Leader* 29, no. 1 (January 2016): 1.

26. Rhea, "Recess"; and Deborah J. Rhea, Alexander P. Rivchun, and Jacqueline Pennings, "The Liink Project: Implementation of a Recess and Character Development Pilot Study with Grades K & 1 Children," *Texas Association for Health, Physical Education, Recreation & Dance Journal* 84, no. 2 (Summer 2016): 14–17, 35.

27. Nicola D. Ridgers, Gareth Stratton, Stuart J. Fairclough, and Jos W. R. Twisk, "Long-Term Effects of a Playground Markings and Physical Structures on Children's Recess Physical Activity Levels," *Preventative Medicine* 44 (2007): 393–397.

28. Stefanie J. M. Verstraete, Greet M. Cardon, Dirk L. R. De Clercq, and Ilse M. M. De Bourdeaudhuij, "Increasing Children's Physical Activity Levels during Recess Periods in Elementary Schools: The Effects of Providing Game Equipment," *European Journal of Public Health* 16 (2006): 415–419.

29. Nicola D. Ridgers, Jo Salmon, Anne-Maree Parrish, Rebecca M. Stanley, and Anthony D. Okely, "Physical Activity during School Recess: A Systematic Review," *American Journal of Preventive Medicine* 43 (2012): 327.

30. Deborah J. Rhea and Irene Nigaglioni, "Outdoor Playing= Outdoor Learning," *Educational Facility Planner* 49, nos. 2–3 (2016): 16–20.

31. Mingguang He, Fan Xiang, Yangfa Zeng, et al., "Effect of Time Spent Outdoors at School on the Development of Myopia among Children in China: A Randomized Clinical Trial," *JAMA* 314, no. 11 (2015): 1142–1148.

32. Harold W. Stevenson and Shin-Ying Lee, "Contexts of Achievement: A Study of American, Chinese, and Japanese Children," *Monographs of the Society for Research in Child Development* 55, nos. 1–2 (1990).

33. Lindsey Turner, Jamie F. Chriqui, and Frank J. Chaloupka, "Withholding Recess from Elementary School Students: Policies Matter," *Journal of School Health* 83 (2013): 533–541.

Critical Thinking

1. As a child during elementary school, how much recess time did you have? What did you spend most of your time doing?

2. Talk to parents about the experiences their elementary school children have regarding recess. Are the parents pleased with the recess time, materials, and experience?

Internet References

Alliance for Childhood
http://www.allianceforchildhood.org/

Recess Makes Kids Smarter
https://www.scholastic.com/teachers/articles/teaching-content/recess-makes-kids-smarter/

Why Kids Need Recess
http://pathwaysoffamilywellness.org/Children-s-Health-Wellness/why-kids-need-recess.html

CATHERINE RAMSTETTER is the founder of Successful Healthy Children, a nonprofit organization focused on school health and wellness. A member of the Ohio chapter of the American Academy of Pediatrics (AAP) Home and School Health Committee, she has researched and written about the importance of recess to children''s development.

ROBERT MURRAY is a professor of human nutrition in the College of Education and Human Ecology at the Ohio State University. A former chair of the Ohio AAP chapter, he was previously a professor in the Department of Pediatrics in the University''s College of Medicine.

Ramstetter, Catherine; Murray, Robert, "Time to Play: Recognizing the Benefits of Recess," *American Educator*, Spring 2017. 17–23. Reprinted by permission of the authors.

Good Thinking! Fostering Children's Reasoning and Problem Solving by Jessica Vick Whittaker

24

Article

Prepared by: Chris J. Boyatzis, *Bucknell University*
Ellen N. Junn, *California State University, Stanislaus*

Good Thinking!
Fostering Children's Reasoning and Problem Solving

JESSICA VICK WHITTAKER

Learning Outcomes

After reading this article, you will be able to:

- Understand how critical thinking and problem solving develop across childhood and appear even in very young children's thinking.

- Describe different research approaches to studying young children's critical thinking and problem solving.

- Evaluate teaching practices for how well they promote problem solving and reasoning in preschool children.

S andy teaches 3- and 4-year-old children in a Head Start classroom. She often asks children to be investigators and to solve problems or questions that arise. For example, during outside time one day, Sandy notices Keira and Amir playing on the slide. Sandy hears Keira say, "Hey, Amir, you're going really fast down that slide! How come I'm not going so fast?" Sandy comments, "Keira, you made a really interesting observation. You noticed that Amir is going down the slide faster than you. Why do you think that might be?" "Well," Keira says thoughtfully, "maybe because his pants are more slippery than mine." Sandra responds, "That is really good thinking! You've made a guess, a hypothesis. Can you think of some way we could test out whether Amir's clothing is making him go faster?"

Keira decides that she can test whether clothing makes a difference by using clothes from the dramatic play area. She finds two pairs of pants: one pair from a wizard outfit that is very shiny and made of what Keira calls "slippery" material, and the other a pair of jeans from the construction worker outfit. They look rough and less slippery. Sandy times Keira as she goes down the slide to see whether the slippery pants make her

go faster. They find that Keira can indeed slide faster with the slippery pants on.

From this experience Keira learns several things. She learns, for example, that the texture of a material—whether it is smooth or rough—affects how quickly or slowly an object (in this case, a person) moves down a ramp. She learns that if she doesn't know the answer to a question she can make a guess and then test that guess to determine if it is correct (she also discovers that another word for *guess is hypothesis*). If something puzzles Keira, she now knows that she can ask her teacher for help and information.

If asked, Sandy could identify particular content areas she supported during this interaction. She could respond that she fostered Keira's knowledge about the physical world and how things work (science), encouraged her thinking about inclined planes (mathematics), and expanded her communication skills by teaching her new words and how to explain her thinking (language). As important as these skills are, however, there was more to this learning experience than just science, mathematics, and language. In this interaction, Sandy encouraged Keira to construct a possible explanation, a hypothesis, and then test that explanation to better understand cause-and-effect relationships. Sandy promoted "good thinking," the ability to logically think and reason about the world.

Critical thinking skills span multiple domains. They include focusing to pursue knowledge, using self-control to define a problem and determine goals, making connections to brainstorm solutions, and communicating to justify actions and share evaluations (Galinsky 2010).

Forty-four percent of the preschool day is spent on learning activities, primarily literacy and writing activities (Early et al. 2005). Too often, such activities focus on skill attainment and not on the critical thinking, reasoning, and problem solving that are foundational to learning and development. Such skills warrant attention, and it is important that teachers foster them *intentionally*. This article summarizes research on the development of preschool children's critical thinking skills and suggests practical, research-based strategies for supporting them.

Reasoning and Problem-Solving Skills

Definitions of critical thinking skills vary, although nearly all include reasoning, making judgments and conclusions, and solving problems (Willingham 2008; Lai 2011). Although it was previously believed that these were higher-order thinking skills that developed only in older children and adults (Piaget 1930), research demonstrates that children reason and problem solve as early as infancy (e.g., Woodward 2009). Between ages 3 and 5, children form complex thoughts and insights, and during the preschool years their cognitive abilities—including logical thinking and reasoning—develop substantially (Amsterlaw & Wellman 2006). These skills enable children to recognize, understand, and analyze a problem and draw on knowledge or experience to seek solutions to the problem (USDHHS 2010). Some researchers conclude that reasoning and problem-solving skills are domain specific (e.g., reasoning skills in science do not necessarily transfer to mathematics); others, however, argue that teachers can foster young children's general critical thinking skills (see Lai 2011 for a review).

Reasoning and problem-solving skills are foundational for lifelong learning. Analyzing arguments, making inferences, reasoning, and implementing decisions to solve problems are important skills across all content areas and thus critical for school success. The ability to efficiently gather, understand, analyze, and interpret information is increasingly necessary to function in school and in the workplace (Schneider 2002). Educators and policy makers, now more than ever, recognize the need to foster critical thinking skills in young children. This is evidenced in the Common Core State Standards, which emphasize the importance of reasoning and problem-solving skills in preparing children for "college, workforce training, and life in a technological society" (NGA Center & CCSSO 2010, 4).

Key Ideas about Children's Thinking

Three key ideas emerge from the research on young children's thinking:

1. Young children are capable of developing reasoning and problem-solving skills.
2. Children's early reasoning and problem-solving skills support their later development and learning.
3. Early childhood educators can foster children's reasoning and problem solving.

Research suggests how these ideas relate to everyday practice.

Young Children can Develop Reasoning and Problem-Solving Skills

Scholars long believed that true logical reasoning does not develop until adolescence (Piaget 1930). However, recent research suggests that logical thinking and reasoning begin in infancy and develop gradually throughout childhood (Gopnik et al. 2004; Hollister Sandberg & McCullough 2010). From infancy on, children pay attention to people's intentions and goals, and infants as young as 6 months old demonstrate rudimentary reasoning skills (Woodward 2009).

Early reasoning skills

Woodward and her colleagues explored how infants make sense of their physical and social worlds and develop reasoning skills (e.g., Hamlin, Hallinan, & Woodward 2008; Cannon & Woodward 2012). The researchers tested whether 7-month-olds would copy an experimenter's actions if they understood the experimenter's intention (Hamlin, Hallinan, & Woodward 2008). Infants were shown two toys, and then they watched as the experimenter reached for one of the toys and grasped it. The experimenter pushed the toys within reach of the infants and said, "Now it's your turn!" Infants reliably touched the same object the experimenter had grasped. This was not the case when the experimenter simply brushed the toy with the back of her hand rather than grasped it (suggesting that the touch was unintentional, not goal directed). In both cases the experimenter's actions drew attention to the object, but infants responded only when they interpreted the experimenter's actions as goal directed. These results, along with others from a series of studies Woodward and colleagues conducted, demonstrate that infants as young as 7 months old can analyze others' intentions and use this information to reason about things in their world (Woodward 2009).

Understanding of causality

Between 9 and 12 months, infants begin to understand that one event or behavior causes another (Woodward 2009), and 2-year-olds are adept at using causality in their thinking (McMullen 2013). Gopnik and colleagues (2000; 2001) designed a series of experiments to explore how young children construct and test explanations for events. They showed children a "magical" light box that glowed when it was activated. Although the experimenter controlled the box, the box appeared to be activated by placing a block on top of it. The experimenter showed

Good Thinking! Fostering Children's Reasoning and Problem Solving by Jessica Vick Whittaker

26

2- to 4-year-old children different blocks, some that turned the box on (the experimenter called these *blickets)* and some that did not (not blickets). The children were asked which block was the blicket. Children as young as 2 were able to draw causal conclusions about which object was the blicket, correctly choosing the block that had "activated" the light. In another experiment with 3- and 4-year-old children, the task was modified so two blocks were placed on the machine and children were asked which block to remove to make the machine stop lighting up. Children correctly predicted which object they should remove from the box to make it stop.

The blicket studies are important because they demonstrate that very young children understand how one thing affects another and that as children get older, their reasoning skills are more sophisticated. Children are increasingly able to generate theories about the causal effects of objects and to test those theories by asking questions and making predictions.

Inductive and deductive reasoning

Understanding cause and effect is an important component of both inductive and deductive reasoning, which develop between the ages of 3 and 6 (Schraw et al. 2011). Young children use *inductive reasoning* when they generalize the conclusions they draw from the consequences of their own behaviors or experiences. *Deductive reasoning* is the process by which individuals use facts or general rules to draw a conclusion, being able to understand the premise "If *P* happens, then *Q* will too" (Schraw et al. 2011).

Three-year-old Maya has a fireplace at home and has learned through experience that fires are hot and should not be touched. When she sees the flame on a gas stove in the kitchen at her early childhood program, she reasons that the stove is also hot and should not be touched. "Hot," she says to her friend. "Don't touch!" Maya uses inductive reasoning in this situation, generalizing and extending her knowledge about fire and heat to a new situation.

> **Although young children's deductive reasoning becomes more sophisticated with age, their development of this reasoning is complex.**

Three-year-old Brandon knows that if it is nighttime, it is time for him to take a bath (if *P*, then *Q*). Through repeated experiences—nighttime (P), then bath (Q)—Brandon connects these two events using deductive reasoning, the basis for making predictions. Inductive and deductive reasoning skills grow

substantially during the preschool years as a result of children's increasing knowledge and varied experiences and interactions with the world around them.

Analogical reasoning

Goswami and Pauen (2005) have spent many years researching how *analogical reasoning,* a form of inductive reasoning that involves making and understanding comparisons, develops in young children (Goswami 1995; Goswami & Pauen 2005). In a series of three experiments, they tested the ability of 3- and 4-year-olds to make comparisons, or relational mappings, based on size (Goswami 1995). An experimenter read *Goldilocks and the Three Bears* to a child, and then said they were going to play a game about choosing cups. The experimenter said, "We are each going to have a set of cups, a daddy-bear-size cup, a mummy-bear-size cup, and a baby-bear-size cup, and you have to choose the same cup from your set that I choose from mine." The experimenter named the cups in her set (e.g., "I'm choosing the Mummy cup") but not in the child's set. To choose the correct cup, the child had to work out the size relationship between the two sets of cups using one-to-one correspondence. Not only did 3- and 4-year-old children choose the correct cup, they could do so even when the positions and colors of their cups were different from those of the experimenter's cups.

However, when experimenters asked 3- and 4-year-olds to make analogies (comparisons) involving concepts rather than physical characteristics (e.g., *A* is hotter than *B* is hotter than *C,* or *A* is louder than *B* is louder than *C*), only the 4-year-olds were successful (Goswami 1995; Goswami & Pauen 2005). Goswami concluded that children as young as 3 can use analogies as a basis for reasoning only if the analogy is based on a familiar structure, such as the characters in *Goldilocks*. This skill develops and becomes more sophisticated over time, doing so rather rapidly during the brief time between ages 3 and 4.

Reasoning with abstract ideas

Research demonstrates that although young children's deductive reasoning becomes more sophisticated with age and that 4-year-olds can reason using abstract ideas, their development of this reasoning is complex. For example, a teacher is working with a small group of children. She says, "We're going to think about some silly stories together. Some of the stories may sound funny, but I want you to think carefully about them. For each story, I'm going to ask you to use your imagination and make a picture in your head. In this story, all cats bark. So the cats that are in your head, are they barking? Are they meowing? Now, Jeremy is a cat. Is Jeremy barking? Is Jeremy meowing? How do you know?" Problems like this actually get more difficult for children as they get older and acquire more real-world experience, because they are more likely to know of counterexamples ("I know a cat that can't 'meow'!"). However, children eventually overcome this and draw the correct conclusions from complex, even absurd, premises (Hollister Sandburg & McCullough 2010).

Children's Early Reasoning and Problem-Solving Skills Support their Later Development and Learning
Cognitive learning

Children's reasoning and problem-solving skills are associated with a range of important literacy learning (e.g., Tzuriel & Flor-Maduel 2010) and mathematics outcomes (Grissmer et al. 2010). In an analysis of six longitudinal data sets, researchers found that general knowledge at kindergarten entry was the strongest predictor of children's science and reading skills and a strong predictor of math skills (Grissmer et al. 2010). General knowledge includes children's thinking and reasoning skills, in particular their ability to form questions about the natural world, gather evidence, and communicate conclusions (USDOE 2002).

Social-emotional learning

Children's reasoning and problem-solving skills are also important components of social and emotional competence. Social problem-solving skills include generating a number of alternative solutions to a conflict and understanding and considering the consequences of one's behaviors (Denham & Almeida 1987; Denham et al. 2012). These skills are linked to children's long-term behavioral outcomes (Youngstrom et al. 2000), school adjustment (Bierman et al. 2008), and academic success (Greenberg, Kusché, & Riggs 2001).

To see how reasoning and problem solving apply to the social-emotional domain, let's return to Sandy's classroom a couple of months after Keira's first experience with creating an experiment to test a hypothesis:

> Keira notices Andy and Eric creating a zoo with animals and blocks in the block area and asks, "Can I play with you?" Andy responds, "No, there's not enough animals for three people!" Upset, Keira says to her teacher, Sandy, "Andy won't play with me because I'm a girl." Sandy bends down to Keira's eye level and says, "Are you sure? I saw you and Andy playing together just this morning on the playground. Can you think of any other reasons Andy might not want to play with you right now?" Keira says, "Well, maybe because there aren't enough animals for me too." Sandy asks Keira where she might find some other animals to add to the zoo. Keira finds several animal puppets in the book area and takes them to the block area.

As this situation demonstrates, children's daily experiences offer opportunities to construct explanations about cause and effect. When teachers provide enriching experiences and materials and support children's interactions with each other, they enable children to develop their reasoning and problem-solving skills. In both scenarios with Keira, Sandy encouraged her to think and to generate hypotheses to solve her questions and problems. In the second scenario, Sandy pointed out that evidence did not support Keira's initial hypothesis and encouraged Keira to problem solve to find a solution. Further, Keira's response provided Sandy insight into Keira's concept of herself in social situations, in particular those involving playing with boys and playing in the block area. From this experience, Keira may begin to learn the importance of producing alternative solutions to interpersonal problems, a key social problem-solving skill (Youngstrom et al. 2000).

Checklist of Teaching Practices and Strategies to Support Preschool Children's Problem Solving and Reasoning

- **Facilitate children's play.** Support children's exploratory play experiences by providing challenging, varied materials that appeal to all of the senses—sight, sound, smell, touch, and taste. Encourage communication during play by extending children's language with their peers and with you. Ask them to talk about their play both during and after their play experiences.
- **Help children understand the difference between guessing and knowing.** A guess, or hypothesis, needs to be tested. Assist children with simple experiments in which they make predictions based on their hypotheses, gather evidence by making observations that they document (e.g., through pictures, dictated stories, graphs), and seek information to help them support or reject their original hypotheses and make conclusions. Do they prove their hypotheses, or do they need to do additional experimenting?
- **Foster categorization skills.** Provide materials that allow children to explore, compare, and sort by a variety of attributes (size, shape, sound, taste, etc.). With younger children, use objects that differ in just one attribute (e.g., balls of different colors). Ask children to describe the similarities and differences and to put the objects into categories. Use and reinforce vocabulary that helps children describe their comparisons (e.g., *short, round, loud, quiet, blue, red,*

smooth, bumpy) and use problem-solving language (e.g., *hypothesis, compare, observe, interpret).* During play, notice how children use materials. Do they sort them? Do they comment on similarities and differences?

- **Encourage children to think before responding.** Help children learn to freeze—to take a moment before answering a question to think about their best or most reasonable response to a problem and how they would test it. With a group of children, discuss different ways they solved a problem to demonstrate that there is often more than one way to do so. Point out that children sometimes think about and approach things differently, but that everyone's ideas should be respected.

- **Model and promote scientific reasoning, using the language of problem solving.** Teachers demonstrate good habits of problem solvers when they encourage children to use their senses to observe the world around them, help children form questions about what they observe and make predictions, share their own thinking and problem-solving processes aloud with children, model and conduct experiments to test predictions, and facilitate discussion about the results of children's experiments.

Early Childhood Educators can Foster Children's Reasoning and Problem Solving

Although children are naturally curious and like to explore, they need adult support to make sense of the world around them. Early childhood educators can foster children's reasoning and problem-solving skills in the context of the developmentally appropriate practices in which they already engage. For example, teachers can provide experiences and materials and engage in interactions that build on children's natural curiosity.

Facilitate children's play

As stated in NAEYC's (2009) position statement on developmentally appropriate practice, "play is an important vehicle for developing self-regulation as well as for promoting language, cognition, and social competence" (14). Play also supports children's reasoning and problem solving (Schulz & Bonawitz 2007; Ramani 2012). Through play, children actively explore their environments, manipulate objects and interact with others, construct knowledge about the way the world works, and learn vital concepts such as cause and effect. Play also provides children opportunities to plan, negotiate, and develop social

perspective-taking skills by considering others' points of view. In the previous scenario, Sandy helped Keira understand why Andy might be hesitant to allow her to join their play and to negotiate a possible solution. Like Sandy, all teachers have an important role in supporting, yet not interfering with, children's play experiences not only by providing materials and opportunities but also by offering suggestions for solving problems.

Scaffold children's understanding of the difference between guessing and knowing

Teachers scaffold children's learning by providing hints, offering a range of answers, and encouraging children to use additional resources. These strategies help children understand the difference between guessing and knowing—and realize that guessing requires testing. The ability to distinguish when there is and is not enough evidence to draw conclusions is fundamental to good problem solving. The more information children have about a particular topic, the better able they are to form reasoned theories and to be confident that those theories are correct. Young children need to learn to find and use evidence to confirm hypotheses, identify trustworthy sources, and reject hypotheses that cannot be supported by evidence.

In addition to these general teaching practices, there are specific strategies that promote preschool children's reasoning and problem-solving skills. These strategies, described in detail in the following three sections, promote "thoughtful decision making" by developing children's planning and reflecting skills (Epstein 2014). (See "Checklist of Teaching Practices and Strategies to Support Preschool Children's Problem Solving and Reasoning" for further explanation of strategies.)

Foster categorization skills

Understanding how to compare and contrast, categorize, and sort enables children to generalize information from one category or situation to another—to reason inductively (Hollister Sandberg & McCullough 2010). Generalizing helps children determine how to approach new objects or events with confidence. For example, 4-year-old Justin was once bitten by a dog and now is afraid of all dogs. During neighborhood walks, his parents have helped him categorize dogs by watching for behavioral signs: a dog with a wagging tail and relaxed demeanor is most likely friendly, but a dog that is barking and has its ears pinned back and teeth bared should be given some space. When they visit the park, Justin generalizes the information he learned about which dogs he can feel safe with based on how he categorizes their behavior.

To promote categorizing, provide children with objects or sets of objects that have contrasting qualities and encourage them to explain how the objects are alike and not alike (Loewenstein & Gentner 2001; Mix 2008; Christie & Gentner

Sample Lesson Plan: Sink or Float

Learning domain: Science Knowledge & Skills, Physical Science (Properties of Materials)

Learning objectives: Children will develop initial understandings of the concept of buoyancy, and will observe and predict whether objects sink or float and classify them accordingly. Children will observe and describe the ways sinking objects can be made to float and floating objects can be made to sink.

Activity setting: Small group

Materials:

- Plastic bottle cap (one per group)
- Cups of water (one per teacher and one per child)
- Objects that float (three to five per group—foam peanuts, plastic bears, etc.)
- Objects that sink (three to five per group—coins, pebbles, solid rubber balls, balls of clay, etc.)
- Pennies (three per group, not plastic)
- Large transparent container of water, such as a glass bowl or an aquarium
- Paper towels

Big idea: The concept of floating and sinking is a tricky one! It is hard to accurately describe the characteristics of an item that will float or sink because the concept of buoyancy may be too advanced for most preschoolers. The goal of the activity is for children to make predictions and then to experiment with, observe, and describe items that float or sink. It is not necessary or appropriate to draw conclusions about buoyancy as a result of this activity.

Planned activity:

1. Say, "Today we are going to learn about objects that float and sink."
2. Demonstrate how to make a floating object sink.
   - Fill a large, transparent container with water. Float an upturned plastic bottle cap in the water. Ask the children to predict what will happen as pennies are placed into the bottle cap "boat." Ask children to describe what happens as each penny is added.
3. Encourage children to experiment with materials that float or sink.
   - Give children cups of water and objects that float or sink.
   - Ask children to describe each object's shape, weight (heavy/light), and material.

- Ask children to predict whether each object will float or sink.
- Ask children to place the objects in the water to see if they float or sink.
- Ask children to group the objects according to whether they float or sink.

Foster categorization skills: The teacher encourages children to sort items according to whether they float or sink.

4. Experiment to make floating items sink and sinking items float.
   - Encourage children to describe the objects that floated.
   - Challenge children to see if they can make those objects sink.
   - As a group, brainstorm ways to make an object float or sink using classroom materials. For example, attach an object that sinks to a foam peanut or shape the clay ball into a boat to make it float; add small blocks or pennies to make a floating object sink.
   - Test the modifications, revising as children offer other ideas.

Model and promote scientific reasoning: Ask children to brainstorm ways to make an object float or sink and then encourage them to test those hypotheses.

5. Say: "Today we learned about things that float and sink." Ask questions such as the following:
   - "Were we able to make something that floated sink? How did we do it? Why do you think that worked?"
   - "Can anyone think of a way we made something that sank be able to float? How?" (e.g., changing a ball of clay or foil into a boat shape can allow it to float)
   - "What was the same or different about the items that were able to float? What was the same or different about the items that were able to sink? Was that *always* the case?"

Scaffold children's understanding of the difference between guessing and knowing: Review with children what was the same or different about the items that floated. Scaffold their understanding of whether there was enough evidence to conclude that the characteristics they identified *always* made the items float or sink.

Adapted, by permission, from M. Kinzie, R.C. Pianta, J. Vick Whittaker, M.J. Foss, E. Pan, Y Lee, A.P. Williford, & J.B. Thomas, *MyTeachingPartner—Math/Science* (Charlottesville: University of Virginia, Curry School of Education, The Center for Advanced Study of Teaching and Learning, 2010), 258–9.

2010). Challenge children to categorize by attributes beyond size and shape; for example, ask them to group objects according to color, width, or function (e.g., "find tools that can cut") (Kemler Nelson, Holt, & Egan 2004). Also, notice how children spontaneously categorize during play; what attributes are they using to categorize in sets they create?

Teachers also foster categorization skills by modeling strategies for children. Children as young as 3 can understand and imitate categorization strategies they see a teacher use without the teacher explicitly stating the strategies (Williamson & Markman 2006; Williamson, Meltzoff, & Markman 2008; Williamson, Jaswal, & Meltzoff 2010). For example, with a group of children watching, Sandy arranges several toys in front of her. Some of the toys make noise and some do not. Without telling children what characteristic she is using to sort, she carefully picks up each toy, shakes it and listens to it, and then puts the toy in the appropriate group. For the last few unsorted toys, she picks them up one at a time and says to a child, "Sort the toys the way I did." To do so, the child must have attended to what Sandy did, understood her goal, and learned her sorting rule as she modeled the strategy (shaking the toys and listening). This requires deeper-level mental processes and more complex problem solving than if Sandy had simply told the children her sorting rule.

Encourage children to brainstorm multiple solutions to problems

Young children tend to act on their first impulse in a situation or on the first thing that comes to mind. But to be good thinkers, they need to develop *inhibitory control,* "the ability to ignore distractions and stay focused, and to resist making one response and instead make another" (Diamond 2006). Inhibitory control helps children regulate their emotions and behavior and problem solve more effectively. Teachers can help children learn this important skill by encouraging them to pause before acting; consider multiple solutions to questions, tasks, or problems; and then choose a solution to try out.

Model and promote scientific reasoning

Scientific reasoning involves constructing hypotheses, gathering evidence, conducting experiments to test hypotheses, and drawing conclusions (Hollister Sandberg & McCullough 2010). It requires children to distinguish between various explanations for events and determine whether there is evidence to support the explanations. Although this is a complex type of reasoning for young children, teachers can support it through modeling and scaffolding. For example, after encouraging children to construct multiple reasonable explanations for events (hypotheses), teachers can help children talk through the steps they will take to test their hypotheses, as Sandy did in

the first scenario with Keira and the slide. As children test their hypotheses, teachers should encourage them to use their senses (i.e., smell, touch, sight, sound, taste) to observe, gather, and record data (e.g., through pictures or charts). Finally, teachers can help children summarize the results of their investigation and construct explanations (i.e., verbalize cause and effect) for their findings. When teachers ask children questions such as "Why do you think that?" or "How do you know?," they help children become aware of their own thinking processes, reflect on the results of their experiments, and evaluate outcomes. (See the sample lesson plan for an example of how teachers support scientific reasoning.)

Conclusion

Children's ability to problem solve and reason is integral to their academic as well as social success. Each day, early childhood teachers support these skills in numerous ways—for example, by facilitating children's play, scaffolding learning, and offering interesting and challenging experiences. With a better understanding of how young children's reasoning and problem-solving skills develop, and a plan for implementing strategies to support them, teachers will become more intentional in helping children become good thinkers.

References

Amsterlaw, J., & H.M. Wellman. 2006. "Theories of Mind in Transition: A Microgenetic Study of the Development of False Belief Understanding." *Journal of Cognition and Development* 7(2): 139–72.

Bierman, K.L., C.E. Domitrovich, R.L. Nix, S.D. Gest, J.A. Welsh, M.T. Greenberg, C. Blair, K.E. Nelson, & S. Gill. 2008. "Promoting Academic and Social-Emotional School Readiness: The Head Start REDI Program." *Child Development* 79(6): 1802–17. www.ncbi.nlm.nih.gov/pubmed/19037591.

Cannon, E.N., & A.L. Woodward. 2012. "Infants Generate Goal-Based Action Predictions." *Developmental Science* 15(2): 292–98. www.ncbi.nlm.nih.gov/pubmed/22356184.

Christie, S., & D. Gentner. 2010. "Where Hypotheses Come From: Learning New Relations by Structural Alignment." *Journal of Cognition and Development* 11(3): 356–73.

Denham, S.A., & C.M. Almeida. 1987. "Children's Social Problem-Solving Skills, Behavioral Adjustment, and Interventions: A Meta-Analysis Evaluating Theory and Practice." *Journal of Applied Developmental Psychology* 8(4): 391–409. http://nichcy.org/research/summaries/abstract29.

Denham, S.A., H.H. Bassett, M. Mincic, S. Kalb, E. Way, T. Wyatt, & Y Segal. 2012. "Social-Emotional Learning Profiles of Preschoolers' Early School Success: A Person-Centered Approach." *Learning and Individual Differences* 22(2): 178–89. www.ncbi.nlm.nih.gov/pmc/articles/PMC3294380.

Diamond, A. 2006. "The Early Development of Executive Functions." Chap. 6 in *Lifespan Cognition: Mechanisms of Change,* eds. E. Bialystok & F.I.M. Craik, 70–95. New York: Oxford University Press.

Early, D., O. Barbarin, D. Bryant, M. Burchinal, F. Chang, R. Clifford, G.M. Crawford, C. Howes, S. Ritchie, M.E. Kraft-Sayre, R.C. Pianta, W.S. Barnett, & W. Weaver. 2005. "Pre-Kindergarten in Eleven States: NCEDL's Multi-State Study of Pre-Kindergarten & Study of State-Wide Early Education Programs (SWEEP): Preliminary Descriptive Report." NCEDL working paper. National Center for Early Development & Learning. http://fpg.unc.edu/sites/fpg.unc.edu/files/resources/reports-and-policy-briefs/NCEDL_PreK-in-Eleven-States_Working-PaperJ005.pdf.

Epstein, A.S. 2014. *The Intentional Teacher: Choosing the Best Strategies for Young Children's Learning.* Rev. ed. Washington, DC: NAEYC.

Galinsky, E. 2010. *Mind in the Making: The Seven Essential Life Skills Every Child Needs.* New York: HarperCollins. Available from NAEYC.

Gopnik, A., C. Glymour, D.M. Sobel, L.E. Schulz, T. Kushnir, & D. Danks. 2004. "A Theory of Causal Learning in Children: Causal Maps and Bayes Nets." *Psychological Review* 111(1): 3–32. www.ncbi.nlm.nih.gov/pubmed/14756583.

Gopnik, A., & D.M. Sobel. 2000. "Detecting Blickets: How Young Children Use Information About Novel Causal Powers in Categorization and Induction." *Child Development* 71(5): 1205–22. www.ncbi.nlm.nih.gov/pubmed/11108092.

Gopnik, A., D.M. Sobel, L.E. Schulz, & C. Glymour. 2001. "Causal Learning Mechanisms in Very Young Children: Two -, Three-, and Four-Year-Olds Infer Causal Relations From Patterns of Variation and Covariation." *Developmental Psychology* 37(5): 620–9. www.ncbi.nlm.nih.gov/pubmed/11552758.

Goswami, U. 1995. "Transitive Relational Mappings in Three- and Four-Year-Olds: The Analogy of Goldilocks and the Three Bears." *Child Development* 66(3): 877–92.

Goswami, U., & S. Pauen. 2005. "The Effects of a 'Family' Analogy on Class Inclusion Reasoning by Young Children." *Swiss Journal of Psychology/Schweizerische Zeitschrift für Psychologie/Revue Suisse de Psychologie* 64(2): 115–24.

Greenberg, M.T., C.A. Kusché, & N. Riggs. 2001. "The P(romoting) A(lternative) TH(inking) S(trategies) Curriculum: Theory and Research on Neurocognitive and Academic Development." *The CEIC Review* 10(6): 22–23, 26. http://files.eric.ed.gov/fulltext/ED455318.pdf.

Grissmer, D., K.J. Grimm, S.M. Aiyer, W.M. Murrah, & J.S. Steele. 2010. "Fine Motor Skills and Early Comprehension of the World: Two New School Readiness Indicators." *Developmental Psychology* 46(5): 1008–117. http://curry.virginia.edu/uploads/resourceLibrary/Research_Brief-Readiness_Indicators.pdf.

Hamlin, J.K., E.V. Hallinan, & A.L. Woodward. 2008. "Do as I Do: 7-Month-Old Infants Selectively Reproduce Others' Goals." *Developmental Science* 11(4): 487–94. www.ncbi.nlm.nih.gov/pubmed/18576956.

Hollister Sandberg, E., & M.B. McCullough. 2010. "The Development of Reasoning Skills." Chap. 10 in *A Clinician's Guide to Normal Cognitive Development in Childhood,* eds. E. Hollister Sandberg & B.L. Spritz, 179–98. New York: Routledge.

Kemler Nelson, D.G., M.B. Holt, & L.C. Egan. 2004. "Two- and Three-Year-Olds Infer and Reason About Design Intentions in Order to Categorize Broken Objects." *Developmental Science* 7(5): 543–9. www.ncbi.nlm.nih.gov/pubmed/15603287.

Lai, E.R. 2011. "Critical Thinking: A Literature Review." Research report. San Antonio, TX: Pearson. http://images.pearsonassessments.com/images/tmrs/criticalthinkingreviewfinal.pdf.

Loewenstein, J., & D. Gentner. 2001. "Spatial Mapping in Preschoolers: Close Comparisons Facilitate Far Mappings." *Journal of Cognition and Development* 2(2): 189–219. http://groups.psych.northwestern.edu/gentner/papers/LoewensteinGentner01.pdf.

McMullen, M.B. 2013. "Understanding Development of Infants and Toddlers." Chap. 3 in *Developmentally Appropriate Practice: Focus on Infants and Toddlers,* eds. C. Copple, S. Bredekamp, D. Koralek, & K. Charner, 23–49. Washington, DC: NAEYC.

Mix, K.S. 2008. "Children's Numerical Equivalence Judgments: Cross-mapping Effects." *Cognitive Development* 23(1): 191–203. www.ncbi.nlm.nih.gov/pmc/articles/PMC2719857.

NAEYC. 2009. "Developmentally Appropriate Practice in Early Childhood Programs Serving Children From Birth Through Age 8." Position statement. Washington, DC: NAEYC. www.naeyc.org/files/naeyc/file/positions/PSDAP.pdf.

NGA Center (National Governors Association Center for Best Practices) & CCSSO (Council of Chief State School Officers). 2010. *Common Core State Standards for English Language Arts and Literacy in History/Social Studies, Science, and Technical Subjects.* Washington, DC: NGA Center & CCSSO. www.corestandards.org/assets/CCSSI_ELA%20Standards.pdf.

Piaget, J. 1930. *The Child's Conception of Physical Causality.* Trans. M. Gabain. New York: Harcourt, Brace.

Ramani, G.B. 2012. "Influence of a Playful, Child-Directed Context on Preschool Children's Peer Cooperation." *Merrill-Palmer Quarterly* 58 (2): 159–90.

Schneider, V. 2002. "Critical Thinking in the Elementary Classroom: Problems and Solutions." Educators Publishing Service. www.eps.schoolspecialty.com/downloads/articles/Critical_Thinking-Schneider.pdf.

Schraw, G., M.T. McCrudden, S. Lehman, & B. Hoffman. 2011. "An Overview of Thinking Skills." In *Assessment of Higher Order Thinking Skills,* eds. G. Schraw & D.H. Robinson, 19–46. Charlotte, NC: Information Age Publishing.

Schulz, L.E., & E.B. Bonawitz. 2007. "Serious Fun: Preschoolers Engage in More Exploratory Play When Evidence Is Confounded." *Developmental Psychology* 43(4): 1045–50. www.ncbi.nlm.nih.gov/pubmed/17605535.

Tzuriel, D., & H. Flor-Maduel. 2010. "Prediction of Early Literacy by Analogical Thinking Modifiability Among Kindergarten Children." *Journal of Cognitive Education and Psychology* 9(3): 207–26.

USDHHS (US Department of Health and Human Services). 2010. "The Head Start Child Development and Early Learning Framework: Promoting Positive Outcomes in Early Childhood Programs Serving Children 3–5 Years Old." www.eclkc.ohs.acf. hhs.gov/hslc/tta-system/teaching/eecd/Assessment/Child%20 Outcomes/HS_Revised_Child_Outcomes_Framework(rev-Sept2011).pdf.

USDOE (US Department of Education). 2002. "Early Childhood Longitudinal Study—Kindergarten Class of 1998–99 (ECLS-K), Psychometric Report for Kindergarten Through First Grade." Working paper. www.nces.ed.gov/pubs2002/200205.pdf.

Williamson, R.A, V.K. Jaswal, & A.N. Meltzoff. 2010. "Learning the Rules: Observation and Imitation of a Sorting Strategy by 36-Month-Old Children." *Developmental Psychology* 46 (1): 57–65. http://ilabs.washington.edu/meltzoff/pdf/10Williamson_ Jaswal_Meltzoff_Rule_Imitation.pdf.

Williamson, R.A., & E.M. Markman. 2006. "Precision of Imitation as a Function of Preschoolers' Understanding of the Goal of the Demonstration." *Developmental Psychology* 42 (4): 723–31. http://bingschool.stanford.edu/pub/emarkman/8.%20 Williamson-Precision%20of%20Imitation.pdf.

Williamson, R.A., A.N. Meltzoff, & E.M. Markman. 2008. "Prior Experiences and Perceived Efficacy Influence 3-Year-Olds' Imitation." *Developmental Psychology* 44 (1): 275–85. www. ncbi.nlm.nih.gov/pubmed/18194026.

Willingham, D.T. 2008. "Critical Thinking: Why Is It So Hard to Teach?" *Arts Education Policy Review* 109 (4): 21–32. www. uvm.edu/~facsen/generaleducation/Critical%20Thinking%20 Article%20-%20Willingham.pdf.

Woodward, A.L. 2009. "Infants' Grasp of Others' Intentions." *Current Directions in Psychological Science* 18 (1): 53–7. http:// web.mit.edu/course/other/i2course/www/devel/wco.pdf.

Youngstrom, E., J.M. Wolpaw, J.L. Kogos, K. Schoff, B. Ackerman, & C. Izard. 2000. "Interpersonal Problem Solving in Preschool and First Grade: Developmental Change and Ecological Validity." *Journal of Clinical Child Psychology* 29 (4): 589–602. www. ncbi.nlm.nih.gov/pubmed/11126636.

Critical Thinking

1. How might preschools do a better job of balancing knowledge development and skills with the cultivation of critical thinking and problem solving?

2. Read the sample lesson plan and critique it: What aspects might work better than others, and why? If you are volunteering or working at an early childhood setting, try to implement small parts of the plan and then share your experience with your class and teacher.

3. There has recently been increased emphasis on academics in preschool settings. Is this good for children? How do the activities described in this article seem to integrate development of critical thinking and problem solving with children's natural play?

Internet References

AboutKidsHealth.com
http://www.aboutkidshealth.ca/En/HealthAZ/LearningandEducation/LiteracyandNumeracy/Pages/spatial-skills-children.aspx

Everydaylife.globalpost
http://everydaylife.globalpost.com/reasoning-activities-preschoolers-45782.html

Jump Start
http://www.jumpstart.com/parents/activities/critical-thinking-activities

National Association for the Education of Young Children
https://www.naeyc.org/files/yc/file/200309/Planning&Reflection.pdf

ParentingScience.com
http://www.parentingscience.com/teaching-critical-thinking.html

Article

Prepared by: Chris J. Boyatzis, *Bucknell University* and
Ellen N. Junn, *California State University, Stanislaus*

The Determinants of Strategic Thinking in Preschool Children

Isabelle Brocas and Juan D. Carrillo

Learning Outcomes

After reading this article, you will be able to:

- Understand preschool children's ability to think strategically yet within limits.
- Describe methods that psychologists use to study preschool children's cognitive skills.

Introduction

Strategic thinking, or the intrinsic ability to anticipate actions and act accordingly, is a cornerstone of rational decision-making. It shapes behavior both in individual situations and in games of strategy. While strategic decision-making in children has received substantial attention in the literature [1–14], little is known about the age at which children start displaying it. For example, tic-tac-toe is popular among preschoolers. However, it is unclear whether children can anticipate multiple steps or whether they are bound to 'play as they go' [3]. Similarly, children are known to display some degree of sophistication in interactions, but behavior in most studied paradigms is likely driven by other-regarding concerns, cultural factors, or by mimicking others' behavior [4, 6, 8, 10, 15–18]. These confounds may hide the contribution of strategic thinking to behavior.

A few recent studies developed paradigms that measure strategic performance in game theoretical settings while controlling for orthogonal concerns [9, 14]. In these studies, children are asked to make decisions and their performance relates to the ability to select an equilibrium strategy. An equilibrium strategy requires acting optimally given an objective, and taking into account that other players are doing the same. These studies suggest that children are not able to strategize, that is to play at equilibrium, before at least 7 years of age. From experimental game theory literature in adults, it is well known that performance in games varies widely across paradigms. Subjects who are able to solve a game requiring a specific number of steps of reasoning may be unable to solve games of similar nature requiring more steps of reasoning [19–22]. This suggests that strategic thinking is multi-faceted and interacts with difficulty. We hypothesize that such effects may have played a role in previous observations in children.

We conjecture that children around 5 years of age exhibit capabilities to think strategically in game theoretic paradigms. On the one hand, by age 5 children have already become less egocentric [23, 24] and have started acquiring the ability to process the intentions of others through Theory of Mind [25–28]. This ability is essential to realize what an opponent might do in a game of strategy. On the other hand, it is still early to perform recursive thinking. Indeed, existing evidence suggests that children are capable of thinking ahead and act accordingly to correct anticipations by 7 years of age [1, 2, 11].

Our main hypothesis is that preschool children are able to think strategically, but their capacity to translate strategic thinking into the ability to solve a task is intimately related to its difficulty. Complexity can come in many forms but it typically relates to pieces of information that need to be processed in order to make a decision. Other things being equal, a multi-stage decision problem is more complex than a one stage problem, a game with multiple options is more complex than a game with only two options, and a game against a real opponent is more complex than a game of chance. It is therefore plausible that, just like adults, the ability of young children to perform strategic reasoning in existing studies is hidden by an excessive complexity of the task.

To test this hypothesis, we present novel experimental tasks specifically designed for preschoolers that allow us to isolate two different aspects of strategic thinking: the ability to perform *logical reasoning* (**LR**) and the ability to perform *anticipatory reasoning* (**AR**). **LR** refers to the minimum level of sophistication necessary to make logical, though possibly myopic, choices. **AR** is the capacity to anticipate future events and use that information to choose the best current course of action. This ability is a simple form of recursive reasoning. We also vary the complexity of our tasks to analyze behavior of children in individual tasks that require simple anticipatory capabilities (**AR-s**), in individual tasks that require complex anticipatory capabilities (**AR-c**), and in games that require taking the perspective of an opponent (**AR-g**).

For analysis, we also investigate the relationship between the ability to think strategically and performance in two paradigmatic tasks of cognitive development in preschool: an egocentrism task and a conservation task. Our egocentrism task helps capture a simple form of perspective taking that is necessary to think strategically. Our conservation task is used to probe logical thinking in a non-strategic setting. This exercise allows us to control for age-related known cognitive developments and to better assess the degree to which preschoolers can think strategically.

2 Design and Methods

To test for strategic thinking, we recruited 74 children from six preschool classes at a private elementary school across two sessions, one in June 2015 and the other in June 2016. All methods were administered in accordance with existing guidelines and protocol was reviewed and approved by the Institutional Review Board at the University of Southern California (UP-12-00528). We obtained written and informed consent from parents of all participants and oral assent from participants themselves. Children were between 53 and 66 months old at the time the study was administered. Two children were excluded due to not completing all tasks. The remaining 72 children (36 females and 36 males) participated in three Strategic Thinking tasks designed to disentangle between **LR** and **AR**, and three Control tasks to capture known developmental characteristics of preschoolers.

Strategic Thinking Tasks

It was essential to find the right level of difficulty for the Strategic Thinking tasks. They had to be easy enough for children 4-5 years of age to solve them and difficult enough to require some degree of anticipation and forward looking reasoning. We designed three novel Strategic Thinking tasks: a Simple individual choice (*Simple*), a Complex individual choice (*Complex*)

and a Game (*Game*), that participants played in this set order. While studies addressing developmental stages of strategic thinking usually consider multiple age-ranges [1–14], our research strategy was different. We instead decided to build several games tailored for preschoolers with varying levels of difficulty. These games were, a priori, too complex to understand for 2-3 years-old children and too simple to execute for 7-8 years-old.

In *Simple*, the experimenter (she) presented three tokens to the participant (he), two red (R) and one yellow (Y), and instructed him to drop all the tokens in a one-column version of the game "Connect 4" (Fig 1). The participant would win if two tokens of the same color never landed next to each other. Before proceeding, the experimenter asked whether the participant was familiar with "Connect 4" and, independently of the answer, provided a demonstration, emphasizing that tokens would fall in the order they were dropped. In *Complex*, the experimenter added two yellow tokens to the same problem and repeated the instructions. Performing the correct sequences in these tasks ('R-Y-R' in *Simple* and 'Y-R-Y-R-Y' in *Complex*) required two distinct calculations. First, the participant had to realize that colors must alternate, which called for myopic logical reasoning and therefore captured **LR**. It is a similar ability as the one necessary to solve pattern recognition problems. After dropping a token, the participant could simply look for a token of the other color. Second, the participant had to start with a token of the color that was most prevalent. This, on the other hand, did require to think ahead and captured **AR**. The participant had to anticipate the future consequences of current actions in order to select the correct color. *Simple* required the simple ability **AR-s**, (if I start with 'Y', then I will be left with 2 'R', so I should start with 'R') while *Complex* required the complex ability **AR-c** (if I start with 'R', then I will drop 'Y', then I will drop 'R', and I will be left with two 'Y', so I should start with 'Y').

In *Game*, the experimenter allocated two tokens to herself and three to the participant (all of the same color). She explained that both players would alternate dropping as few or as many tokens as they wished, starting with the participant, and that the person who put the last token would win. She also explained that she would try to win. This game is an extremely simplified version of the Hit-N game [29, 30] and the optimal strategy for the experimenter is to always put one token when it is her turn. Therefore, the participant would win only if he also put exactly one token at each turn. This task required **LR** because the participant had to think logically and realize that, in order to keep his advantage, he should never drop more tokens than his rival in the previous turn. This task also required **AR-g**, the ability to anticipate the possible futures after dropping 1, 2 or 3 tokens, which necessitated not only to think ahead but also to take the other player's perspective.

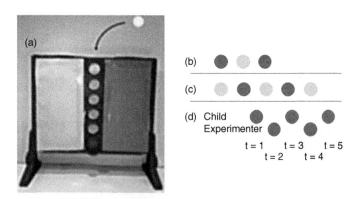

Figure 1   Strategic thinking tasks.
(a) One-column "Connect 4" game; (b) In *Simple*, the child must drop tokens in the order Red-Yellow-Red; (c) In *Complex*, the child must drop tokens in the order Yellow-Red-Yellow-Red-Yellow; (d) In *Game*, the child must put exactly one token at each turn.

https://doi.org/10.1371/journal.pone.0195456.g001

The two individual choice tasks *Simple* and *Complex* were introduced to the children as problems they needed to solve while *Game* was framed as a game against the experimenter with a set of rules. Even though the children were not acquainted with those problems, they were familiar with the material we used and they were invited to play rather than answer abstract questions. We wanted to avoid proposing conceptual tasks, as it is known that familiarity with context and experience significantly affects children's performance [31, 32]. At the same time, we wanted to be able to measure children's intrinsic ability to solve new problems, so we opted for tasks that differed from known games.

Notice that, contrary to standard practices in Psychology, we intentionally decided against counterbalancing the Strategic Thinking tasks to avoid confusing participants. Indeed, there was a natural order to explain the tasks, starting with the simple individual, then moving to the complex individual and finishing with the game against the experimenter. There is a priori no fundamental reason why the order between an individual task and the game should have any effect on behavior, as performance in one did not provide information on how to play the other. Furthermore, tasks were very short and children were given as much time as they needed to relax between tasks to prevent fatigue. By contrast, the order between the two individual tasks could potentially have had a performance effect, since learning to play one of them could provide guidance on how to play the other. We should therefore take this into consideration when interpreting the results.

Control Tasks

Our Control tasks were borrowed and adapted from traditional literature. They consisted of one egocentrism task [23, 24,

33–35] that tested perspective-taking (*Ego*) and two conservation tasks [36] –a non-motivated task with blocks (*Blocks*) and a motivated task with bracelets or bouncy balls (*Toys*). In the egocentrism task, a wall divided two figurines facing each other. We asked each participant if the figurines could see each other. In the conservation tasks, we presented participants with 2 rows: one with 6 objects, and the other with 5 objects. First, we spaced the objects in such a way that the row featuring 5 objects was shorter. We then manipulated the spacing of the objects in front of the child so that the row featuring 5 objects was longer. In the non-motivated version, we asked participants "which line has more blocks?" once before the manipulation and once after. In the motivated task, we asked "which line of toys do you want to bring home and keep?" again before and after the manipulation. The egocentrism task *Ego* captured a very primitive form of Theory of Mind. The conservation tasks *Blocks* and *Toys* captured logical thinking abilities that are known to develop gradually and are not yet fully acquired in preschool. These tasks are useful to study the relationship between logical thinking and the context in which questions are asked. In particular, questions are abstract in the non-motivated version while they are meaningful in the motivated version.

The entire procedure was performed one-on-one between the experimenter and the participant and took 10 to 15 minutes. At the end of each task, children were debriefed on their performance, although the majority realized by themselves whether they had "won" or not. Children who did not complete a Strategic Thinking task successfully could try again if they wished. However, given the endogeneity and heterogeneity in their decision to try again, we report here only the results of their first decision in each task. In addition to the line of bracelets or bouncy balls they decided to keep in *Toys*, children could choose several other toys to bring home (die-cast cars, erasers, trading cards, figurines, poppers, etc.) as a token of our appreciation.

3 Results
3.1 Aggregate Analysis
The proportions of correct choices in the Strategic Thinking and Control tasks are represented in Fig 2.

Individual Choice Tasks
65.3% of the children solved *Simple* while only 31.9% solved *Complex* and 25.0% solved both. If participants were to choose randomly at each step, they would complete *Simple* with probability and *Complex* with probability $\frac{2}{3} \times \frac{1}{2} = 0.33$, and therefore both tasks with probability $\frac{3}{5} \times \frac{1}{2} \times \frac{2}{3} \times \frac{1}{2} = 0.1\ 0.03$. Our

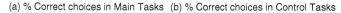

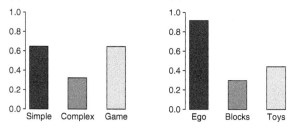

Figure 2   Strategic thinking tasks.

(a) Strategic thinking tasks: Proportions of correct choices in *Simple, Complex* and *Game*; (b) Control tasks: Proportions of correct choices in *Ego, Blocks* and *Toys*.

https://doi.org/10.1371/journal.pone.0195456.g002

findings are inconsistent with this hypothesis (test for equality of proportions, 95% confidence interval [0.54, 0.75], p-value < 0.001 for *Simple*; 95% confidence interval [0.22, 0.43], p-value < 0.001 for *Complex*; 95% confidence interval [0.16, 0.36], p-value < 0.001 for both tasks).

As an alternative hypothesis, it is plausible that participants understood the need to alternate but did not know which token to choose first. If they were to randomly choose the first token only and alternate thereafter, they would complete *Simple* with probability 0.66 and *Complex* with probability 0.6, and hence both tasks with probability 0.4. While we cannot reject this was the case in *Simple* (test for equality of proportions, 95% confidence interval [0.53, 0.75], p-value = 0.80), participants did not play according to this strategy in *Complex* (test for equality of proportions, 95% confidence interval [0.22, 0.43], p-value < 0.001) nor across tasks (test for equality of proportions, 95% confidence interval [0.16, 0.36], p-value = 0.009). Overall, participants' performance was better than random and worse than randomly choosing the first token and alternating thereafter.

To better assess the contribution of chance to the overall performance of our participants, we identified children who were able to alternate in both tasks: given any starting color, children were categorized as able to alternate if they chose a different color in the second step and kept alternating until it was not possible to do so (as in sequence 'R-Y-R-Y-Y' for instance). We found that 62 children alternated in both tasks. 75.8% of these children completed *Simple* while only 37% completed *Complex*. Children who demonstrated the ability to alternate chose the correct color in the first step more often than random in *Simple* (test for equality of proportions, 95% confidence interval [0.64, 0.85], p-value = 0.01) and less often than random in *Complex* (test for equality of proportions, 95% confidence interval [0.26, 0.50], p-value = 0.0002). Taken together, these results indicate that, on aggregate, while chance may have accounted for some successes, it is unlikely to be a driving

force. It is more likely that many children realized that they had to alternate but failed to anticipate with clarity their future moves in order to choose the first token.

Last, it shall be noted that some participants may have transferred knowledge of how to play *Simple* (start with the color most prevalent, then alternate) to their behavior in *Complex*. This means that observed variations in performance may not be entirely driven by changes in difficulty. Given our order of play, the decrease in success between *Simple* and *Complex* constitutes a lower bound of the pure effect of difficulty on choice.

Game Task

Among our participants, 52.8% successfully completed *Game*. Note that a necessary condition to win was to drop only one token in the first round. If participants were to play randomly in the first round (i.e., dropping 1, 2 or 3 tokens with equal probability), they would win with at most probability 0.33, a hypothesis not supported by the data (test for equality of proportions, 95% confidence interval [0.41, 0.64], p-value < 0.001). Also, among the participants who did not solve *Game*, 20 (58.8%) dropped 3 tokens, and 11 (32.3%) dropped 2 tokens in their first turn. Only 3 children started off correctly by dropping 1 token. This means that children who did not solve *Game* made almost invariably a mistake in the first round.

Perspective of Others

66 out of 72 children (91.7%) correctly answered *Ego*. This is a higher fraction than in the early literature with preschoolers [23] but comparable to the results obtained in follow-up studies [24]. It indicates very little evidence of egocentrism in our participants. Children were also fast in providing their answers, and could articulate their reasoning ('they can't see each other because there is a wall between them'). The overwhelming majority of children were able to take the perspective of others, indicating that failure to complete *Game* was unlikely due to developmental differences in the ability to take a different perspective.

Conservation

As in earlier literature [36], more children correctly solved the motivated conservation task than the non- motivated conservation task (44.0% for *Toys* vs. 30.5% for *Blocks*, McNemar test, chi-squared = 4.66, df = 1, p- value = 0.031). Children who answered correctly did so by counting the number of items. None of them applied a conservation reasoning. These results indicate that children in our sample were typical preschoolers.

The main conclusion of this aggregate analysis is that children do not play randomly. They often behave as if they understand the importance of alternating colors in *Simple* and *Complex*. At the same time, they sometimes act as if they fail to anticipate future moves when making current choices in *Complex* and *Game*.

3.2 Performance Across Tasks and Classification Analysis

The previous results suggest that not all children behave equally. We hypothesize here that aggregate results hide developmental differences across children: some children are able to strategize in all tasks while others are still struggling with the most difficult situations. To investigate this possibility and assess heterogeneity in behavior, we represent the distribution of correct choices across Strategic Thinking tasks (Fig 3).

Strategic Thinking and Complexity

27.8% of the children (20) solved neither *Simple* nor *Complex*, 40.3% (29) solved only *Simple* and 25.0% (18) solved both *Simple* and *Complex* (only 6.9% (5) solved *Complex* but not *Simple*). Among the children who solved *Simple* but not *Complex*, 93% started *Complex* with 'R' and kept alternating colors until they could not anymore (sequence 'R-Y-R-Y-Y'). This

(a) Distribution of correct answers

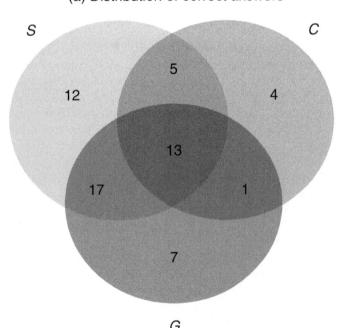

G

(13 participants did not solve any task)

Figure 3 Strategic thinking tasks: Venn diagram showing the number of subjects who solved the different combinations of *Simple* (S), *Complex* (C) and *Game* (G).

https://doi.org/10.1371/journal.pone.0195456.g003

Table 1 Classification of Children According to their Behavior in *Simple* and *Complex*

strategic thinkers	limited strategic thinkers	alternators	randomizers
LR & AR-s & AR-c	LR & AR-s	LR	none
18 children	27 children	13 children	9 children

https://doi.org/10.1371/journal.pone.0195456.t001

indicates that these subjects were not playing randomly. On the other hand, among subjects who picked the wrong initial color in *Simple* (sequence 'Y-R-R'), only 20% completed *Complex* correctly while 65% switched color for the initial token of *Complex* and ended up with the sequence 'R-Y-R-Y-Y'. These results suggest that many subjects were able to perform the color alternation required by **LR**. Failure was often due to inability to anticipate the correct starting color, or inability to perform **AR**. Table 1 provides a classification of the children according to their logical reasoning and anticipatory reasoning capabilities, after excluding 5 participants who are difficult to categorize due to their success in *Complex* and failure in *Simple*. Children who were able to alternate and solve both *Simple* and *Complex* (they performed **LR**, **AR-s** and **AR-c**) were classified as "strategic thinkers". Children who were able to alternate but only solved *Simple* (they performed **LR** and **AR-s** only) were classified as "limited strategic thinkers". Children who were able to alternate but did not solve any task (they performed **LR** only) were classified as "alternators". Last, children who were not able to alternate in any task (they acted as if they had not yet acquired any of the relevant abilities) were classified as "randomizers".

This classification reveals a large heterogeneity, reflecting different developmental stages. The next relevant issue is to investigate how children in different groups performed across our two contexts: individual decisions vs. game.

Strategic Thinking Across Contexts

We first investigated whether performance in individual tasks was predictive of performance in *Game*. A Probit regression with the binary variable "success in *Game*" as the dependent variable showed that performance in *Simple* was a significant predictor of performance in *Game* after controlling for demographic variables (Table 2—left). By contrast, performance in *Complex* was not a significant predictor. This result is consistent with the fact that the completion rate of *Game* fell between that of *Simple* and *Complex*, and that these tasks

Table 2 Probit Regressions of Success in *Game*

	Game
Simple	0.86 (0.35)*
Complex	0.23 (0.34)
Age	− 0.04 (0.04)
Gender	− 0.12 (0.31)
Constant	2.31 (2.71)
AIC	101.41
	Game
Start	**0.49 (0.38)**
LR *ability*	− 1.30 (0.47)**
Age	− 0.04 (0.04)
Gender	− 0.17 (0.32)
Constant	3.17 (2.79)
AIC	**95.91**

* = 5% significance (st. error in parenthesis).

** = 1% significance (st. error in parenthesis).

https://doi.org/10.1371/journal.pone.0195456.t002

Table 3 Probit Regression of Success in *Toys* (Top) and in *Complex* (Bottom)

	Toys
Start	0.77 (0.37)*
LR *ability*	0.33 (0.40)
Age	0.04 (0.05)
Gender	− 0.35 (0.31)
Constant	− 2.85 (2.70)*
AIC	**91.00**
	Complex
Toys	0.71 (0.34)*
Blocks	0.13 (0.36)
Age	0.08 (0.04)
Gender	0.13 (0.33)
Constant	-5.46 (2.76)*
AIC	**91.00**

* = 5% significance (st. error in parenthesis).

https://doi.org/10.1371/journal.pone.0195456.t003

were correctly performed by an overlapping, but non-nested subset of children (Fig 3): *Complex* was perceived as more difficult than *Game* by many.

We also found that 72.2% of "strategic thinkers", 63.0% of "limited strategic thinkers" and 46.2% of "alternators" solved *Game*. By contrast, only 11.1% of "randomizers" solved *Game*. These proportions were significantly different (4-sample test for equality of proportions, $\chi^2 = 10.27$, df = 3, p-value = 0.016). This suggests that being able to perform **AR** in the individual tasks (especially **AR-c**) transferred to *Game*, though only partially. Moreover, not being able to perform **LR** in the individual tasks was a predictor of not succeeding in *Game*. A probit regression of success in *Game* confirmed that the inability to solve **LR** (dummy variable **LR** *ability*) was a significant predictor of not being able to solve *Game*, while the ability to solve both individual tasks (dummy variable *Strat*) was not, again after controlling for demographic variables (Table 2— right).

These results taken together indicate that the ability to play at equilibrium in *Game* was inherently related to the ability to think logically (**LR**) and to make simple anticipations (**AR-s**) in individual tasks.

Strategic Thinking and Conservation

Interestingly, we found that performance in the motivated conservation task was related to performance in the strategic thinking tasks: 66.7% of "strategic thinkers" were able to solve *Toys*

compared to 29.6%, 46.2% and 33.3% of the "limited strategic thinkers", "alternators" and "randomizers" respectively. A probit regression of success in *Toys* showed that the ability to solve both *Simple* and *Complex* (dummy variable *Strat*) was a significant predictor of solving *Toys*, after controlling for demographic variables (Table 3—left). This suggests that the ability to solve the motivated conservation task is related to the distinctive ability to solve *Complex*.

To assess the relationship between performance in *Complex* and *Toys*, we ran a Probit regression with "success in *Complex*" as the dependent variable. This exercise showed that performance in the motivated conservation task was indeed a significant predictor of performance in the complex individual task after controlling for demographic variables (Table 3—right).

Overall, the ability to solve the arguably most difficult task *Complex* was associated with the ability to rely on intrinsic motivation to overcome the tendency to fail conservation questions.

3.3 Strategic Thinking and Age

The existence of developmental differences in our sample suggested that age, even within our short window, may have played a role in the decisions of participants. We investigated performance in all our tasks as a function of age. We first noted that differences in the conservation tasks were not related to age, again confirming that children in our sample were typical preschoolers.

Table 4 Average age of Children in each Category

Strategic Thinkers	Limited Strategic Thinkers	Alternators	Randomizers
LR & AR-s & AR-c	LR & AR-s	LR	none
60.3 months	59.1 months	57.4 months	56.9

https://doi.org/10.1371/journal.pone.0195456.t004

Children who solved *Simple* were on average older than those who did not (59.5 vs. 57.5 months, two-sample t-test, t = -2.390, df = 50.84, p-value = 0.021). The age-effect was marginal between those who solved *Complex* and those who did not (60 vs. 58.3, two-sample t-test, t = -1.863, df = 38.17, p-value = 0.070). Children who solved both tasks were also significantly older than those who solved neither of them (60.3 vs. 57.2, two-sample t-test, t = 2.788, df = 33.45, p-value = 0.008). In contrast with the individual tasks, we found no significant age difference between children who solved and did not solve *Game* correctly (58.8 vs. 58.9, two-sample t-test, t = 0.120, df = 69.14, p-value = 0.904).

Table 4 reports the average age of children in each category. Age was decreasing in the number of abilities that were correctly implemented. In particular, "strategic thinkers" were significantly older than "alternators" (two-sample t-test, t = 2.183, df = 26.42, p-value = 0.038) and "randomizers" (two-sample t-test, t = 2.959, df = 23.51, p-value = 0.007).

A multinomial Probit regression confirmed that being classified as "strategic thinker" was positively and significantly associated with age (reference category "randomizers", coefficient for age in the "Strategic Thinker" category = 0.061, p-value< 0.05) after controlling for gender.

3.4 Strategic Thinking and Gender

We did not find any effect of gender in our study. Female and male solved *Simple*, *Complex* and *Game* at similar rates (all tests for equality of proportions, p-value > 0.05). Within each category, the proportion of females was also similar to the proportion of males (4-sample test for equality of proportions, $\chi^2 = 3.493$, df = 3, p-value = 0.322). Similarly, performance in the two conservation tasks was very similar (all tests for equality of proportions, p-value > 0.05). These results are also consistent with the regressions reported in Table 2, indicating that performance in the different tasks are correlated but they are not affected by gender.

4 Discussion

Our analysis provided evidence that children understood the need to apply logical reasoning, **LR**, in the individual decision-making tasks *Simple* and *Complex*, but many failed to implement anticipatory reasoning, **AR**, in the most difficult tasks *Complex* and *Game*. Our classification analysis revealed a large heterogeneity reflecting different developmental stages: a few participants were able to apply these abilities across contexts while many others struggled with the second, and some did not acquire any. In particular, the ability to play at equilibrium in *Game* was inherently related to the ability to think logically (**LR**) and to make simple anticipations (**AR-s**) in individual decision-making tasks. Interestingly, the ability to solve the arguably most difficult task *Complex* was associated with the ability to answer conservation questions in a motivated context. A few comments are in order regarding these results.

Individual tasks *Simple* and *Complex* were designed to require the ability to perform **LR** and **AR**, but *Complex* was more challenging. In particular, it necessitated more attention to process the information contained in the extra tokens (**AR-c** vs. **AR-s**). The decrease in success between *Simple* and *Complex* together with the significant effect of age on performance suggests that children around 5 years of age are learning to think strategically. The results are consistent with research correlating performance in games with age and difficulty [37] as well as with the well-documented gradual development of executive functions [38, 39]. As executive functions and attention-related mechanisms develop, children learn how to integrate more elements in their decision-making in an efficient way; they progressively learn how to solve simple then complex individual tasks that require anticipation and forward looking behavior. Our results are also consistent with the literature on problem-solving and planning strategies which suggests that young children are able to attend to a limited number of features of the problem. As they grow, they become able to incorporate more information and solve larger problem [40–42]. These ideas are also reminiscent of the fact that young children exhibit centration, the tendency to focus on one salient aspect of a situation, a tendency they overcome only gradually [43].

It was unclear a priori which of *Game* and *Complex* would exhibit a higher success rate. *Game* was cognitively less demanding than *Complex* as it required fewer steps of reasoning (it was relatively easy to discard the alternatives of dropping 2 or 3 tokens). At the same time, it was more challenging because some future moves were left to the discretion of the opponent. While the overall difficulty of *Game*, measured by the likelihood of success, was somewhere between that of *Simple* and *Complex*, the game and individual tasks were correctly performed by an overlapping, but non-nested subset of children. Indeed, among the subjects who did not solve *Simple*, a significant fraction answered *Game* correctly (32.0%). Conversely, among the subjects who successfully solved *Complex*, a significant fraction did not answer *Game* correctly (36.4%). This suggests that the individual and game tasks required related, but different sets of cognitive skills. Interestingly, we also observed that among participants who solved *Game*, 95% realized that colors had to alternate in *Complex*, suggesting that only subjects who were able to perform **LR** were also able to solve *Game*. We also noted that performance in *Game* was predicted by performance in *Simple*. Taking these results together, strategic thinking in *Game* was supported by the ability to perform **LR** and **AR-s**. In turn, this suggests that the inability to select equilibrium strategies in interactive settings may be simply due to limitations of logical reasoning rather than to under-developed Theory of Mind.

Performance in *Complex* was predicted by success in *Toys*. It has been hypothesized that young children, those who are not yet verbally fluent, fail conservation tasks such as *Blocks* because they use a misleading perceptual strategy and answer the question "which line is longer" rather than "which line has more blocks". This is referred to as the 'length-equals-number' heuristic [44, 45]. Recent neuroimaging studies have shown that success in conservation tasks requires the involvement of structures that inhibit the length-equal- number strategy and allow the manipulation of numerical information [46]. These structures are not yet fully developed in preschool children and number conservation is not automatic. It is plausible that motivation facilitates success because it helps children activate attentional processes that are still developing [47, 48]. The fact that success in *Complex* was predicted by success in *Toys* suggests the existence of a common underlying cognitive process that helps both decisions. Given the previous discussion, it is plausible that both complex anticipation and motivated conservation (which is inherently also a complex task for a preschooler) require the involvement of attention-executive processes. In the context of our study, the ability to solve a complex task correlates with the ability to solve a different complex task.

Supporting Information

	A	B
1	S1. Dataset	
2		
3	Keys	
4		
5	id	Subject id
6	Gender	gender F, M
7	Age	Age in months
8	SimpleSequence	Sequence in Simple task
9	SimpleCorrect	Correct sequence 1 = yes, 0 = no
10	ComplexSequence	Sequence in Complex task
11	ComplexCorrect	Correct sequence 1 = yes, 0 = no
12	GameSequence	Sequence in Game task (correct is 1-1-1-1-1)
13	GameCorrect	Game correct 1 = yes, 0 = no
14	LegoAnswer	Egocentrism task answer: yes or no (no is correct)
15	ConservationLegoQ1	Line pointed in question 1 Lego task
16	ConservationLegoQ2	Line pointed in question 2 Lego task
17	ConservationToyQ1	Line pointed in question 1 Toy task
18	ConservationToyQ2	Line pointed in question 2 Toy task
19		
20	'na' refers to cases where the child did not provide any articulated answer	

keysdata.

References

1. Eliot J, Lovell K, Dayton CM, McGrady B. A further investigation of children's understanding of recursive thinking. Journal of Experimental Child Psychology. 1979;28(1):149–157.

2. Shultz TR, Cloghesy K. Development of recursive awareness of intention. Developmental Psychology. 1981;17(4):465–471.

3. Crowley K, Siegler RS. Flexible Strategy Use in Young Children's Tic-Tac-Toe. Cognitive Science. 1993;17(4):531–561.

4. Harbaugh WT, Krause K, Liday S, Vesterlund L. Trust in children. Trust and reciprocity: interdisciplinary lessons from experimental research. 2003; p. 302–322.

5. Sutter M. Outcomes versus intentions: On the nature of fair behavior and its development with age. Journal of Economic Psychology. 2007;28(1):69–78.

6. Fehr E, Bernhard H, Rockenbach B. Egalitarianism in young children. Nature. 2008;454(7208):1079–1083. pmid:18756249

7. Brosig-Koch J, Heinrich T, Helbach C. Exploring the Capability to Backward Induct–An Experimental Study with Children and Young Adults; 2012.

8. Fehr E, Glätzle-Rützler D, Sutter M. The development of egalitarianism, altruism, spite and parochialism in childhood and adolescence. European Economic Review. 2013;64:369–383.

9. Sher I, Koenig M, Rustichini A. Children's strategic theory of mind. Proceedings of the National Academy of Sciences. 2014;111(37):13307–13312.

10. Jordan JJ, McAuliffe K, Warneken F. Development of in-group favoritism in children's third-party punishment of selfishness. Proceedings of the National Academy of Sciences. 2014;111(35):12710–12715.

11. Tecwyn EC, Thorpe SK, Chappell J. Development of planning in 4-to 10-year-old children: Reducing inhibitory demands does not improve performance. Journal of experimental child psychology. 2014;125: 85–101. pmid:24858446

12. Blake PR, Rand DG, Tingley D, Warneken F. The shadow of the future promotes cooperation in a repeated prisoner's dilemma for children. Scientific reports. 2015;5. pmid:26417661

13. Czermak S, Feri F, Glätzle-Rützler D, Sutter M. How strategic are children and adolescents? Experimental evidence from normal-form games. Journal of Economic Behavior & Organization. 2016;. https://doi.org/10.1016/j.jebo.2016.04.004

14. Brocas I, Carrillo JD. The development of rational thinking from Kindergarten to adulthood. LABEL Discussion Paper 2017.01; 2017.

15. Gummerum M, Hanoch Y, Keller M. When child development meets economic game theory: An interdisciplinary approach to investigating social development. Human Development. 2008;51(4):235–261.

16. Kagan S, Madsen MC. Experimental analyses of cooperation and competition of Anglo-American and Mexican children. Developmental Psychology. 1972;6(1):49.

17. Paulus M. It's payback time: Preschoolers selectively request resources from someone they had benefitted. Developmental psychology. 2016;52(8):1299. pmid:27359157

18. Kenward B, Hellmer K, Winter LS, Eriksson M. Four-year-olds' strategic allocation of resources: Attempts to elicit reciprocation correlate negatively with spontaneous helping. Cognition. 2015;136:1–8. pmid:25490123

19. Schotter A, Weigelt K, Wilson C. A laboratory investigation of multiperson rationality and presentation effects. Games and Economic Behavior. 1994;6(3):445–468.

20. Costa-Gomes M, Crawford VP, Broseta B. Cognition and behavior in normal-form games: An experimental study. Econometrica. 2001;69(5):1193–1235.

21. Camerer C. Behavioral game theory: experiments in strategic interaction. Princeton University Press; 2003.

22. Brocas I, Carrillo JD, Wang SW, Camerer CF. Imperfect choice or imperfect attention? Understanding strategic thinking in private information games. The Review of Economic Studies. 2014; p. 944–970.

23. Piaget J, Inhelder B. The Child's Conception of Space. Routledge and Kegan Paul, Ltd., London, England; 1956.

24. Hughes M. Egocentrism in preschool children. Edinburgh University; 1975.

25. Wimmer H, Perner J. Beliefs about beliefs: Representation and constraining function of wrong beliefs in young children's understanding of deception. Cognition. 1983;13(1):103–128. pmid:6681741

26. Wellman HM, Cross D, Watson J. Meta-analysis of theory-of-mind development: the truth about false belief. Child Development. 2001;72(3):655–684. pmid:11405571

27. Wellman HM, Liu D. Scaling of theory-of-mind tasks. Child Development. 2004;75(2):523–541. pmid:15056204

28. Apperly IA, Butterfill SA. Do humans have two systems to track beliefs and belief-like states? Psychological Review. 2009;116(4):953–970. pmid:19839692

29. Bouton CL. Nim, a game with a complete mathematical theory. The Annals of Mathematics. 1901;3(1/4):35–39.

30. Gneezy U, Rustichini A, Vostroknutov A. Experience and insight in the Race game. Journal of Economic Behavior & Organization. 2010;75(2):144–155.

31. Hatano G, Inagaki K. Desituating cognition through the construction of conceptual knowledge. Context and cognition: Ways of learning and knowing. 1992; p. 115–133.

32. Meadows S. The child as thinker: The development and acquisition of cognition in childhood. Routledge; 2006.

33. Newcombe N. The development of spatial perspective taking. Advances in child development and behavior. 1989;22:203–247. pmid:2688376

34. Newcombe N, Huttenlocher J. Children's early ability to solve perspective-taking problems. Developmental psychology. 1992;28(4):635.

35. Frick A, Möhring W, Newcombe NS. Picturing perspectives: development of perspective-taking abilities in 4-to 8-year-olds. Frontiers in psychology. 2014;5:386. pmid:24817860

36. Mehler J, Bever TG. Cognitive capacity of very young children. Science. 1967;158(3797):141–142. pmid:6054816

37. Brocas I, Carrillo JD. Strategic Thinking and Iterated Dominance in Young Children. LABEL Discussion Paper 2018-01; 2018.

38. Diamond A, Taylor C. Development of an aspect of executive control: Development of the abilities to remember what I said and to "Do as I say, not as I do". Developmental Psychobiology. 1996;29(4):315–334. pmid:8732806

39. Carlson SM. Developmentally sensitive measures of executive function in preschool children. Developmental Neuropsychology. 2005;28(2):595–616. pmid:16144429

40. Deloache JS, Brown AL. The early emergence of planning skills in children. In: Making sense: The child's construction of the world. New York, NY, US: Methuen; 1987. p. 108–130.

41. Gardner W, Rogoff B. Children's deliberateness of planning according to task circumstances. Developmental Psychology. 1990;26(3):480.

42. Hudson JA, Fivush R. Planning in the preschool years: The emergence of plans from general event knowledge. Cognitive Development. 1991;6(4):393–415.

43. Crain W. Theories of development: Concepts and applications. Psychology Press; 2015.

44. Houdé O. Inhibition and cognitive development: Object, number, categorization, and reasoning. Cognitive Development. 2000;15(1):63–73.

45. Houdé O, Guichart E. Negative priming effect after inhibition of number/length interference in a Piaget-like task. Developmental Science. 2001;4(1):119–123.

46. Poirel N, Borst G, Simon G, Rossi S, Cassotti M, Pineau A, et al. Number conservation is related to children's prefrontal inhibitory control: an fMRI study of a Piagetian task. PloS One. 2012;7(7):e40802. pmid:22815825

47. Gerstadt CL, Hong YJ, Diamond A. The relationship between cognition and action: performance of children 3 1/2—7 years old on a stroop-like day-night test. Cognition. 1994;53(2):129–153. pmid:7805351

48. Rueda MR, Fan J, McCandliss BD, Halparin JD, Gruber DB, Lercari LP, et al. Development of attentional networks in childhood. Neuropsychologia. 2004;42(8):1029–1040. pmid:15093142

Critical Thinking

1. What are some ways that preschoolers can think more strategically and logically than was previously believed?
2. What is a strength and a limitation of the methods used to study preschoolers' strategic thinking?
3. How might parents and teachers of preschool-aged children help develop children's strategic thinking?

Internet References

Bustle
Tools To Enhance Young Children's Thinking
https://nceln.fpg.unc.edu/sites/nceln.fpg.unc.edu/files/resources/ToolstoEnhanceYoungCHildrensThinking.pdf
Virtual Lab School
https://www.virtuallabschool.org/preschool/cognitive/lesson-2

Brocas, Isabelle and Carrillo, Juan D. "The determinants of strategic thinking in preschool children." PLOS One, May 31, 2018.

Article

Prepared by: Chris J. Boyatzis, *Bucknell University* and
Ellen N. Junn, *California State University, Stanislaus*

Quality 101: Identifying the Core Components of a High-quality Early Childhood Program

Simon Workman and Rebecca Ullrich

Learning Outcomes

After reading this article, you will be able to:

- Discuss the benefits to children of having access to quality early childhood education.

- Identify skills a quality leader will possess to create and foster a high-quality and developmentally appropriate learning environment.

Every day, millions of American families go through a familiar ritual: dropping off their young child at childcare or preschool. And while there are many reasons why parents choose a particular program—cost, location, the teachers, shared values, and the program's specific focus—one thing is universal: As parents walk away from the classroom in the morning to start their own day, each of them hopes that they have made the right decision and that their child will have a rich and fulfilling day, supported by a loving and affectionate caregiver.

Unfortunately, parents often have very few childcare options and limited ways to really know the quality of care their child is receiving. The level to which basic needs are met—keeping the child well fed, safe, and clean—is usually easy to verify, but determining if one's child is engaging sufficiently and is participating in age-appropriate learning activities is much harder to ascertain.

The need for high-quality early childhood education has never been greater. Increasingly, children are growing up in families where all available parents are working—out of necessity as well as choice. Furthermore, research continues to affirm the short- and long-term benefits for children who participate in high-quality early learning programs.[1] However, parents face significant barriers when searching for high-quality care. Waitlists are long and employers are inflexible, high-quality programs are expensive, and parents often lack the necessary tools to evaluate program quality. Many families live in childcare "deserts," and even when programs are available, quality is not well-regulated or supported by local, state, or federal policies, putting it out of reach for most families.[2]

This childcare crisis has received increased attention in recent years, from policy makers, political candidates, and voters.[3] However, there remains a critical need to better understand the components of high-quality programs to ensure policy solutions adequately support and promote access to quality for all families. To that end, this issue briefly highlights three core indicators of high-quality early childhood programs and identifies six structural supports that are necessary to achieve and maintain high quality. These indicators and supports provide a roadmap for policy makers as they develop solutions to the current childcare crisis and can also serve as a guide for parents seeking to make the best and most informed choices for their child.

Why Does Quality Matter?

A large body of research has demonstrated the critical importance of the first three years of a child's life.[4] The experiences and interactions children have in these early years significantly affects brain development and helps to establish the foundation for future learning.[5] Warm and responsive interactions

Quality 101: Identifying the Core Components of a High-quality Early Childhood Program by Simon Workman and Rebecca Ullrich

44

can create a nurturing and stable environment that enables the development of secure attachments between children and their caregivers—both those within and beyond their families. These attachments support children as they develop a sense of self and begin to understand their emotions, and they lay the foundation for establishing successful relationships at later ages.[6] With an estimated 6 million young children enrolled in childcare, it is clear that early learning programs, and the people who work in them, have a critical role to play in child development—a role that complements parents.[7] Furthermore, this crucial development must be supported from infancy, when brain development is at its peak. Waiting until children enter preschool or kindergarten to introduce these vital interventions is simply too late.

The positive effects of high-quality early childhood programs on specific, short- and long-term outcomes for children, families, and communities, have been quantified by numerous research studies.[8] In the short to medium term, children enrolled in high-quality early learning programs are less likely to need special education services during their K-12 years, are less likely to commit juvenile offenses, and more likely to graduate from high school. In the long term, those participating children are more likely to be employed and less likely to be dependent on government assistance.[9] The positive effects are larger, and more likely to be sustained, when programs are high quality.[10] In addition, the impact is greatest for children from low-income families.[11] Differences in children's cognitive abilities by income are evident at only nine months old and significantly widen by the time children are two years old.[12] Children living in poverty are more likely to be subject to stressful home environments—which can have lifelong impacts on learning, cognition, and self-regulation—while parents living in poverty have limited resources to provide for their families and high barriers to access affordable, high-quality childcare.[13] High-quality early learning programs staffed by warm and responsive adults can help mitigate these effects, offering a safe and predictable learning environment that fosters children's development.[14]

Despite evidence of the positive impact of high-quality early childhood education for all children, it remains out of reach for most low- and moderate-income families.[15] The average price of center-based care in the United States accounts for nearly 30 percent of the median family income, and only 10 percent of childcare programs are considered high quality.[16] Publicly funded programs—such as Head Start, Early Head Start, childcare, and state pre-K programs—are primarily targeted at low-income families, but limited funding for these programs severely hinders access.[17] This lack of access to high-quality early childhood education perpetuates the achievement gap, evidenced by the fact that only 48 percent of low-income children are ready for kindergarten, compared with 75 percent of moderate- or high-income children.[18]

Moderate-income families are typically ineligible for these publicly funded programs, but at the same time, such families struggle to afford the high cost of care in the private sector.[19] This leaves parents facing a series of difficult choices, including prioritizing childcare expenses over other household necessities; settling for low-quality childcare that fits their budget; patching together multiple informal care options; or leaving the workforce altogether.[20] To ensure that all children can realize the gains that come from attending high-quality early childhood programs, policy solutions need to focus on improving program supports and creating funding strategies that will increase access to high-quality programs for children from all backgrounds.

What Does High Quality Look Like?

All states have regulations or licensing standards that childcare providers must meet in order to legally operate in the state. These regulations provide a baseline standard and are primarily focused on protecting children from harm rather than on advancing child development and early learning.[21] While these standards are critically important to children's well-being—mitigating risks from inadequate supervision, poor building and hygiene standards, and unsafe practices—they do not address the comprehensive needs of young children. As such, meeting licensing requirements serves only as a baseline providing the fundamental components necessary for operation rather than an indication of program quality. In addition, states have varying requirements when it comes to determining exactly which providers need to be licensed, often making exemptions for faith-based programs or based on the number of nonrelative children served. As a result, significant numbers of children attend license-exempt programs that are not required to meet even the minimum licensing standard.[22]

Moreover, the key to a high-quality program is what happens inside the classroom or family childcare home, namely the interactions that take place between the teacher and child.[23] In a high-quality program, teachers engage children with learning strategies that are tailored to the age of the child and use an appropriate curriculum to structure the learning experience.[24] A variety of supports are needed to facilitate these interactions so that high-quality teaching and learning can occur. As such, the quality of an early childhood program is dependent on the following three key factors.

Interpersonal Interactions

The learning environment created by a teacher is critical to the quality of an early childhood program.[25] The experiences that a child has in their earliest years shape their development, and teachers play an important role in creating those experiences. A well-trained and highly skilled teacher tailors their interactions to fit the needs of the child—using responsive language, engaging all children in classroom activities, fostering independence, and creating a language-rich environment.[26] Effective early childhood teachers proactively prevent and redirect challenging behavior and respond to children's needs with respect, warmth, and empathy. The experiences children have with teachers in their earliest years can also set the tone for their interactions with teachers in later grades and thus are crucial to promoting positive attitudes about school and approaches to learning.[27]

Physical Environment

Children need a physical setting—both inside and outdoors—where they can play, explore, and learn safely. The learning environment needs to include engaging and developmentally appropriate materials and be arranged to promote independence and exploration based on children's different stages of development. For example, infants need to interact with their environment in a very physical way, examining cause and effect relationships by touching and feeling objects. The environment should therefore include toys made of different materials that are small enough to be picked up by an infant.

Toddlers and preschoolers use objects in more complex combinations and engage in sociodramatic play with one another. Their environment needs toys that spark the imagination, such as play kitchens, and that can engage them in problem solving such as puzzles.[28] Learning centers—clearly defined areas set aside in a learning environment where children can have easy access to materials and engage in independent and self-directed learning activities—can be an effective way to organize and support developing abilities, encourage interactions, create opportunities for role playing, and promote literacy skills.[29]

In addition to the indoor learning environment, children need access to outdoor space where they can move and engage with the natural world. Outdoor play has positive impacts on health and has been shown to combat childhood obesity and help develop stronger immune systems.[30] Research also shows that children who play outdoors regularly have more active imaginations, lower stress levels, and have greater respect for themselves and others.[31]

Program Support Structure

A high-functioning operating environment is an essential element of a quality early childhood program. This administrative operational support takes a number of forms. First, programs need effective leaders who can provide instructional support to teachers as well as sound business management to the overall program.[32] These multiple leadership functions are complex and often need to be fulfilled by more than one person. Second, external to the immediate program, programs need a series of structural supports, including access to professional development, quality improvement resources, stable and sufficient funding streams, and a pipeline of well-trained teachers. These external supports recognize that early childhood programs do not operate in a vacuum and rely on the wider early childhood system.[33]

All three factors need to be in place to ensure quality. A well-resourced classroom is not sufficient without an effective teacher to harness those resources. Meanwhile, an effective teacher is not sustainable without a support system to manage the business, support instruction, and provide professional development.

How States Measure Quality in Early Childhood

While there is no single definition of high quality and therefore no single measurement tool to determine and compare early childhood program quality across the United States, there are a number of tools that are widely used to assess and report the quality of early childhood programs.

Environment rating scales: The Early Childhood Environment Rating Scale, or ECERS for children ages 3–5, the Infant/Toddler Environment Rating Scale, and the Family Child Care Environment Rating Scale are standardized tools used to measure process quality at the classroom level. The measures contain multiple items on which programs are rated, organized into seven subscales. These subscales include ratings of the space and furnishing, personal care routines, the activities and interactions that take place in the classroom, and how the program engages with families. Ultimately, these tools are designed to assess the various interactions that occur in the learning environment—for example, between staff and children and among children themselves, the interactions children have with materials and activities, and the structures that support these interactions such as the space and the schedule.[34]

CLASS: The Classroom Assessment Scoring System, or CLASS, is an observation tool that assesses the interactions between teachers and children that affect learning and development. CLASS has separate scales for different age groups, reflecting the differences in how infants, toddlers, and preschoolers learn. The infant observation has just one domain while the pre-K observation has three domains. The observation assesses the quality of relationships, routines, the organization of the physical environment, and the way language is used, and interactions are facilitated to prompt children to think critically.[35]

National accreditation: Accreditation is a voluntary process that programs can use to help improve their level of quality and to demonstrate to families—both currently enrolled and prospective—that the program has gone above and beyond what is required by state regulation and achieved a specified level of quality.[36] To achieve these accreditations, programs need to engage in extensive self-study and go through an external validation process.[37] While these accreditations do differ, most contain a number of common standards. For example, they generally include standards related to the learning environment, teacher and child interactions, staff qualifications, professional development, and family engagement, among others.[38]

QRIS: All states either have a quality rating and improvement system, or QRIS; a pilot; or are in the planning process for a QRIS.[39] QRIS are designed to assess, improve, and communicate the level of quality in early childhood education settings.[40] Programs are assessed on multiple elements and receive a rating reflecting their level of quality—usually on a scale of 1–3 or 1–5. While there is not one single QRIS in use across the United States, each state has a unique QRIS reflecting their own priorities and context. Many QRIS do include environmental observations such as ECERS or CLASS as part of their assessment activities, and these scores factor into overall QRIS rating. Other elements of the rating might include family engagement activities, child assessments, and program management. Many QRIS also waive some requirements for programs with national accreditation, or automatically grant programs a certain QRIS rating as a result of their national accreditation.

What Components Are Necessary to Achieve and Maintain High Levels of Quality?

In addition to a core set of health and safety requirements, the three factors discussed above make up the key elements of a high-quality program.[41] In order to achieve and maintain these elements of high quality, early childhood programs need access to a number of key structures and supports, many of which can be aided by policy. While each program's pathway to quality will be unique, the following six elements represent the core components that are necessary for a quality program and are areas where policy makers should look to be supportive.

1. Professional and Stable Teacher Workforce

The workforce is the most critical component of quality in an early childhood program. All teachers need to have a foundational knowledge of child development and be able to lead activities that promote children's learning at various ages. This important role requires that teachers have formal education and training in early childhood education.[42]

Moreover, the early childhood workforce needs compensation that reflects the importance of their work and the expertise necessary to educate the nation's youngest children. Providing professional compensation and benefits, comparable to kindergarten teachers, helps recruit and retain effective and educated teachers and promotes a stable healthy learning environment for children.[43]

In addition, programs need to be staffed at a level that allows for teacher–child ratios that are appropriate for the age of the children and the size of the group, such as those required for programs accredited by the National Association for the Education of Young Children.[44] Low teacher–child ratios enable teachers to focus on the individual needs of the children and engage them in meaningful interactions.[45] This means having both an adequate number of teachers specifically assigned to a classroom, as well as providing sufficient substitutes or floaters to cover for breaks, planning time, and paid leave.

The early childhood education workforce should also reflect the growing diversity of the child population, ensuring that children have teachers they can relate to and role models that reflect their own backgrounds.[46]

2. Effective Leadership

Early childhood program administrators are responsible for a broad range of tasks, requiring many different competencies.[47] First, programs need instructional leaders with a solid understanding of child development and teaching and learning strategies. Instructional leaders support teachers with lesson planning and curriculum implementation, behavior management strategies, and professional development.

Second, programs need leaders with sound business management skills. The majority of early childhood programs are private businesses, and similar to any other small business, their long-term stability is reliant on adequate business management and the implementation of good budgetary practices.[48] Programs require clear enrollment, financial, and personnel policies and need leaders who can implement these policies in a fair and consistent manner.[49]

Finally, program administrators must be skilled in organizational management and relationship building. In addition to fostering relationships with families and the community, leaders play a key role in creating a positive atmosphere inside the program, which can minimize teacher turnover, increase program efficiency, and allow teachers to focus on the children.[50]

These multiple administrative roles need to be staffed sufficiently, which ideally includes more than one person, given the varied skill sets required.[51] In smaller programs—with limited capacity to employ multiple administrators—leaders need to be supported in their various roles through access to external technical assistance, leadership resources, and targeted professional development.

3. Age-appropriate Curriculum

All early childhood programs should adopt a research-based curriculum that is developmentally, culturally, and linguistically relevant for all children.[52] Curricula can provide a guiding philosophy for program activities, including teacher interactions and the design of the physical indoor and outdoor environment. Curricula also help teachers effectively structure and sequence classroom activities, target particular activities to build skills or meet development milestones, and build on prior learning and experiences. Curricula provide varying levels of flexibility to individual teachers; some provide highly structured models for teachers to implement, while others offer guiding principles and expect teachers to determine the best way to implement.[53]

There are a large number of curricula available for programs to choose from, with some of the best known models being the Creative Curriculum, HighScope Curriculum, and Tools of the Mind.[54] Research has found a positive impact on early achievement scores and socioemotional behavior when

Components of an Effective Curriculum

The National Center on Quality Teaching and Learning has identified 13 components that need to be present in an effective curriculum[57]:

1. Grounded in child development principles
2. Evidence-based
3. Shows effects on child outcomes
4. Comprehensive across learning domains
5. Depth for each covered learning domain
6. Specific learning goals
7. Well-designed learning activities
8. Responsive teaching
9. Supports for individualized instruction
10. Culturally and linguistically responsive
11. Ongoing assessments
12. Professional development opportunities
13. Family involvement materials

programs intentionally apply a curriculum that is supported by professional development, coaching, and sufficient resources.[55] Programs should adopt a curriculum that best fits their program philosophy and ensure teachers receive professional development and ongoing support to adequately incorporate the curriculum into their practice. It is also important that a curriculum is adopted for all age groups, not just preschoolers. Infants and toddlers need a curriculum that focuses on their need to explore and discover the world around them, guided by supportive and responsive caregivers.[56]

4. Comprehensive Family Engagement Activities

A high-quality program recognizes that families are essential to children's educational success and has policies in place to engage families in children's learning. Programs need to develop family engagement strategies that encourage families to participate in their child's learning and promote two-way communication, enabling parents to share with teachers the unique strengths and talents of their child.[58] Strategies must also be responsive to family needs, recognizing the increasing diversity of the child population and the specific needs that arise as a result. Engaging with families in an inclusive and reciprocal way can help providers understand a family's culture and values, which can inform the development of culturally responsive learning experiences.[59]

Family engagement often involves providing feedback on children's progress and discussing how parents can sustain learning activities at home.[60] This can take many forms, including regular parent–teacher conferences; daily communications between teachers and families, for example through daily report sheets and e-mails; monthly newsletters; parent-in-classroom events; family open nights; and other events intended to build a community that includes children, families, teachers, and program leaders. High-quality family engagement activities can help build trusting and positive relationships between teachers and families, which can help address any concerns—such as behavior problems or developmental delays—and better coordinate a response before issues become significant and affect children's learning.[61]

5. Multilevel Continuous Quality Improvement System

Achieving high quality in an early childhood program is not a onetime milestone. Programs must constantly monitor, reflect, and revise policies and practices to ensure that they maintain quality. In addition to measuring children's developmental progress, it is important that structures are also in place to assess the overall program, individual classrooms, and employees, using data to inform positive and proactive improvements.[62]

Quality 101: Identifying the Core Components of a High-quality Early Childhood Program by Simon Workman and Rebecca Ullrich

48

Given that data show many programs are not currently operating at high quality, it is critically important that quality improvement supports are available to help programs increase and then maintain quality.[63] Quality improvement supports can take many forms—including formal training opportunities, mentor programs, coaching, communities of practice, and informal networks of support—and can be accessed through state or national technical assistance providers or by local networks.[64] Most states have a QRIS, which can be a mechanism for directing quality improvement supports. In many QRIS, providers can access professional development and coaching opportunities and can receive financial incentives to purchase materials or equipment.[65] While QRIS offers a promising framework for accessing continuous quality improvement supports, these systems are still in the formative stages and are often under-resourced, resulting in supports being insufficient to sustain increased quality.

6. Sustainable and Sufficient Set of Funding Mechanisms

In order to support the highly qualified workforce, the safe and engaging physical and learning environment, and the stable business infrastructure necessary to achieve and maintain high quality, programs need to be able to access funding that supports the actual cost of operation.[66] Many public funding streams are insufficient to support the costs of high quality, and low- and middle-income families struggle to afford the cost of tuition at high-quality programs. In order to ensure high-quality programs are available to all children, public funding needs to be sufficient to cover the costs of quality and provide families with help to afford the cost of private tuition.

In addition, funding needs to be stable so that programs can make staffing and other business decisions based on anticipated income that is not subject to annual appropriations or fluctuations due to child absences. The total funding available to a program therefore needs to be adequate to cover the actual cost of operating at high quality and secure enough for programs to make plans beyond the short term.[67]

7. High Quality Should Be Accessible for All Children

These six elements are key to achieving and maintaining high quality in all early childhood settings. Given the huge variation in early childhood programs in the United States, there is not a one-size-fits-all approach to quality, and quality is not restricted to one program type. Family childcare homes, childcare centers—both for-profit and nonprofit—and public schools can all provide high-quality early childhood education for children of all ages. While targeted supports or modifications to

standards might be required to take into account specific circumstances, the focus on children's learning, development, and overall well-being can be maintained in all these childcare settings. For example:

- Curricula can be implemented for infants and toddlers, not just preschoolers.
- Family childcare providers could access quality improvement supports through family childcare provider networks.
- Small programs might access administrative supports through a shared services alliance.
- Rural private providers might partner with public schools or Head Start/Early Head Start programs to leverage services and supports.
- Providers serving predominantly low-income or dual language learners can tailor family engagement activities to take into account the unique needs of their populations.

Neither the demographic background of a child and family nor the type of facility in which the child is enrolled should be a barrier to accessing high-quality programs. However, programs need support to achieve and maintain quality. The six elements outlined above offer a roadmap to policy makers and stakeholders that allow them to focus on the key structures necessary to support high quality.

Conclusion

The need for high-quality early childhood education has never been greater, but programs are increasingly out of reach for a majority of Americans. As policy makers at the federal, state, and local levels develop strategies to address the childcare crisis, they must simultaneously focus on the importance of quality. To achieve the goal of increasing access to high-quality programs for all children, it is vital that families and policy makers fully understand what quality looks like and what structures are needed to support it. The quality indicators identified in this issue brief can serve as a roadmap for policy makers to ensure the key supports are in place to help programs achieve and maintain quality and to help families access those high-quality programs.

Acknowledgments

The authors would like to thank Harriet Dichter and Anne Mitchell for their insights and feedback on previous drafts of this issue brief, as well as our colleagues Katie Hamm and Rachel Herzfeldt-Kamprath at American Progress for their comments and edits.

Notes

1. Bureau of Labor Statistics, *Employment Characteristics of Families Summary* (U.S. Department of Labor, 2016), available at http://www.bls.gov/news.release/famee.nr0.htm; See, for example, Jorge Luis Garcia and others, "The Life-cycle Benefits of an Influential Early Childhood Program." HCEO Working Paper 2016-035 (The University of Chicago, 2016), available at https://econresearch.uchicago.edu/sites/econresearch.uchicago.edu/files/Garcia_Heckman_Leaf_etal_2016_life-cycle-benefits-ecp_r1.pdf.

2. Rasheed Malik and others, "Child Care Deserts: An Analysis of Child Care Centers by ZIP Code in 8 States" (Washington: Center for American Progress, 2016), available at https://www.americanprogress.org/issues/early-childhood/reports/2016/10/27/225703/child-care-deserts/; National Institutes of Health, *The NICHD Study of Early Child Care and Youth Development: Findings for Children up to Age 4 1/2 Years* (U.S. Department of Health and Human Services, 2016), available at https://www.nichd.nih.gov/publications/pubs/documents/seccyd_06.pdf.

3. Emily Parker, Bruce Atchison, and Emily Workman, "State Pre-K Funding for 2015–2016 Fiscal Year: National trends in state preschool funding" (Denver: Education Commission of the States, 2016), available at http://www.ecs.org/ec-content/uploads/01252016_Prek-K_Funding_report-4.pdf; Hillary for America, "Early Childhood Education," available at https://www.hillaryclinton.com/issues/early-childhood-education (last accessed September 2016); Donald J Trump for President, Inc., Fact Sheet: Donald J. Trump's New Child Care Plan," available at https://www.donaldjtrump.com/press-releases/fact-sheet-donald-j.-trumps-new-child-care-plan (last accessed September 2016).

4. For a compilation of evidence, see Coalition for Evidence-Based Policy, "Social Programs That Work: Prenatal/Early Childhood," available at http://evidencebasedprograms.org/about/early-childhood (last accessed October 2016); Hirokazu Yoshikawa and others, "Investing In Our Future: The Evidence Base on Preschool Education" (Ann Arbor, MI: Society for Research in Child Development; New York: Foundation for Child Development, 2013), available at http://www.srcd.org/sites/default/files/documents/washington/mb_2013_10_16_investing_in_children.pdf.

5. Harvard University Center on the Developing Child, "InBrief: The Science of Early Childhood Development" (2007), available at http://developingchild.harvard.edu/resources/inbrief-science-of-ecd/.

6. National Scientific Council on the Developing Child, "Young Children Develop in an Environment of Relationships." Working Paper 1 (Harvard University, 2004), available at http://developingchild.harvard.edu/wp-content/uploads/2004/04/Young-Children-Develop-in-an-Environment-of-Relation-ships.pdf.

7. Bureau of the Census, *Who's Minding the Kids? Child Care Arrangements: Spring 2011* (U.S. Department of Commerce, 2013), available at https://www.census.gov/prod/2013pubs/p70-135.pdf.

8. For a complication of evidence, see Coalition for Evidence-Based Policy, "Social Programs That Work"; Yoshikawa and others, "Investing in Our Future." While much of this research focused on preschool programs for three- and four-year-olds, a number of studies have demonstrated the benefits of early childhood programs for infants and toddlers. One of the most well respected and frequently cited studies—the Abecedarian Project—included children from birth to five-year-olds, and a National Institute of Child Health and Human Development study found positive effects on cognitive and language development for children six months and older who attended a childcare center. For more, see Coalition for Evidence-Based Policy, "Social Programs That Work: Abecedarian Project," available at http://evidencebased-programs.org/1366-2/abecedarian-project (last accessed September 2016); National Institutes of Health, *The NICHD Study of Early Child Care and Youth Development.*" In addition, numerous studies of home visiting programs—which focus on supports for pregnant women and young infants—have found long-term benefits, including significant gains in school readiness and achievement. See Washington State Institute for Public Policy, "Return on investment: Evidence-based options to improve statewide outcomes" (2012), available at http://www.wsipp.wa.gov/ReportFile/1102/Wsipp_Return-on-Investment-Evidence-Based-Options-to-Improve-Statewide-Outcomes-April-2012-Update_Full-Report.pdf; U.S. Department of Health and Human Services, Office of Child Care, "Child Development and School Readiness," available at http://homvee.acf.hhs.gov/Outcome/2/Child-Development-and-SchoolReadiness/3/1 (last accessed August 2016).

9. Lynn A. Karoly and James H. Bigelow, "The economics of investing in universal preschool education in California" (Santa Monica, CA: Rand Corporation, 2005), available at http://www.rand.org/content/dam/rand/pubs/mono-graphs/2005/RAND_MG349.pdf.

10. Yoshikawa and others, "Investing in Our Future."

11. Ibid.

12. National Center for Education Statistics, "Early Childhood Longitudinal Program (ECLS): Birth Cohort (ECLS-B)," available at https://nces.ed.gov/ecls/birth.asp (last accessed April 2016).

13. Jack P. Shonkoff and others, "The Lifelong Effects of Early Childhood Adversity and Toxic Stress," *Pediatrics* 129 (1) (2012), available at http://pediatrics.aappublications.org/content/129/1/e232.full.pdf; Amar Hamoudi and others, "Self-Regulation and Toxic Stress: A Review of Ecological, Biological, and Developmental Studies of Self-Regulation and Stress" (Washington: U.S. Department of Health and Human Services, 2015), available at https://www.acf.hhs.gov/sites/default/files/opre/acf_report_2_rev_022415_final_508.pdf; Harvard University Center on the Developing Child, "Tackling Toxic Stress," available at http://developingchild.harvard.edu/science/key-concepts/toxic-stress/tackling-toxic-stress/ (last accessed March 2016); Heather Sandstrom and Sandra Huerta, "The Negative Effects of Instability on Child Development:

A Research Synthesis" (Washington: Urban Institute, 2013), available at http://www.urban.org/sites/default/files/alfresco/publication-pdfs/412899-The-Negative-Effects-of-Instability-on-Child-Development-A-Research-Synthesis.PDF; Malik and others, "Child Care Deserts"; Patrice L. Engle and Maureen M. Black, "The Effect of Poverty on Child Development and Educational Outcomes" (San Luis Obispo, CA: California Polytechnic State University; Baltimore: University of Maryland Baltimore, 2008), available at http://digitalcommons.calpoly.edu/cgi/viewcontent.cgi?article=1002&context=psycd_fac; Federal Interagency Forum on Child and Family Statistics, *America's Children: Key National Indicators of Well-Being 2002* (U.S. Department of Commerce, 2002), available at https://www.childstats.gov/pdf/ac2002/ac_02.pdf.

14. Ross A. Thompson and Ron Haskins, "Early Stress Gets under the Skin: Promising Initiatives to Help Children Facing Chronic Adversity" (The Future of Children, 2014), available at http://futureofchildren.org/publications/docs/24_01_Policy_Brief.pdf.

15. Karen Schulman and W. Steven Barnett, "The Benefits of Prekindergarten for Middle-Income Children" Policy Report (New Brunswick, NJ: National Institute for Early Education Research, 2005) available at http://nieer.org/policy-issue/policy-report-the-benefits-of-prekindergarten-for-middle-income-children (last access October 2016); Marcia Meyers and more, "Inequality in Early Childhood Education and Care: What Do We Know?" In Kathryn M. Neckerman, ed., *Social Inequality* (New York: Russell Sage Foundation, 2004).

16. Jessica Troe, "Early Learning in the United States" (Washington: Center for American Progress, 2016), available at https://www.americanprogress.org/issues/early-childhood/report/2016/07/19/141234/early-learning-in-the-united-states/.

17. Head Start programs on average only have enough capacity to serve 4 in 10 eligible children. The federal childcare subsidy program, which subsidizes care for children from low-income families, only serves 1 in 6 eligible children. See The Heller School for Social Policy and Management, "Head Start's Capacity to Serve Eligible Low-Income Children," available at http://www.diversitydatakids.org/files/Policy/Head Start/Capacity/Participation POIs/Head Start's Capacity to Serve Eligible Low-Income Children.pdf; Office of the Assistant Secretary for Planning and Evaluation, *Estimates of Child Care Eligibility and Receipt for Fiscal Year 2011* (U.S. Department of Health and Human Services, 2015), available at https://aspe.hhs.gov/report/estimates-child-care-eligibility-and-receipt-fiscal-year-2011.

18. Danielle Ewen and Rachel Herzfeldt-Kamprath, "Examining Quality Across the Preschool-to-Third Grade Continuum" (Washington: Center for American Progress, 2016), available at https://www.americanprogress.org/issues/early-childhood/reports/2016/01/28/128439/examining-quality-across-the-preschool-to-third-grade-continuum/.

19. Katie Hamm, "Early Childhood." In Carmel Martin, Andy Green, and Brendan Duke, eds., "Raising Wages and Rebuilding Wealth: A Roadmap for Middle-Class Economic Security" (Washington: Center for American Progress, 2016) available at https://www.americanprogress.org/issues/economy/reports/2016/09/08/143585/raising-wages-and-rebuilding-wealth/.

20. Michael Madowitz, Alex Rowell, and Katie Hamm, "Calculating the Hidden Cost of Interrupting a Career for Child Care" (Washington: Center for American Progress, 2016), available at https://www.americanprogress.org/issues/early-child-hood/report/2016/06/21/139731/calculating-the-hidden-cost-of-interrupting-a-career-for-child-care/.

21. Licensing standards are typically related to items such as staff credential and training requirements; employee background checks; maximum group sizes and adult–child ratios; immunization requirements for children; and health and safety procedures, such as hand-washing, diapering, and maintaining daily attendance records. For more details, see Office of Child Care, Trends in Child Care Center Licensing Regulations and Policies for 2014, (U.S. Department of Health and Human Services, 2015), available at https://childcareta.acf.hhs.gov/resource/research-brief-1-trends-child-care-center-licensing-regulations-and-policies-2014.

22. Across all states, 15 percent of children receiving state childcare subsidies are enrolled in providers that are license-exempt. In eight states and territories, at least 35 percent of children participate in license-exempt providers. See Office of Child Care, *Supporting License-Exempt Family Child Care* (U.S. Department of Health and Human Services, 2015), available at https://childcareta.acf.hhs.gov/sites/default/files/public/supporting_exempt_fcc.pdf.

23. In this brief, the word "teacher" is used to describe the lead adult that is primarily responsible for the children in their care. As such, this term includes both center- and school-based teachers as well as family childcare providers.

24. Andrew J. Mashburn and others, "Measures of Classroom Quality in Prekindergarten and Children's Development of Academic, Language, and Social Skills" *Child Development* 79 (3) (2008): 732–749, available at http://files.webydo.com/175519/Masburn_CLASS.pdf.

25. Ibid.; Robert C. Pianta and Megan W. Stuhlman, "Teacher–Child Relationships and Children's Success in the First Years of School," *School Psychology Review* 33 (3) (2004): 444–458, available at http://pages.erau.edu/~andrewsa/Project_2/Christian_John/DuneProject/Teaching.pdf.

26. The National Center on Quality Teaching and Learning, "Improving Teacher–Child Interactions: Using the CLASS in Head Start Preschool Programs" (2013), available at http://eclkc.ohs.acf.hhs.gov/hslc/tta-system/teaching/docs/using-the-class.pdf.

27. Pianta and Stuhlman, "Teacher–Child Relationships and Children's Success in the First Years of School."

28. Rebecca Isbell, "An Environment that Positively Impacts Young Children," Earlychildhood News, available at http://www.earlychildhoodnews.com/earlychildhood/article_view.aspx?ArticleID=334 (last accessed September 2016).

29. TeacherVision, "Learning Centers," available at https://www. teachervision.com/learning-center/new-teacher/48462.html (last accessed October 2016); Gayle M. Stuber, "Centering Your Classroom: Setting the Stage for Engaged Learners" (National Association of Early Childhood Specialists in State Departments of Education, 2007), available at https://www. naeyc.org/files/yc/file/200707/OfPrimaryInterest.pdf.

30. Ingunn Fjortoft, "Landscape as Playscape: The Effects of Natural Environments on Children's Play and Motor Development" *Children, Youth and Environments* 14 (2) (2004): 21–44, available at http://www.springzaad.nl/litdocs/ landscape_as_playscape_the_effects_of_natural_environ-ments_on_childrens_play_and_motor_development.pdf.

31. Hillary L. Burdette and Robert C. Whitaker, "Resurrecting Free Play in Young Children: Looking Beyond Fitness and Fatness to Attention, Affiliation, and Affect," *JAMA Pediatrics* 159 (1) (2005): 46–50, available at http://archpedi.jamanet-work.com/ article.aspx?articleid=485902.

32. Charles Kivunja, "Leadership in Early Childhood Education Contexts: Looks, Roles, and Functions" *Creative Education* 6 (2015): 1710–1717, available at http://file.scirp.org/pdf/ CE_2015091611423350.pdf.

33. Elliot Regenstein and Katherine Lipper, "A Framework for Choosing a State-Level Early Childhood Governance System" (Boston: BUILD Initiative, 2013), available at http://www. buildinitiative.org/Portals/0/Uploads/Documents/Early%20 Childhood%20Governance%20for%20Web.pdf; Julia Coffman, "A Framework for Evaluating Systems Initiatives" (Boston: BUILD Initiative, 2007), available at http://www.buildinitiative. org/Portals/0/Uploads/Documents/Framework%20for%20 Evaluating%20Systems%20Initia-tives.pdf.

34. University of North Carolina at Chapel Hill, Frank Porter Graham Child Development Institute, "Environment Rating Scales," available at http://ers.fpg.unc.edu/ (last accessed September 2016).

35. Teachstone, "CLASS Domains & Dimensions," available at http://teachstone.com/classroom-assessment-scoring-system/ class-domains-dimensions/ (last accessed September 2016).

36. Among the most well-known accreditation bodies are the National Association for the Education of Young Children, the National Early Childhood Program Accreditation, the National Accreditation Commission for Early Care and Education Programs, the National Association for Family Child Care, the Council on Accreditation, and the American Montessori Society.

37. National Center on Child Care Quality Improvement, *National Accreditation Organizations for Early Childhood Programs* (U.S. Department of Health and Human Services, 2011), pp. 1–3, available at https://qrisguide.acf.hhs.gov/files/National_ Accred.pdf.

38. U.S. Department of Health and Human Services, National Center on Early Childhood Quality Assurance, "National

Program Standards Crosswalk Tool," available at https://qris-guide.acf.hhs.gov/crosswalk/ (last accessed October 2016).

39. QRIS National Learning Network, "Current Status of QRIS in States: January 2017," available at http://qrisnetwork.org/sites/ all/files/maps/QRISMap_0.pdf (last accessed February 2017).

40. Anne W. Mitchell, "Stair Steps to Quality: A Guide for States and Communities Developing Quality Rating Systems for Early Care and Education" (United Way, 2005), available at http://www.earlychildhoodfinance.org/downloads/2005/ MitchStairSteps_2005.pdf.

41. For example, employee background checks and first aid training, adult–child ratios and safe equipment, and environmental health standards. For more, see Early Childhood Development Interagency Coordination, *Caring for our Children Basics: Health and Safety Foundations for Early Care and Education* (U.S. Department of Health and Human Services, 2015), available at http://www.acf.hhs.gov/sites/ default/files/ecd/caring_for_our_children_basics.pdf.

42. Institute of Medicine and National Research Council, "Transforming the Workforce for Children Birth Through Age 8: A Unifying Foundation" (Washington: The National Academies Press, 2015), available at http://www.nap.edu/catalog/19401/ transforming-the-workforce-for-children-birth-through-age-8-a.

43. Marcy Whitebrook, Deborah Phillips, and Carollee Howes, "Worthy Work, STILL Unlivable Wages: The Early Childhood Workforce 25 Years after the National Child Care Staffing Study" (Berkeley, CA: Center for the Study of Child Care Employment, 2014), available at http://cscce.berkeley.edu/ files/2014/ReportFINAL.pdf; National Institute for Early Education Research, "Preschool Policy Matters," Issue 2, December 2004, available at http://nieer.org/wp-content/ uploads/2016/08/2.pdf.

44. National Association for the Education of Young Children, "Teacher–Child Ratio Chart," available at http://www.naeyc. org/academy/files/academy/file/Teacher_Child_Ratio_Chart. pdf (last accessed January 2017).

45. Organisation for Economic Co-operation and Development, "Encouraging Quality in Early Childhood Education and Care (ECEC), Research Brief: Working Conditions Matter," available at http://www.oecd.org/education/school/49322250.pdf (last accessed September 2016).

46. Mary E. Dilworth and Marcus J. Coleman "Time for a Change: Diversity in Teaching Revisited" (Washington: National Education Association, 2014), available at http://www.nea. org/assets/docs/Time_for_a_Change_Diversity_in_Teaching_ Revisited_(web).pdf; Leo Casey and others, "The State of Teacher Diversity in American Education" (Washington: Albert Shanker Institute, 2015), available at http://www. shankerinstitute.org/resource/teacherdiversity.

47. Mary L. Culkin, "Administrative Leadership." In Sharon L. Kagan and Barbara T. Bowman, eds., *Leadership in Early*

Quality 101: Identifying the Core Components of a High-quality Early Childhood Program by Simon Workman and Rebecca Ullrich

52

Care and Education (Washington: National Association for the Education of Young Children, 1997).

48. Denise M. Scott, "Early Childhood Leaders on Leadership" (Washington: National Association for the Education of Young Children, 2005), available at https://www.naeyc.org/files/yc/file/200501/Scott.pdf.

49. Data from the National Survey of Early Care & Education shows that nearly 60 percent of teachers and caregivers work in a nonpublic setting and only 16 percent of children enrolled in center-based early childhood programs are attending a program run by a government agency. See National Survey of Early Care and Education, "Number and Characteristics of Early Care and Education (ECE) Teachers and Caregivers: Initial Findings from the National Survey of Early Care and Education (NSECE)" (2013), available at http://www.acf.hhs.gov/sites/default/files/opre/nsece_wf_brief_102913_0.pdf; National Survey of Early Care and Education, "Characteristics of Center-based Early Care and Education Programs," available at http://www.acf.hhs.gov/sites/default/files/opre/characteristics_of_cb_fact_sheet_final_111014.pdf (last accessed October 2016); Alliance for Early Childhood Finance, "The Iron Triangle: A Simple Formula for Financial Policy in ECE Programs," available at http://www.earlychildhoodfinance.org/downloads/2010/IronTriangle_10.2010.pdf (last accessed October 2016).

50. Clive R. Belfield, "The Fiscal Impacts of Universal Pre-K: Case Study Analysis for Three States." Working Paper 6 (Flushing, NY: Queens College, 2006), available at http://citeseerx.ist.psu.edu/viewdoc/download?doi=10.1.1.603.4632&rep=rep1&type=pdf.

51. For example, some programs have an educational coordinator or identify master teachers, in addition to the program director, while others employ business managers to handle the administrative side of the program.

52. National Association for the Education of Young Children and the National Association of the Early Childhood Specialists in State Departments of Education, "Early Childhood Curriculum, Assessment, and Program Evaluation," available at http://www.naeyc.org/files/naeyc/file/positions/pscape.pdf (last accessed September 2015).

53. Stacie G. Goffin, "The Role of Curriculum Models in Early Childhood Education" (Champaign, IL: ERIC Clearinghouse on Elementary and Early Childhood Education, 2000), available at http://files.eric.ed.gov/fulltext/ED443597.pdf.

54. The National Center on Quality Teaching and Learning, "Preschool Curriculum Consumer Report" (2015), available at https://eclkc.ohs.acf.hhs.gov/hslc/tta-system/teaching/practice/docs/curriculum-consumer-report.pdf.

55. Greg J. Duncan and others, "Boosting School Readiness: Should Preschools Target Skills or the Whole Child?" (Irvine, CA: Irvine Network on Interventions in Development, 2015), available at http://inid.gse.uci.edu/files/2011/03/Duncan_etal_Preschool_JHRsubmit.pdf; Yoshikawa and others, "Investing in Our Future."

56. Desalyn De-Souza, "Infant & Toddler Curriculum & Individualization" (2015), available at http://www.nysecac.org/files/3614/2184/7874/Infant_Toddler_Curriculum_NYS_Infancy_Conference_Curriculum.pdf.

57. The National Center on Quality Teaching and Learning, "Preschool Curriculum Consumer Report."

58. Linda C. Halgunseth and others, "Family Engagement, Diverse Families, and Early Childhood Education Programs: An Integrated Review of the Literature" (Washington: National Association for the Education of Young Children; The Pew Charitable Trusts, 2009), available at https://www.naeyc.org/files/naeyc/file/research/FamEngage.pdf.

59. *Policy Statement on Family Engagement: From the Early Years to the Early Grades* (U.S. Department of Health and Human Services and U.S. Department of Education, 2016), available at https://www2.ed.gov/about/inits/ed/earlylearning/files/policy-statement-on-family-engagement.pdf.

60. Linda C. Halgunseth and others, "Family Engagement, Diverse Families, and Early Childhood Education Programs."

61. The National Center on Parent, Family, and Community Engagement, *Understanding Family Engagement Outcomes: Research to Practice Series, Families as Lifelong Educators* (U.S. Department of Health and Human Services, 2016), available at http://eclkc.ohs.acf.hhs.gov/hslc/tta-system/family/docs/rtp-series-families-as-lifelong-educators.pdf.

62. Debi Mathias, "Chapter 8: Impact of the Early Learning Challenge on State Quality Rating and Improvement Systems." In BUILD Initiative, *Rising to the Challenge: Building Effective Systems for Young Children and Families*, available at http://www.buildinitiative.org/Portals/0/Uploads/Documents/Chapter8Mathias.pdf (last accessed August 2016).

63. Kathryn Tout and others, "A Blueprint for Early Care and Education Quality Improvement Initiatives: Final Report" (Minneapolis: Child Trends, Inc., 2015) available at http://www.childtrends.org/wp-content/uploads/2015/03/2015-07BlueprintEarlyCareandEd.pdf.

64. QRIS National Learning Network, "Continuous Quality Improvement Framework—Supported Resources and Initiative," available at http://qrisnetwork.org/sites/all/files/materials/Continuous%20Quality%20Improvement%20Framework%20-%20Supported%20Resources%20and%20Initiatives_0.docx (last accessed November 2016).

65. QRIS Compendium, "A Catalog and Comparison of Quality Rating and Improvement Systems (QRIS)," available at http://qriscompendium.org/ (last accessed October 2016).

66. groundWork Ohio, "The Dollars and Cents of Early Learning: Investing in Success" (2016), available at http://www.early-childhoodfinance.org/dev/wp-content/uploads/2016/03/Dollars-and-Cents-FINAL-031416.pdf; Louise Stoney, "Financing High-Quality Center-Based Infant-Toddler Care: Options and Opportunities" (Fairfax, VA: ICF International, 2015), available at https://earlyeducatorcentral.acf.hhs.gov/sites/default/

files/public/resources/Financing%20High%20Quality%20
Center%20Based%20Infant%20Toddler%20Care%20
Options%20and%20Opportunities.pdf.

67. Alliance for Early Childhood Finance, "The Iron Triangle:
A Simple Formula for Financial Policy in ECE Programs,"
available at http://www.earlychildhoodfinance.org/down-
loads/2010/IronTriangle_10.2010.pdf (last accessed October
2016); Margie Wallen and Angela Hubbard, "Blending and
Braiding Early Childhood Program Funding Streams Toolkit:
Enhancing Financing for High-Quality Early Learning
Programs" (Chicago: Ounce of Prevention Fund, 2013)
available at www.theounce.org/pubs/policy-pubs/NPT-Blended-
Funding-Toolkit.pdf.

Critical Thinking

1. What are the most important criteria to consider when
evaluating an early childhood setting?

2. Describe three of the components of an effective early
childhood curriculum.

Internet References

Six Keys to Maintain a High-Quality Early Childhood Program
https://www.waterford.org/keys-to-high-quality-early-childhood-program/

The Building Blocks of High-Quality Early Childhood Education Programs
https://learningpolicyinstitute.org/product/building-blocks-high-quality-early-childhood-education-programs

The 10 NAEYC Program Standards
https://families.naeyc.org/accredited-article/10-naeyc-program-standards

SIMON WORKMAN is the Associate Director of Early Childhood Policy
at the Center for American Progress.

REBECCA ULLRICH is a Policy Analyst for the Early Childhood Policy
team at the Center.

Workman, Simon; Ullrich, Rebecca, "Quality 101: Identifying the Core Components of a High-Quality Early Childhood Program," Center for American Progress, February 13, 2017.
This article was created by the Center for American Progress (www.americanprogress.com). Used with permission.

Article   Prepared by: Chris J. Boyatzis, *Bucknell University* and
Ellen N. Junn, *California State University, Stanislaus*

What Homeschooling Actually Looks Like

Most parents don't plan to homeschool their kids. Many decide to try this method later on for a variety of reasons.

SARAH RIVERA

Learning Outcomes

After reading this article, you will be able to:

- Appreciate the personal reasons some families have for removing their children from public education and home-schooling them instead.

- Understand the difference between so-called "first choice" and "second choice" homeschoolers.

- Describe some differences in states' requirements for homeschooling.

Why Some Take the Plunge

"I *never* thought I would do it. I really enjoyed school," said Cyndi Miller, a mother who taught her daughter, Aurelia, at home from sixth to eighth grade. "I had a lot of respect for teachers. I'd worked as a substitute."

Because of a move, her daughter was going to have to change schools in sixth grade and asked her mom to teach her at home just for a year until junior high. The district they lived in had notoriously bad junior highs, so they stuck with homeschooling.

Cyndi was concerned about the social aspects of middle school, as well. "I envisioned her having a hard time peer-wise. I dreaded that whole middle school experience for her." Aurelia was studious and shy, and while mature, she was still very much a child. People warned Cyndi that homeschooling would make her daughter socially awkward, particularly when

she went on to public high school after being homeschooled for several years; but the opposite proved true.

"She developed a real sense of confidence. She really embraced herself." When Aurelia got to high school, she found a good group of friends. She was in honors programs and achieved a 4.0 GPA. Initially, Aurelia was intimidated by the size of the school, but she managed to get used to it.

Grades were hard for her, too. "She'd come home with a 95 percent and be disappointed," said the Cyndi.

Another family decided that they had to get out of the education rat race.

"Living in New York City, there is a huge pressure to get your kid into the right school, and it starts when you are pregnant. [There] is this insanity for both public and private school. We just felt like we weren't going to enjoy our children's childhood if we were worrying about their future all the time," said Leslie Burby, a mother of two who lives in New York City.

She and her husband also had learned from others' experiences at competitive schools. "We had friends who had eight-year-olds. They were having three-hour homework assignments in elementary school," said Leslie. "Homework in those days [ten years ago] was a good thing. Parents saw it as getting their kids ready for Harvard."

They also were concerned about how their son, Henry, now a homeschooled high school senior, would do in kindergarten. He had a huge vocabulary, but no interest in reading or learning to read. He was an "advanced thinker," but not a reader. As it was, they read to him *a lot*. He started reading when he was nine. "He was able to do it [at] his own pace." Henry scored a 770 on his verbal SAT and is applying to honors programs in college for next fall.

Another couple living in a highly regarded school district was told by classroom volunteers that their sons spent most of their school days reading because they finished their assignments so quickly. They took their boys out of school and started teaching them at a pace that challenged them. They relied heavily on online courses, such as those offered by Khan Academy, and also enrolled their kids in classes at the local community college.

First Choice vs. Second Choice Homeschoolers

The above cases involve parents who make the choice to homeschool because their kids are highly motivated and their schools don't meet their children's needs. These kinds of engaged parents are termed second choice homeschoolers, because their first choice was sending their kids to a school. First choice homeschoolers are parents who want to homeschool their kids from the get-go, for pedagogical or religious reasons.

"[Homeschooling] used to be an act of dissent," said Rachel Coleman, executive director of the Coalition for Responsible Home Education (CHRE). "It's now just seen as one more educational option." Coleman and other former homeschooled children founded CHRE to advocate for basic safeguards for the social and educational well-being of children.

As more families join the homeschool movement, it gets easier to find support. There are a great variety of online curricula. Many schools are allowing homeschooled kids to take individual classes at schools and join clubs as well as sports teams.

State Requirements

According to the National Home Education Research Institute, about 2.2 million students—three percent of all school-age children—are homeschooled. Homeschoolers are a fast-growing education sector. There is talk that the Common Core is also driving some parents out of the schools, as they seek to avoid what they view as a one-size-fits-all educational trend.

Most homeschooling parents aren't able to test their children to gauge how they are doing. One parent wanted to administer a state assessment to her daughter, but the school district wouldn't allow it because they said the tests were just for school students.

The requirements for homeschooling vary by state. Families can find out what requirements there are where they live through the Home School Legal Defense Association.

"You can literally do nothing," said Cyndi. She submitted her lesson plans and certification, all of which were returned to her. She was told that the only thing they needed was the signed form. Cyndi knew a mother who called her year of homeschooling her elementary-aged son "the year of G.I. Joe" because the child didn't want any schooling, even at home, and spent most of his time playing with his G.I. Joe toys. Another homeschooling family had a strong emphasis on gardening. *Only gardening.*

Coleman said these situations are not uncommon in homeschooling. One girl said that her parents hadn't taught her anything beyond fourth-grade content. Another boy reported that his mother tried to teach him algebra when he was 14 but gave up, and his math studies went no further. Beyond that, some parents use homeschooling to isolate and abuse children. While these are certainly the worst-case scenarios, they do underscore the fact that there is often little oversight for homeschooling families. While some parents teach their middle schoolers calculus, others may allow their children's math abilities to languish.

Finding Materials

For many homeschooling families, the homeschooling setting enables them to tailor their teaching to their children's needs.

Still, many new homeschooling parents have anxiety about providing clear and comprehensive instruction. "The one variable that people talk about is structure, especially their first year or two," said Brian Ray, president of the National Home Education Research Institute (NHERI) based in Salem, Oregon, which advocates for homeschooling.

Most start with a curriculum package at home and then start adding different bits as they go along and learn the ropes. The Burbys tried the online courses, but their kids missed human interaction.

Cyndi researched textbooks and found highly regarded, rigorous curricula. "We didn't get away from textbooks," she said.

Playing the Roles of Teacher and Parent

It's not easy for parents to assume the role of teacher.

"I have heard a lot of parents say, 'No way, I couldn't be patient enough [to homeschool],'" said Ray, a parent who opted to homeschool his kids. "It is going to change you as a parent. It is going to reveal some weaknesses in your character." He said he often finds parents who say that they—the parents—are having a blast studying history as they teach it. They find they have better relationships with their kids because they are also their teachers. There is no confusion about what a child is learning and what is going on at school.

"I put a lot of hours into reading ahead of her, making my own notes," [said] Cyndi, who works full-time.

Summers and weekends are no longer school-free for homeschooling families. They are often used as additional time for other lessons. Leslie met with other homeschooling mothers ("it's usually the moms") in her neighborhood for two hours each week to plan their homeschooling agendas. They developed intensive curricula around things such as the Silk Road and Greek and Roman history. They followed state guidelines with about six other families and spent at least one day a week together, during which they would give their kids a classroom experience.

"We didn't let them lie on the floor," she said. They worked out how they should speak in the group, whether raising hands or just waiting for a turn to speak. They would take field trips to museums and art classes, and they would avail their kids of educational programs that were funded through endowments.

Both of the mothers worked extensively with their children on writing.

"You are still their primary English teacher," said Leslie.

Cyndi said they worked on poetry, short stories, and essays. Her daughter learned very quickly that if she handed in something that wasn't up to par, her mother would make her re-do it. She said she didn't just give her a grade, never to address the assignment again. On the contrary, each assignment "was more how it works in the real world," she said. You don't get grades; you get suggestions for revisions. "She would do it again, and she would surpass my expectations."

The Burbys also had a younger son, Henry, who wanted to go to public high school. He got into a music-oriented school and was there for a year. Although he found it hard to get to school by 7:30 A.M. to get through the metal detectors, to have lunch at 10:30 A.M., and to receive instruction in the school's basement, he enjoyed negotiating New York City on his own and making a diverse group of friends.

He ultimately lasted just a year at the school and decided to go back to homeschooling. He seemed to have a different take on school than many of his peers; he thought that being at school was a privilege and learning was fun. Henry felt that his homeschooling group saw education in the same way he did and preferred taking classes with them. He also found many of his classmates disrespectful in their interactions with teachers. Even though he left the school, he still hangs out with his old high school friends. He's re-reading "Catch 22" because, as he tells it, he missed so much of it the first time around. "He's so excited by it. He wants to read it aloud to us," his mother said.

Sources

Coalition for Responsible Home Education. "The Case for Oversight." Retrieved from Coalition for Responsibile Home Education.

Coalition for Responsible Home Education. "How Have Scholars Divided Homeschoolers into Groups." Retrieved from Coalition for Responsible Home Education.

Home School Legal Defense Association "My State." Retrieved from Home School Legal Defense Association.

National Center for Educational Statistics. "Fast Facts: Homeschooling." Retrieved from National Center for Education Statistics.

Ray, Brian D. "Research Facts on Homeschooling." Jan. 1, 2014. National Home Education Research Institute. Retrieved from National Home Education Research Institute.

Critical Thinking

1. How does this article help you understand the varied reasons why parents would want to homeschool their children? Would you want to homeschool your child? What are some pros and cons for doing so?

2. How does this article help you appreciate the challenges parents face in their dual role of "teacher" and "parent"?

Internet References

Association for Supervision and Curriculum Development, ASCD
http://www.ascd.org/publications/educational-leadership/sept94/vol52/num01/Why-Parents-Choose-Home-Schooling.aspx

EducationWeek.org
http://www.edweek.org/ew/issues/home-schooling/

Homeschool.com
http://www.homeschool.com/

NationalHomeEducationResearchInstitute.com
http://www.nheri.org/research/research-facts-on-homeschooling.html

PublicSchools.org
http://www.publicschools.org/homeschooling-pros-cons/

Article

Prepared by: Chris J. Boyatzis, *Bucknell University* and
Ellen N. Junn, *California State University, Stanislaus*

Why the Danes Encourage Their Kids to Swing Axes, Play with Fire, and Ride Bikes in Traffic

JENNY ANDERSON

Learning Outcomes

After reading this article, you will be able to:

- Describe the Danes' attitudes about free play for children and how they set up play activities for their children. Why do they advocate that their children engage in free play activities considered my many in America to be dangerous (e.g., playing with saws, building fires).

- Cite the positive outcomes that these Danish free play activities have for their children.

- What other societal benefits and perks does the Danish government provide to their parents that may also produce positive outcomes for their children?

Heidi Vikkelsø Nielsen needed to find an image to show what childhood looks like in her country. The former teacher and current professor of education in Denmark settled on one of a young girl gleefully wielding a very sharp saw. "I think it captures perfectly how we think about childhood," she says.

Adults appreciate that children learn by doing, not by being taught, she adds. So adults—both teachers and parents—generally get out of the way to let children do what they love: run, jump, climb, dig, hide, run, and, apparently, do some light carpentry.

At a forest playground on the outskirts of Copenhagen, kids are encouraged to build fires. At an urban playground in the city, kids cycle around a mini-version of Copenhagen with kid-sized bike lanes, pint-sized street lights, and mini-walkways. As a

school principal told Nielsen: "We are trying to embrace the child in an adult world."

As many university heads, school reformers, and fed-up parents clamor for more free play for children, Denmark offers an appealing example of what child-led care and early education looks like. Independence is favored over "learning," care is emphasized over "teaching," and over-supervision—helicoptering—is considered a sure-fire path to preventing kids from acquiring essential life skills.

We don't want to disturb the child with all this learning.

"There's a high focus on play especially, free play," says Nielsen. When you walk into a *vuggestue* (nursery) or *dagpleje* (daycare), caregivers are hands-off, with less structured activity and more child-led exploring. This is different from many UK and US early-care systems, which often prioritize school readiness, making kids spend more time at desks learning numbers and letters, which means less time doing whatever catches their fancy. In Denmark, "academic learning is almost frowned upon," Nielsen notes. "We don't want to disturb the child with all this learning."

Nature plays a significant role, with natural materials prominent in Danish playgrounds, instead of all the plastic and rubber often used elsewhere. Risky play is encouraged, and injuries almost expected. There is a distinction between getting hurt and seriously hurt, though. "I think a broken arm is seriously hurt," Nielsen says.

"Bruises are seen as how you experience life," she explains. "You fall, you get up." Professionals would not be punished—or sued—for a child coming home with the requisite bumps and bruises of childhood.

Tim Gill, author of *No Fear: Growing up in a risk averse society* and a long-time play advocate in the UK, says Copenhagen and other Danish cities are leading the way internationally to create distinctive, challenging public playgrounds and schoolyards. "Water, fallen trees, hillocks [berms], ditches and other risky elements are common ingredients," he says. The approach reflects Danes' love of nature and their desire for children to interact with it. "The Danes trust their children to take responsibility for themselves from an early age, with spaces that feed children's appetite for adventure and nurture their resilience and self-reliance."

Some playgrounds are staffed, so there are adults to bring out equipment for kids and show them how to use it. "They manage items like bikes, axes, or balls," says Jeff Risom, chief innovation officer at Gehl Architects in Copenhagen. "There's a teaching element," he notes, like showing kids how to use a knife for whittling or an ax to chop wood.

Danes come from a starting point that children need to play, so schools and the government find ways to create structures that encourage this, from building playgrounds and public spaces that encourage risky play, to providing after-school care that focuses on freedom, not skills to get into university or a high-paying job. Indeed, some CEOs now argue that more free play is exactly what kids will need to survive and thrive in the age of AI, when machines do the computations and humans will be needed to be, well, human.

Institutions Matter

Nielsen admits that it's not just the country's prevailing philosophy that makes Denmark's approach so novel: it's the role of the welfare state. For one thing, parents are paid, quarterly, for having children, on a sliding scale that diminishes with age, up until the child turns 17.

Maternity leave starts four weeks before birth, continues for 14 weeks after birth, and then another 32 weeks can be shared between partners. Fathers get two weeks of paternity and whatever is chosen to share. A nurse comes to check up on new mothers at home, and support is offered to those who struggle with breastfeeding.

By age one, most children go into care, which is affordable, local, high-quality and hands-off. It is even cheaper if you are poorer, or parenting alone. Even private schools are subsidized, with 71% of the cost covered.

As a result, Denmark has one of the highest female labor participation rates in the world—76.1%, according to the OECD. "The concept of a stay-at-home-mother does not really exist in Denmark due to parental leave system," says Nielsen.

When kids enter school in Denmark, they can sign up for after-school clubs that keep them occupied until parents are done with work. Rather than hone their piano, math, or Mandarin skills, these clubs also simply let children play.

On a windy Monday afternoon at a playground outside of the Guldberg school in Nørrebro, one of Copenhagen's poorer neighborhoods, children are jumping on small trampolines and talking to us strangers—what are we looking at, why are we here, and would we like to see them bicycle full speed? They climb on high structures and most are not wearing coats. "They know if they are cold," says Nielsen. There are no grownups around; in the corner of the playground, there is a building which houses the after-school club. Our guide says the adults are inside.

Child's Play

Research supports Denmark's approach. Meghan Talarowski, an American landscape designer, conducted a massive study on playground use in the US and UK, using video to track how 18,000 visitors used the playgrounds. Comparing playgrounds of similar size (one-quarter to three-quarters of an acre) and population density (50,000 to 175,000 people in a square mile area) in London, San Francisco, Los Angeles, and New York, she discovered that the London playgrounds had 55% more visitors, 14% more adults, and children and teens were 16–18% more physically active. One reason, she concluded, was that the London playgrounds used more natural materials and promoted riskier play.

"Besides accommodating adults, the London playgrounds think outside the box," her report concluded. "They use diverse materials and non-prescriptive, riskier play structures that lead to lower costs and lower injury rates than U.S. playgrounds, which is counter intuitive, given our intense focus on safety in the last few decades."

American playgrounds, she countered, have reached "peak safety." "We have created a nation of overly expensive, homogeneously safe, and insidiously boring play spaces," she wrote. In her study, half of the children studied were found in just four areas: climbing, swinging, or in sand or grass.

Gill, the author, reflects on numerous reports published this autumn concluding that girls in the UK are less happy than they used to be, and wonders whether a lack of choice may be at the heart of their growing unhappiness. "We know children value their everyday freedoms and choices," he says, referencing the 2013 Children's Society Good Childhood studies, which showed that simply having choice in life had the highest correlation to kids' reported well-being. Indeed, studies suggest children have less everyday freedom than they used to. "I think it's entirely reasonable to think that—amongst other things—less everyday freedom means less happy children," Gill says.

Glorifying social care and education systems in small, rich, homogenous countries like Denmark can be both instructive and annoying. Every country must adapt to its own reality, and nobody has got it exactly right.

For her part, Nielsen thinks Denmark's hands-off approach in the early years, when children are learning to negotiate social settings, can be problematic. Some kids, including those from poorer backgrounds, she argues, may not have well-developed social skills; without guidance, they might fail to develop it. "It is almost like a lord of the flies," she says.

Denmark's education system is also rarely extolled as being a global leader, like Finland's or Estonia's. The state spends a lot of money to get mediocre international test results. But new OECD research (pdf) shows educational social mobility is relatively high, meaning the poorest kids have a shot at getting a good education, unlike in many other places, where neighborhoods determine students' destinies. The other advantage Danish children have in their crucial early years is the time, and space, to just play.

Critical Thinking

1. Do you think that if Americans adopted the Danish model of free play that includes activities with dangerous elements (such as building fires, playing with saws) that it would work in this country? Why or why not?

2. If you moved in Denmark, would you like to have your children learn to engage in the Danish free play activities described in this article? Explain why or why not.

3. Based on the research presented in this article, compare and contrast the playgrounds and activities found in Denmark, London and the United States. What the benefits and possible negative consequences of these differences?

Internet References

The Junk Playground of New York City
https://www.theatlantic.com/education/archive/2016/08/the-junk-playground-of-new-york-city/495371/

"Junk playgrounds" show the value of free play for kids (Video)
https://www.treehugger.com/culture/junk-playgrounds-show-value-free-play-kids-plas-madoc-guardian.html

Landing Lightly: Playgrounds Don't Have to Hurt
https://www.nsc.org/home-safety/safety-topics/child-safety/playgrounds

Save Emdrup Adventure Playground | Love Outdoor Play
https://rethinkingchildhood.com/tag/denmark/

Social and Emotional Development

Prepared by: Chris J. Boyatzis, *Bucknell University* and
Ellen N. Junn, *California State University, Stanislaus*

UNIT

Social and Emotional Development

One of the truisms about our species is that we are social animals. From birth, each person's life is a constellation of relationships, from family at home to friends in the neighborhood, school, the community, and beyond. This unit addresses how children's social and emotional development is influenced by important relationships with parents, peers, and teachers.

When John Donne in 1623 wrote, "No man is an island, entire of itself . . . any man's death diminishes me, because I am involved in mankind," he implied that all humans are connected to each other and that these connections make us who we are. Early in this century, sociologist C. H. Cooley highlighted the importance of relationships with the phrase "looking-glass self" to describe how people tend to see themselves as a function of how others perceive them. Personality theorist Alfred Adler, also writing in the early 20th century, claimed that personal strength derived from the quality of one's connectedness to others: The stronger the relationships, the stronger the person. The notion that a person's self-concept arises from relations with others also has roots in developmental psychology. As Jean Piaget once wrote, "There is no such thing as isolated individuals; there are only relations." The articles in this unit respect these traditions by emphasizing the theme that a child's emotional and social development occurs within the context of relationships.

Consequently, this second unit highlights the significant milestone of early childhood involving a child's ability to interact effectively with peers, socialize, communicate successfully, begin to understand ethics and morality, and play effectively with peers. Many studies now point to the importance of encouraging children to engage in reflective, mindful, kind, peaceful, and contemplative behaviors that ideally should include nature or outdoor activities and environments. Other studies focus on understanding how culture and healthy peer interaction can deeply shape children's socio-emotional well-being and how adults and teachers can serve as models for caring and pro-social behavior for children. Unfortunately, a variety of other factors may pose challenges for young children, such as growing up poor or minority, suffering from childhood trauma, being shy, being bullied, or coping with other environmental pressures. Children who face these challenges may suffer negative outcomes in later childhood and even adulthood, but new interventions, programs, and a better understanding of protective factors are making it possible and easier for educators, parents, and professionals to help ameliorate these negative conditions for children.

Thus, our hope is that the research and stories in this section will provide teachers, parents, and others with guidance and information on how they might better safeguard and enhance the future success of their children and students to help in building a stronger social–emotional understanding of themselves and others.

Early Sympathy and Social Acceptance Predict the Development of Sharing in Children by Tina Malti et al.

62

Article

Prepared by: Chris J. Boyatzis, *Bucknell University* and
Ellen N. Junn, *California State University, Stanislaus*

Early Sympathy and Social Acceptance Predict the Development of Sharing in Children

TINA MALTI ET AL.

Learning Outcomes

After reading this article, you will be able to:

- Identify how sympathy develops in childhood and describe sex differences in the behavior.

- Analyze how sympathy may be related to altruistic behaviors and antisocial behaviors.

Introduction

Sharing is a fascinating activity of the human species and a focus of interest in various disciplines including psychology, economics, and evolutionary science. It exemplifies the willingness to take the welfare of others into account and thus represents "other-regarding" preferences [1]. Investigating the developmental antecedents of such "other-regarding" preferences will ultimately help in understanding the roots of fairness, caring, and cooperation in human social interaction [1], [2]. Here we use sharing resources with anonymous others as an empirical indicator of "other-regarding" preferences [1] and one subtype of prosocial behavior.

Prosocial behaviors have been studied by psychologists for decades [3]. Most of these studies have focused on other forms of prosocial behavior, such as children's instrumental or altruistic helping or providing emotional support for needy others. These behaviors are either measured experimentally [4], [5] or assessed through observations [6], parent reports or teacher reports [7], [8]. More recently the behavioral economics approach of evaluating sharing with anonymous others, such as the Dictator Game, has become an interdisciplinary paradigm to

study other-regarding preferences [9], [10]. Sharing resources with anonymous others, like other forms of prosocial behavior (e.g., instrumental or altruistic helping), is based on a concern for others' needs and goals and the motivation to assist them [11]. Yet, sharing resources with anonymous others in the Dictator Game incurs real tangible costs for the actor, whereas the efforts associated with measures of prosocial behavior are generally low-cost (see [12]). Furthermore, whereas many experimental, observational, and questionnaire measures of prosocial behavior cannot be easily operationalized for different age groups, the strength of using the behavioral economic paradigm lies in the fact that the same experimental instrument (i.e., the Dictator Game) can be used across wide range of age groups which maximizes the ability to draw meaningful comparisons across development [13]. Because proposers in a one-shot dictator game only interact once with an anonymous other player who cannot reciprocate or punish in a future round of the game, their positive offers have been interpreted as altruistic or have been attributed to their fairness concerns [13].

Only a few experiments have investigated children's other-regarding preferences in this paradigm [9], [10], [14], [15], and whether younger children are self-serving or prefer equality in resource allocations is still debated [10], [16] . A recent experiment examining sharing has shown that 7- to 8-year- olds, but not 3- to 4-year olds, prefer equal resource allocations when sharing with friends and acquaintances [1]. There have not been any empirical studies that have examined the social-emotional antecedents of children's sharing resources with anonymous others.

All of the studies that assessed sharing resources with behavioral economic tasks, such as the Dictator Game, have relied on cross-sectional data sets composed of children who vary in age. Thus, although there is some limited evidence that children's other-regarding preferences increase from early-to-middle childhood, it is not known if this developmental increase applies to all children equally or if some children have these preferences from early on. If the latter is true, it remains an open and intriguing question in what characteristics children with early-existing other-regarding preferences might differ from children who develop these preferences in middle childhood.

In order to measure how children's willingness to share resources with others develops over time, and to understand which factors influence these other-regarding preferences, longitudinal data sets are necessary [17]. In order to assess individual stability of sharing across development we investigated 175 Swiss children (85 girls) in a longitudinal-experimental study. The children were assessed at 6 years of age, 7 years of age, and 9 years of age with the Dictator Game, a paradigmatic economics task of prosocial sharing behavior with an anonymous other (see below).

We focused on two socio-emotional antecedents of sharing, namely sympathy and social acceptance. The question of whether children's other-regarding preferences are rooted in sympathy is striking, as recent experiments suggest that non-human primates are able to sympathize with others, especially if these others are members of their immediate social group [18], [19]. Such in-group preference has also been observed in preschool-children [20].

Sympathy entails feelings of concern for the other person based on an understanding of that person's circumstances [21], [22]. Sympathy (i.e., other-oriented concern), like empathy (i.e., emotional contagion), involves the comprehension or apprehension of another's affective state. Unlike empathy, however, sympathy primarily entails other-oriented concern and not the experience of the same or a similar emotion as the other [23]. In this way, sympathy entails a degree of distancing between the self and the other that is not present in empathy [21]. Sympathy has been posited by theorists to be an important motive of morally relevant, prosocial behavior [24], and it might be an antecedent of sharing resources with anonymous others [25]. In contrast, empathy might not lead to prosocial behavior, because it can either lead to sympathy for another or personal distress. Thus, empathy would relate positively to prosocial behavior only in specific situations [26]. In addition, empathic overarousal can lead to feelings of being overwhelmed so that one cannot be concerned with the needy other [22].

We investigated whether developmental processes in sharing with anonymous others depend on the earlier propensity to sympathize with anonymous others who are not members of the immediate social group. The focus on the early social-emotional roots of humans' other-regarding preferences is new and fascinating because philosophers and psychologists have argued that social emotions play a role in the development of prosocial behaviors and are important motivators for prosociality in general [21]. Previous psychological and economic research has mostly focused on the cognitive antecedents of other-regarding preferences, such as theory of mind.

Sharing may not only be influenced by the capacity to sympathize with anonymous others, but also by the extent to which one feels socially accepted by others, especially peers [27], [28]. Peer acceptance is important to children's social, emotional, and behavioral development, because it provides opportunities to learn and interact with children, which in turn promotes development [29]. Humans need to feel a sense of acceptance and belonging to develop an other-orientation [30]. We examined if sharing valuable resources with others relies on early feelings of being accepted by peers; does a child's need for acceptance predict how they will subsequently share with anonymous others?

Sharing seems also to differ across gender. There is evidence that females are more averse to unequal sharing than males [31]. Yet, it is not known when these gender differences in other-regarding preferences emerge in humans. The few existing findings on early gender differences in sharing are inconsistent. Some studies show no differences, and others show that females share more generously than males in some age groups [32], [33]. If indeed there are evolutionarily-derived gender differences in sharing, then it is likely that they evolve early in life.

We studied children's sharing when they were 6, 7 and 9 years of age. According to Fehr et al. [1], at the age of 6, unequal, self-serving distributions should dominate, whereas by the age of 9, about half, or more, of the participants should show equal allocations. At each of the three time points, sharing behavior was assessed in a one-shot experiment with anonymous interaction partners [8], [9], [10], [33]. We presented children with identical stickers and asked them to distribute the stickers, in any way they want among themselves and an anonymous child of the same age and gender (see Materials and Methods). Via standardized questionnaires, we asked primary caregivers to report on their children's sympathy towards anonymous distressed others at each time point, as well as on their children's feelings of social acceptance. We also obtained these reports from the children themselves and from the children's classroom teachers through the same standardized questionnaire at each time point. Multi-informant measures have been shown to be the most reliable sources of information on children's social-emotional skills [34]. In order to control for variables known to be of influence on other-regarding preferences [3], we collected information about the family's socioeconomic status (SES) and obtained the children's intelligence quotient.

Results

The descriptive statistics of all study variables, as well as the correlation coefficients across all main study variables, are presented in Table 1.

Overall, 43% of the children shared evenly across all assessment points. Fifty-seven percent of the children were not willing to equally allocate resources at least one time point. We used unconditional latent growth modeling in Mplus (version 6.11) to test if there was growth in sharing, and if there was variability among the children in their growth curves [35]. The unconditional linear growth model provided good fit to the data, $AIC = -881.06$, $BIC = -862.07$. Both the intercept and slope factors were significant for the sharing model, Intercept Est. = 0.45, $SE = 0.01$, $p<.001$, and Slope Est. = 0.01, $SE = 0.01$, $p<.01$, respectively. We found an increase in children's sharing from the age of 6 to 9 years (see Figure 1), and there was significant variability among children in the intercept and linear slope.

We found a strong gender effect in sharing. On average, girls shared more than boys at 6 years of age, $F(1, 174) = 6.20$, $p = .01$, $\eta 2 = .04$, and at 7 years of age, $F(1, 174) = 6.02$, $p = .02$, $\eta 2 = .03$. In contrast, girls and boys did not differ in the number of stickers shared when they were 9 years of age, $F(1, 174) = 3.41$, ns (see Figure 1).

Next, to test our hypothesis regarding the effects of sympathy and social acceptance on the development of sharing, we estimated two latent growth curve models with time-varying and time-invariant covariates. The time-varying covariate was matched to the later outcome. In other words, sympathy and social acceptance at 6 years of age was matched to sharing at 7 years of age, and sympathy and social acceptance

Table 1   Means (Standard Deviations), Ranges and Spearman Correlation Coefficients of the Main Study Variables

	M(SD)	Range	1	2	3	4	5	6	7	8	9	10	11
1. Sharing at T1 (Age 6)[a]	.44 (.16)	0–1											
2. Sharing at T2 (Age 7)[a]	.47 (.10)	0–.83	.15*										
3. Sharing at T3 (Age 9)[a]	.48 (.07)	0–.92	.09	.12									
4. Sympathy at T1 (Age 6)	.54 (.16)	0–.92	.04	.11	.04								
5. Sympathy at T2 (Age 7)	.61 (.13)	.17–92	.13	.14	.12	.23**							
6. Sympathy at T3 (Age 9)	.68 (.14)	.22–1	.15	.23**	.17*	.29**	.48**						
7. Social acceptance at T1 (Age 6)	4.14 (.65)	1.96–6	.01	.12	.18*	.26**	.21**	.15					
8. Social acceptance at T2 (Age 7)	4.17 (.71)	2.13–6	.10	.00	−.02	.10	.39**	.22**	.51**				
9. Social acceptance at T3 (Age 9)	4.04 (.90)	1–6	.20**	.04	−.11	.09	.30**	.36**	.41**	.56**			
10. Intelligence quotient (T1)	97.1 (11.71)	74–132	.05	.05	.01	.22**	.07	.13	.22**	.11	.05		
11. Socioeconomic status (T1)	5.78 (2.45)	1–10	−.09	.08	.09	.14	.07	.15	.16*	.09	.07	.22**	
12. Gender (T1)	-	-	.17*	.18*	.20**	.17*	.27**	.26**	.17*	.14	.19*	.03	.07

**p<.01, *p<.05.

[a]Sharing scores represent proportional scores.

Notes. T1 = Time 1. T2 = Time 2. T3 = Time 3.

doi:10.1371/journal.pone.0052017.t001

https://doi.org/10.1371/journal.pone.0052017.t001

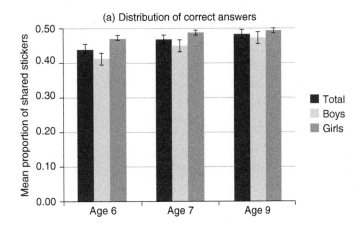

Figure 1 Development Trend of Children's Sharing from 6 to 9 Years as a Function of Gender.

The figure shows mean proportion scores of shared stickers as a function of age and gender (N=175). Growth curve modeling indicates that there is a significant increase in sharing over time, Intercept Est.=0.45, SE=0.01, p<.001, and Slope Est.=0.01, SE=0.01, p<.01. Proportions of shared stickers at each time point are calculated separately for boys and girls and compared using one-way ANOVAs. At Time 1 (age 6) and Time 2 (age 7), girls share significantly more stickers than boys, F(1, 174)=6.00, p=.02 , η2=.03, and F(1, 174)=6.07, p=.02, η2=.03, respectively. At Time 3 (Age 9), boys catch up, and the difference between the number of stickers shared by girls and boys is not significant, F(1, 174)=2.65, p=.11. Error bars represent SEM; *p<.05.

https://doi.org/10.1371/journal.pone.0052017.g001

at 7 years of age was matched to sharing at 9 years of age. The time-varying covariates were estimated to have a direct effect on the later-time sharing indicator [8]. Gender, verbal intelligence, and SES were added as time-invariant covariates and were used to predict the intercept and slope factors in the models.

The model for sympathy and sharing fit the data very well (Table 2). There were time-specific effects of sympathy at Time 1 on sharing at Time 2 (p<.01) and sympathy at Time 2 on sharing at Time 3 (p<.05), indicating that sympathy at Time 1 and Time 2 predicted an increase in levels of sharing at subsequent time points. This finding held even after controlling for gender, child intelligence, and SES. The model also indicated that after adding the time-varying sympathy variables, the initially significant time effect (i.e., increase in sharing with age) remained significant. This finding indicates that sympathy at Time 1 and Time 2 predicted growth above and beyond the trajectory captured by the growth factor; however, it did not fully account for the general increase in sharing with age. Gender predicted initial level of sharing; that is, girls showed higher initial levels of sharing than boys. Gender did not predict growth.

In contrast, the latent growth curve analysis yielded no significant effects of social acceptance on the increase in sharing. However, a regression analysis indicated that sharing at Time 2 was predicted by social acceptance at Time 1 (β = .16, p<.05). This finding held even after controlling for sharing at Time 1,

Table 2 Parameter Estimates (Standard Errors) for the Latent Growth Curve Models with Time-Varying Covariates for Effects of Sympathy on the Development of Sharing

	Sharing
Mean Intercept	0.29 (0.07)***
Mean Slope	0.15 (0.03)***
Intercept Variance	0.00 (0.00)
Intercept/Slope Covariance	−0.36 (.10)***
Slope Variance	0.01 (0.00)
Time-Varying Covariates	
Sympathy T1 - Sharing T2	0.06 (0.02)**
Sympathy T2 - Sharing T3	0.08 (0.04)*
Time-Variant Covariates	
Gender at T1[a]	0.05 (0.02)**
Verbal Intelligence at T1[a]	0.00 (0.01)
SES at T1[a]	−0.01 (0.00)
model fit	
χ^2/df	8.58/9
RMSEA	0.00
SRMR	0.03

Notes. [a]Coefficients for the time invariant covariates are reported for the intercept only. None of the covariates showed significant slope effects.

T1 = Time 1. T2 = Time 2. T3 = Time 3.

***p<.001, **p<.01, *p<.05,

doi:10.1371/jornal.pone.0052017_t1002

https://doi.org/10.1371/journal.pone.0052017.t002

gender, child intelligence, and SES (R^2 = .07, F(5, 174) = 2.43, p<.05). Sharing at Time 3 was not significantly predicted by earlier social acceptance (see Table 3).

Discussion and Conclusions

Given the pivotal role that other-regarding preferences play in fairness, caring, and cooperation, it is important to understand how they develop in humans [36]. Sharing has been regarded as an important indicator of other-regarding preferences. Notably, we found that children share more, and thus become less self-focused and more other-oriented, from 6 to 9 years of age. Studies have shown that instrumental helping (i.e., helping another individual achieve its instrumental goal) develops in early childhood [5], that young children share after having worked together to earn a reward [37], and that 7- to 8-year-olds, but not 3- to 4-year-olds, prefer equal resource allocations when sharing with friends [1].

Table 3   Results of the Hierarchical Linear Regression Analyses Predicting Sharing at Time 2 and Time 3 by Earlier Social Acceptance

Sharing Time 2			Sharing Time 3		
Independent variables	**β**	**R^2/F for stop**	**Independent variables**	**β**	**R^2/F for stop**
Step1[a]		.04/ 2.27	Step1*		.03/1.54
Gender	.18*		Gender	.13	
IQ	.06		IQ	−.04	
SES	.03		SES	.08	
Step 2		.07/ 2.43*	Step 2		.07/1.83
Social acceptance T1	.16*		Social acceptance T1/T2	.18*/−.10	
Sharing T1	.08		Sharing T1/T2	.12/−.13	

Notes. * Control variables.

T1 = Time 1. T2 = Time 2. T3 = Time 3.

*p<.05.

doi: 10.1371/journal.pone.0052017.t003

https://doi.org/10.1371/journal.pone.0052017.t003

Our findings document that sharing equally with anonymous others increases from middle to late childhood. In addition, we show that for a substantial number of children, other-regarding preferences seem to exist from the age of 6 and remain highly stable across middle childhood. For others, however, social-emotional factors (i.e., sympathy, social acceptance) might play a central role in developing other-regarding preferences. The developmental process in other-regarding preferences is likely due to children's growing concern with norms of fairness and caring [38], [39], [40]. Additionally, as children move from middle to late childhood, they may also learn that fairness and caring help them in earning respect and acceptance by their peers [29]. The latter may be the reason why they increasingly share resources with others.

Whether young children show either selfish or other-regarding preferences from early on may be due to differences in sympathy: Sympathy towards anonymous distressed others strongly predicted subsequent sharing, even after controlling for earlier sharing, intelligence, and family SES. These findings implicate that human sharing is critically shaped by the earlier propensity to sympathize with anonymous others. Evolutionary theories suggest that one of the driving forces behind altruism is sympathy, especially if members of one's immediate social groups are involved [41]. In the present study, we demonstrated that concern for anonymous others in distress might be an important human capacity which leads to other-regarding preferences. According to psychological theories, sympathy is important for prosocial behavior, as feeling negative emotions when someone else is experiencing distress increases the likelihood of caring [24]. It is likely that these feelings result, in part,

from processes of understanding others' emotions (i.e. affective perspective-taking skills). Since perspective-taking skills develop over the course of middle childhood, children may increasingly care about others' feelings and, as a result, act more prosocially towards them [38], [42].

The development of other-regarding preferences might also be due to differences in social acceptance. Our findings indicate that social acceptance at 6 years of age strongly predicted sharing at 7 years of age, even after controlling for earlier sharing, intelligence, and family SES. These findings are striking as they implicate that children's sharing is critically shaped by whether they feel accepted by others earlier on. Psychological theories emphasize the need for belonging as one of the core human needs [27], [28]. Our findings provide evidence for the notion that being accepted by others at the kindergarten age leads to increased willingness to share valuable resources with others at the elementary-school age. This latter finding suggests that feelings of being socially accepted during the transition from kindergarten to elementary school, a time when children have to adjust to a new environment and new social groups, are particularly important for the development of other-regarding preferences.

Our results showed that important gender differences exist with respect to other-regarding preferences. Younger girls tended to share more than boys, but this gender difference disappeared when children got older. Thus, it seems that gender may play an important role in the emergence of sharing [43] in early and middle childhood. These results can be interpreted in different ways: Socialization theories assume that children become increasingly aware of their social reputation when they move from middle to late childhood [29]. Hence, both boys and girls may increasingly try to maintain a positive peer reputation by behaving prosocially [29].

Studies in the behavioural economic paradigm have usually assessed age-differences in other-regarding preferences among cross-sectional samples. Compared to cross-sectional studies, longitudinal data sets, such as the one analyzed in the current study, offer the advantage of assessing individual stability of sharing resources across development. Other psychological research investigated the development of prosocial behavior and related socio-emotional abilities longitudinally in toddlers and preschool children. For example, Zahn-Waxler and colleauges (1992) found that some aspects of sympathy, such as expressing concern for a person hurting her finger and attempts to comprehend the distress of this person, increased significantly in children assessed at 14 and 20 months of age, but that the frequency of prosocial acts (i.e., helping or comforting the distressed person) remained stable [4]. Knafo and Plomin (2006) showed that parents rated their children as significantly more prosocial at age 3 than at age 2 [7]. Taken together, these studies indicate that, beginning in toddlerhood, prosocial behavior increases over middle to later childhood. Further longitudinal studies should assess sharing with the same instrument over a wide age range (from toddlerhood to adolescence).

Our results revealed that the ability to sympathize with others and the feeling of being socially accepted were longitudinally predictive of increased sharing, but no cross-sectional relations were found in the multivariate analyses. These results suggest that sympathy and social acceptance play an important role in children's early orientation towards the needs of others -an orientation that predicts generous sharing behavior later in development. The surprising finding that sympathy predicts later, but not concurrent, increases in sharing, may be due to the difference in salience that competing motivations to share or not share (e.g., motivations based on concerns of fairness or morality versus motivations based on hedonism) have at different stages of development. Existing research documents cross-sectional relations between sharing valuable resources with sympathy in 4-year-olds only, but not in 8- and 12-year-olds ([23], see also [44]). Research also demonstrates that hedonistic concerns (i.e., a focus on obtaining desired outcomes for the self) exert a powerful influence over prosocial dilemmas, including decisions to share or not share, in early childhood [45], [46]. Prosocial decisions later in childhood, however, increasingly incorporate more differentiated concerns including those of fairness and morality, as well as concerns over reciprocity, need, merit, and social reputation [15], [23]. It may be the case that sympathy at the age of 6, though not salient enough to overcome hedonistic motivations to keep resources for the self, may predispose children to consider the needs and feelings of others in the face of competing concerns later in development. Similarly, social

acceptance at the age of 6 may predispose children to share valuable resources later in development because being accepted by peers early in development may create subsequent trust in others, which has been shown to lead to an increase in sharing from early childhood to adulthood [47], and which is related to a more pro-social and less antisocial orientation towards peers later in development [48]. However, the effects for the findings on social acceptance were very small in size. Thus, these interpretations admittedly have to remain speculative. Clearly, future research is warranted to validate our findings.

In conclusion, the fact that children increasingly shared valuable resources with others shows that human children strongly develop other-regarding preferences from middle to late childhood. These preferences develop earlier in girls than in boys, but there are no gender differences in other-regarding preferences by late childhood and early adolescence [10]. Our finding regarding sharing being predicted by the early ability to sympathize with anonymous others demonstrates that sharing may be rooted in a human tendency to feel for others who are suffering, even if they are strangers. In addition, children's sharing was in part driven by feelings of social acceptance, which indicates that an orientation towards others may also depend on feeling happy and safe in the company of others. These findings have important implications for clinical interventions aimed at increasing an orientation towards others and at decreasing antisocial behavior in children.

Materials and Methods
Ethics Statement

The current study consisted of non-invasive and unconstrained child interviews; these interviews were conducted in separate rooms at schools and at home. According to the current regulations in the canton of Zurich in Switzerland (the so-called "Regulations of the Ethics Commission for Psychological Research", 2011), there is no requirement for an ethics committee approval. According to this regulation (Article 5, paragraph 1), this study is exempted from requiring formal ethical approval. The study fully complies with the ethics guidelines given by this legal regulation (see Article 8, paragraph 2). The regulation is based on the "Ethical Principals of Psychologists and Code of Conduct" (as outlined in the so-called "Ethical Guidelines for Psychologists of the Swiss Society for Psychology, as amended on October 13, 2003) and the ethical standards of the American Psychological Association (APA). Only children for whom parental written informed consent was obtained participated in the study. The interviews began after receiving permission from the schools. The data were analyzed anonymously.

Participants

The data were taken from the first three waves of a Swiss longitudinal study concerning social development from childhood to adolescence. A random sample of kindergarten children and their primary caregivers was drawn from residents of the canton of Zurich in Switzerland. Written informed consent was obtained from the primary caregivers. Interviews were conducted at T1 with 175 children and 175 primary caregivers. One- hundred and sixty-three of the primary caregivers (93%) filled in a supplementary questionnaire. The children had an average age of 6.10 years ($SD = 0.19$). There were 85 girls (48.6%) and 90 boys (51.4%). Of the primary caregivers, 98% gave written consent to contact the child's kindergarten teacher, and 133 of the corresponding kindergarten teachers filled in a questionnaire (77%). The great majority of participants were White. At the second assessment (T2), interviews were carried out with 158 children; one child refused to participate and one mother refused to let the child participate because the child was too shy.

Consent to contact the teacher at T2 was obtained from 154 parents (96%), and 140 teachers (91%) filled in a questionnaire. At T2, the children had an average age of 7.08 years ($SD = 0.20$).

At the third assessment (T3; two years after T2), 141 interviews and 139 interviews were carried out with children and primary caregivers, respectively. One hundred and thirty-four (96%) of the primary caregivers completed a supplementary questionnaire that measured the child's social development and the primary caregiver's parenting style. Consent to contact the teacher at T3 was obtained from 141 parents (100%), and 130 teachers (93%) filled in a questionnaire. The average age of the children at T3 was 9.17 ($SD = 0.21$).

Sample attrition effects were tested by comparing the primary caregivers at T1 ($N = 175$) whose children dropped out with those whose children dropped out at T2 (N = 15) and T3 (N = 21) on demographic variables (i.e., highest primary caregiver education, marital status) and the study variables at T1. Children who dropped out at T2 had caregivers who were more likely to lack a significant other (25% of the caregivers were single) than children who stayed in the sample (7% of the caregivers were single) at T2, $\chi^2(1, 175) = 4,44$, $p < .05$. No other variables were related to attrition status. Although retention in the study was high, there were some missing data. Therefore, single imputation was carried out to estimate the values for the missing data points using the expectation maximization method (SPSS Version 19).

Procedure

The first assessment was conducted during the spring of 2006. The second and third assessments were completed 1 and 2 years later respectively, using the same procedure as the one used at T1. There were three sessions for each child at T1, each lasting approximately 60 minutes: one at home consisting of a computer-assisted personal interview (CAPI) and video recording (observation) of the child's interaction with the primary caregiver, and two sessions in quiet rooms at the kindergarten or school) using paper-and-pencil tests and video recording. The interviewers were undergraduate psychology students who had been intensively trained in the relevant interview techniques.

Measures
Sharing Behaviour

At all assessment points, spontaneous sharing behavior was measured by using the dictator game, a sharing task developed in experimental economics [9]. In the present study, participants had to share six identical stickers between themselves and another anonymous child of the same age and gender at T1 and T2. At T3, they shared twelve identical stickers. For data analysis, proportional scores were created by computing the number of shared stickers divided by the total number of stickers.

Sympathy

At all assessment points, children's sympathy was assessed by (a) teachers' ratings, (b) mothers' ratings, and (c) self-ratings [49].

At T1–T3, the teachers and mothers rated the child's sympathy on five items [49] using a six-point scale. For teacher-rated sympathy, Cronbach's $\alpha = .92$ at T1, .90 at T2, and .97 at T3. For mother-rated sympathy, Cronbach's $\alpha = .83$ at T1, .85 at T2, and .88 at T3.

At T1–T3, children rated their sympathy on a scale containing five items (from [49]; e.g., "When I see another child who is hurt or upset, I feel sorry for him or her"). The children were asked whether the sentence was like him/her or not, and, if so, how much (0=*not like him/her*; 1=*sort of like him/her*; 2=*like him/her*). Cronbach's α for the sympathy scale was .67 at T1, .73 at T2, and .74 at T3.

Social Acceptance

At all assessment points, children's social acceptance was assessed by (a) teachers' ratings, (b) mothers' ratings, and (c) self-ratings [50], [51], [52].

At T1–T3, the teachers and mothers rated the child's social acceptance on five items using a six-point scale. The items were taken from the Strengths and Difficulties Questionnaire and a questionnaire on peer relations [50], [51]. For teacher-rated social acceptance, Cronbach's $\alpha = .79$ at T1, .82 at T2, and .87 at T3. For mother-rated social acceptance, Cronbach's $\alpha = .75$ at T1, .80 at T2, and .72 at T3.

At T1–T3, children rated their social acceptance on six items of the Pictorial Scale of Perceived Competence and Social

Acceptance (from [52]; e.g., "This boy has friends to play with, and this boy has no friends to play with. Which boy are you more like?"). The children were asked to report which child they were more like, and the degree to which they were like the child in the picture (*sort of true for me; really true for me*). Thus, items were scored on a 4-point scale. Cronbach's α for the social acceptance scale was .69 at T1, .85 at T2, and .60 at T3.

Because the primary caregivers', teachers', and children's ratings of sympathy were predominantly significantly associated with each other at each time point, and to reduce the number of measures and increase reliability [53], they were averaged into overall scales labelled "sympathy at T1", "sympathy at T2", and "sympathy at T3". The same was done for the primary caregivers', teachers', and children's ratings of social acceptance, and the overall scales were labeled "social acceptance at T1", "social acceptance at T2", and "social acceptance at T3".

Intelligence Quotient

The children's intelligence was measured at T1 using the "verbal intelligence" section of the German version of the Hamburg-Wechsler Intelligence Test (HAWIK-III).

Family Socioeconomic Status

For socioeconomic background, we coded both the primary caregivers' and their partners' highest educational attainment. Responses were coded 1 (primary or lower secondary education), 2 (vocational training), 3 (vocational college), 4 (baccalaureate degree or higher vocational diploma), and 5 (university degree). Education scores, which served as an index of socioeconomic status (SES), were then computed. Higher scores indicated higher SES.

Author Contributions

Conceived and designed the experiments: TM. Performed the experiments: TM. Analyzed the data: TM MPC. Contributed reagents/materials/analysis tools: TM MB. Wrote the paper: TM MG MK MPC MB.

References

1. Fehr E, Bernhard H, Rockenbach B (2008) Egalitarianism in young children. Nature 454: 1079–1083.
2. Olson KR, Spelke E-S (2008) Foundations of cooperation in young children. Cognition 108: 222–231.
3. Eisenberg N, Spinrad TL, Sadovsky A (2006) Empathy-related responding in children. In Killen M, Smetana J, editors. Handbook of moral development. Mahwah, NJ: Lawrence Erlbaum. 517–549.
4. Zahn-Waxler C, Radke-Yarrow M, Wagner E, Chapman M (1992) Development of concern for others. Dev Psychol 28: 126–136.
5. Warneken F, Tomasello M (2006) Altruistic helping in human infants and young chimpanzees. Science 311: 1301–1303.
6. Eisenberg N, Guthrie IK, Murphy BC, Shepard SA, Cumberland A (1999) Consistency and development of prosocial dispositions: A longitudinal study. Child Dev 70: 1360–1372.
7. Knafo A, Plomin R (2006) Prosocial behavior from early to middle childhood: Genetic and environmental influences on stability and change. Dev Psychol 42: 771–786.
8. Malti T, Gummerum M, Keller M, Buchmann M (2009) Children's moral motivation, sympathy, and prosocial behavior. Child Dev 80: 442–460.
9. Benenson JF, Pascoe J, Radmore N (2007) Children's altruistic behavior in the dictator game. Evol Hum Behav 28: 168–175.
10. Gummerum M, Keller M, Takezawa M, Mata J (2008) To give or not to give: Children's and adolescents' sharing and moral negotiations in economic decision situations. Child Dev 79: 561–576.
11. Warneken F, Tomasello M (2007) Helping and cooperation at 14 months of age. Infancy 11: 271–294.
12. Eisenberg N, Fabes R (1998) Prosocial development. In W. Damon (Editor-in-Chief) & N. Eisenberg (Vol. Ed.), Handbook of child psychology: Vol. 3. Social, emotional, and personality development (5th ed). New York: Wiley. 701–778.
13. Gummerum M, Hanoch Y, Keller M (2008) When child development meets economic game theory: An interdisciplinary approach to investigating social development. Hum Dev 51 235–261.
14. Sutter M (2007) Outcomes versus intentions: On the nature of fair behavior and its development with age. J Econ Psychol 28: 69–78.
15. Almås I, Alexander W, Sørensen CEØ, Tungodden B (2010) Fairness and the Development of Inequality Acceptance. Science 328: 1176–1178.
16. Harbaugh WT, Krause K (2000) Children's altruism in public good and dictator experiments. Econ Inq 38: 95–109.
17. Singer JD, Willett JB (2003) Applied longitudinal data analysis: Methods for studying change and event occurrence. New York: Oxford University Press. 627 p.

18. Jensen K, Hare B, Call J, Tomasello M (2006) What's in it for me? Self-regard precludes altruism and spite in chimpanzees. Proc Biol Sci 273: 1013–1021.

19. Vonk J, Brosnan SF, Silk JB, Henrich J, Richardson AS, et al. (2008) Chimpanzees do not take advantage of very low cost opportunities to deliver food to unrelated group members. Anim Behav 75: 1757–1770.

20. Gummerum M, Takezawa M, Keller M (2009) The influence of social category and reciprocity on adults' and children's altruistic behaviour. Evol Psychol 7: 295–316.

21. Eisenberg N (2000) Emotion, regulation, and moral development. Annul Rev Psychol 51: 665–697.

22. Hoffman M (2000) Empathy and moral development: The implications for caring and justice. Cambridge: Cambridge University Press. 325 p.

23. Ongley SF, Malti T (2012) The role of moral emotions in children's sharing. Manuscript submitted for publication.

24. Eisenberg N (1986) Altruistic cognition, emotion, and behavior (Hillsdale, NJ: Erlbaum).

25. Knafo A, Zahn-Waxler C, Van Hulle C, Robinson JL, Hyun Rhee S (2008) The developmental origins of a disposition toward empathy: Genetic and environmental contributions. Emotion 8: 737–752.

26. Eisenberg N, Miller P (1987) Empathy, sympathy, and altruism: empirical and conceptual links. In Eisenberg N, Strayer J editors, Empathy and its development. Cambridge: Cambridge University Press. 292–316.

27. Maslow A (1943) A theory of human motivation. Psychol Rev 50: 370–396.

28. Ryan RM, Deci EL (2002) An overview of self-determination theory. In Deci EL, Ryan RM, editors. Handbook of self-determination research. New York: University of Rochester. 3–33.

29. Rubin KH, Bukowski W, Parker JG (2006) Peer interactions, relationships, and groups. In Damon W, Lerner RM, Eisenberg N editors. Handbook of child psychology: Vol.3, Social, emotional, and personality development. New York: Wiley. 571–645.

30. Hart C, Yang C, Nelson L, Robinson CC, Olsen JA, et al. (2000) Peer acceptance in early childhood and subtypes of socially withdrawn behaviour in China, Russia and the United States. Int J Behav Dev 24: 73–81.

31. Houser D, Schunk D (2009) Social environments with competitive pressure: Gender effects in the decisions of German school children. J Econ Psychol 30: 634– 64.

32. Zhou L, Huangfu G, Keller M, Mou Y, Danzhi C (2008) The development of Chinese children's decision-making in ultimatum and dictator games. Acta Psychol Sin 40: 402–408.

33. Leman PJ, Keller M, Takezawa M, Gummerum M (2009) Children's and adolescents' decisions about sharing money with others. M Soc Dev 18: 711–727.

34. Piacentini JC, Cohen P, Cohen J (1992) Combining discrepant information from multiple sources: are complex algorithms better than simple ones? J Abnorm Child Psychol 20: 51–63.

35. Muthén LK, Muthén BO (2010) Mplus User's Guide, 6 ed (Muthén & Muthén, Los Angeles).

36. Brosnan SF (2011) A hypothesis of the co-evolution of cooperation and responses to inequity. Front Neurosci 5: 43.

37. Warneken F, Lohse K, Melis A, Tomasello M (2011) Young children share the spoils after collaboration. Psychol Sci 22: 267–273.

38. Malti T, Ongley SF (in press) The development of moral emotions and moral reasoning. In Killen M, Smetana J editors. Handbook of moral development. New York: Taylor & Francis.

39. Watson M (2003) Learning to trust: transforming difficult elementary classrooms through developmental discipline (Jossey-Bass, CA, San Francisco).

40. Fehr E, Fischbacher U, Gächter S (2002) Strong reciprocity, human cooperation, and the enforcement of social norms. Hum Nat 13: 1–25.

41. de Waal FBM (2008) Putting the altruism back into altruism: The evolution of empathy. Annul Rev Psychol 59: 279–300.

42. Flavell JH (2004) Theory-of-mind development: Retrospect and prospect. Merrill Palmer Q 50: 274–290.

43. Croson R, Gneezy U (2009) Gender differences in preferences. J Econ Lit 47: 1–27.

44. Gummerum M, Hanoch Y, Keller M, Parsons K, Hummel A (2010) Preschoolers' allocations in the dictator game. The role of moral emotions. J Econ Psychol 31 25– 34.

45. Arsenio W, Gold J, Adams E (2006) Children's conceptions and displays of moral emotionsIn Killen M, Smetana J editors. Handbook of moral development. Mahwah, NJ: Lawrence Erlbaum. 581–610.

46. Malti T, Krettenauer T (2012) The relation of moral emotion attributions to pro- and antisocial behavior: A meta-analysis. Child Dev. Early online publication, 24 September 2012.

47. Sutter M, Kocher M (2007) Trust and trustworthiness across different age groups. Gam Econ Behav 59(2): 364–382.

48. Malti T, Averdijk M, Ribeaud D, Rotenberg K, Eisner MP (2012) "Do you trust him?" Children's trust beliefs and developmental trajectories of aggressive behavior in

an ethnically diverse sample. J Abnorm Child Psych. In press.

49. Eisenberg N, Fabes RA, Murphy BC (1996) Parents' reactions to children's negative emotions: Relations to children's social competence and comforting behavior. Child Dev 67: 2227–2247.

50. Goodman R (1997) The Strengths and Difficulties Questionnaire: A research note. J Child Psychol Psyc 38: 581–586.

51. Perren S, Alsaker F (2006) Social behavior and peer relationships of victims, bully victims, and bullies in kindergarten. J Child Psychol Psyc 47: 45–57.

52. Harter S, Pike R (1984) The pictorial scale of perceived competence and social acceptance for young children. Child Dev 55: 1969–1982.

53. Rushton JP, Brainerd CJ, Pressley M (1983) Behavioral development and construct validity: The principle of aggregation. Psychol Bull 94 18–38.

Critical Thinking

1. What are some differences and similarities between sympathy, empathy, and altruism?
2. Why might sympathy increase at different ages?
3. Should parents and schools "train" children to be sympathetic? What kinds of problems might be reduced if they did so?

Internet References

Empathy or Sympathy: Do You Care More about Your Child's Feelings or Your Own?
https://www.advantage4parents.com/article/empathy-vs-sympathy-do-you-care-more-about-your-childs-feelings-or-your-own/

How to Foster Sympathy in Your Children at a Young Age
https://lifehacker.com/how-to-foster-sympathy-in-your-children-at-a-young-age-1787091654

Malti, Tina. et al., "Early Sympathy and Social Acceptance Predict the Development of Sharing in Children." PLOS One, December 13, 2012.

Friend or Foe? Early Social Evaluation of Human Interactions by Marine Buon et al.

72

Prepared by: Chris J. Boyatzis, *Bucknell University* and
Ellen N. Junn, *California State University, Stanislaus*

Article

Friend or Foe? Early Social Evaluation of Human Interactions

Marine Buon et al.

Learning Outcomes

After reading this article, you will be able to:

- Describe how infants and young children can distinguish between the goals and actions of helpful and non-helpful actors and agents.

- Explain some methods scientists use to study young children's evaluations and judgments of interactions.

- Consider how identifying helpful and non-helpful actions may set the stage for moral judgments.

Introduction

Humans seem unique in their ability to help, cooperate and communicate with their conspecifics [1], [2], and also to harm, defect and deceive them [3], [4]. Therefore, the ability to discriminate potentially benevolent from malevolent agents would seem important for survival, not only in adulthood but also in early childhood or even infancy. Congruent with this view, recent developmental studies indicate that infants do not only represent agents' actions, goals and intentions [5]–[7], but also evaluate them: using non-verbal dependent measures, several studies have showed that young toddlers and even preverbal infants are able to *evaluate* some actions as either positive or negative and express *social preferences* towards agents as a function of the valence of their actions.

In a seminal study, Premack and Premack [8] showed 52-week-old infants interactions between pairs of 2D balls on a computer screen. In the habituation phase of the experiment, infants saw one ball performing either a negative action towards another ball (hitting or preventing the ball to achieve its goal) or a positive action (caressing or helping). Infants habituated to a positive action, but not to a negative action, showed a dishabituation response (as measured by looking times), when presented with a novel instance of a negative action (hitting). This suggests that 52-week-old infants are able to categorize actions along their positive or negative valence across differences in the low-level kinematic characteristics of the actions.

More recent studies went a step further by exploring whether infants are able to socially *evaluate* an agent as a function of his/her performed action. Hamlin, Wynn and Bloom [9] showed that 6- and 10-month-old preverbal infants prefer an agent whose action is congruent rather than incongruent with the goal of another agent climbing towards the top of a hill (see also [10], [11] for results with younger infants and other social scenarios). Nineteen-month-olds [12] and even 16-month-olds [13], [14] have also been shown to be sensitive to the fair/unfair allocation of resources among distinct individuals. Vaish, Carpenter & Tomasello [15] showed that young preschoolers are more prone to help an agent who did not intend to destroy another's property than an agent who intended to perform this action, whatever the consequences of their actions (see [16] for similar results regarding physical harm; see also [17], [18] for the distinction between various benevolent/malevolent actions whatever the consequences).

Although infants show clear evidence of being able to socially evaluate the agents of some malevolent/benevolent actions, it remains to be established whether this ability stems from a generic capacity to evaluate an agent as a function of the *valence* of his/her action, as suggested by Premack and Premack [8], or whether it rests on a collection of domain-specific social evaluation systems [19]. It is possible that some pairs of benevolent/malevolent actions are more primitive or essential for survival than others and that agents who perform them are therefore evaluated more robustly and earlier by young infants than others. For example, the survival of young infants might depend more upon the contrast between harming and comforting than upon the contrast between fair and unfair allocations of resources. Even if there is a single action evaluation system in infants, it is clear that no simple set of perceptual cues can characterize the contrast between malevolent and benevolent actions in general. For example, the detection of a contrast between harming and comforting relies on the ability to perceive qualitative changes in individuals' *emotional* or *physical* states. The detection of a contrast between helping and hindering actions requires the ability to understand an agent's *goal* and whether this goal has been achieved or not. The detection of unfair distributions depends on the joint abilities to track the number and quality of recipients, the fraction of the commodity allocated to them, and some standard for assessing what counts as a *fair* distribution. The detection of a violation of a property right (the destruction of another's property, for example) requires that infants have some understanding of the concept of *ownership* (or at least attachment) of an agent towards some inanimate objects, and that they keep track of them in third-party exchanges. Given that these situations implicate cognitive mechanisms of different complexity, it is unlikely that the corresponding evaluative capacities all emerge at the same time in human infants. It is therefore of considerable theoretical interest to establish separately, in each of these domains, the emergence of evaluative capacities in young infants.

In this paper, our aim is to investigate whether the ability to distinguish and socially respond to the harm/comfort contrast is achieved by the age of 10 months. Surprisingly, this contrast has, so far, not been studied independently. Smetana [20], Leslie and collaborators [17] et al. (2006), Weisberg & Leslie [18] and Vaish and collaborators [15] have studied preschoolers' responses to situations of harm but they were mixed with violations of property rights. Nelson [16], Zelazo, Helwig & Lau [21] and others studied situations of harm independently, but they did not explore whether toddlers or even infants would socially evaluate benevolent/malevolent agents. Premack and Premack [8] showed that 52-week-old infants seem able to generalize from a harmful/comforting contrast to a helpful/hindering one, but they did not test whether infants are able to evaluate the agent of these actions. Hamlin et al. [9] showed that 10-month-old infants prefer a pro-social to an anti-social agent, but only for the hindering/helping contrast. Therefore, it is plausible that 10-month-old infants should be able to discriminate a harmful from a comforting agent, but it has not been tested yet whether they prefer the latter over the former.

One of the difficulties in studying a pure benevolent/malevolent contrast, and in particular a contrast like harm/comfort, is to construct a situation where infants' or toddlers' reactions depend on their conceptual understanding of the agents' action or intentions, and not on the mere presence of superficial cues of positive or negative valence. For example, in Vaish's study

[15], the malevolent agent performs an anti-social action: he intentionally destroys the property of another character. In addition, he emits "mildly aggressive vocalizations". As infants are able to discriminate different emotional expressions by an early age [22], [23] express preferences for positive emotions (happiness) over negative ones (sadness and anger) [24], the fact that the agent who intends to perform a bad action emits "mildly aggressive vocalizations" makes it difficult to know which aspect of the situation the toddler is reacting to (the superficial negative cues vs. the negative valence of the act of destruction). Similarly, in Hamlin's experiment [9], after the puppet has been helped, it jumps up and down till the end of the sequence; this could be interpreted as a state of excitement. By contrast, after the puppet has been hindered, it rolls end-over-end down the hill and then remains immobile till the end of the sequence; this could be interpreted as a depressed state. The differences in the puppets' motions in the final part of the sequences may reflect differences in underlying emotional or physical states, and could partially contribute to infants' evaluations, irrespective of whether they understand helping and hindering at a conceptual level.

The purpose of our paper is to investigate the preferences of preverbal human infants when confronted with a contrast involving only harming and comforting. In order to enhance the ecological validity of cues available to infants, we embodied this contrast in movie clips using human agents performing simple actions (threatening and pushing to the ground, raising and comforting), rather than animated geometric shapes. As indicated above, the contrast between harming and comforting is particularly difficult to study, because it inherently incorporates a change in the victim's emotional state, which is confounded with the anti-social versus pro-social nature of the action. In order to mitigate this confound, we equated the average emotional state of the human victims across all situations: in the harm condition, the victim is first happy, then sad; in the comfort condition, she is first sad, then happy. Thus, the absolute amount of positive/negative cues is matched, and the only possible cue relevant to evaluating the victim's emotional state is in the *change of state* associated to the agent's action. We then equated the actions and expressions of the anti-social and pro-social agents by using a cross-over, internal control design, in which the two agents each performed a pair of actions, one positive, one negative. Critically, the 'pro-social' agent directed his positive action towards a human "patient" and his negative action towards a non-human "patient" (an inanimate object), while the 'anti-social' agent did the opposite. In this way, the two agents exhibited the same overall amount of positive and negative emotions and the only way to distinguish them is to track the agent's actions in conjunction with the human versus non-human status of the patient.

To examine whether toddlers and infants distinguish and socially respond to the harm/comfort contrast, we conducted two experiments. In Experiment 1, we tested 29-month-olds using verbal questionnaires designed to explore toddlers' absolute evaluations of each agent taken individually as well as their preference toward one agent over another. In experiment 2, we tested the preferences of preverbal 10-month-olds for one agent over another using a non-verbal toy choice task previously used by Kinzler, Dupoux and Spelke [25].

Experiment 1

In this experiment, 29-month-old toddlers saw short films involving two distinct adult agents: the anti-social agent and the pro-social agent. Each of these agents performed a pair of actions: one directed towards a human patient and the other towards an inanimate object. The anti-social actor threatened and pushed a little girl, and he caressed a backpack resting on a stool. Conversely, the pro-social agent comforted the little girl, and he threatened and pushed the backpack. The agents were two adult males and the human patient was a female child. The inanimate object was chosen so as to match the size of the human patient. In both pairs of positive and negative actions, we took care of matching both the bodily movements and emotional displays of agents of both types. Therefore, the only factor distinguishing the pro-social from the anti-social agents was how their two actions (positive vs. negative) were paired with the two targets (human patient vs. inanimate object) and the targets' subsequent reactions (emotional changes for the human patient, and no visible changes for the inanimate object). In this experiment, the dependent variable was the response to verbal questionnaires administered through a puppet. As toddlers of this age tend to give inconsistent responses to the same questions, we used a total of 9 questions some of them regarding each agent individually and the others allowing the child to compare the two agents. We then combined the responses into absolute valence indexes (composed of the responses given by toddlers to the individual questions) and a relative valence index (composed of the responses given by toddlers to the comparative questions).

Method
Stimuli

We designed four action scripts representing all possible combinations of the two action-types (harm/comfort) and two patients (human patients/inanimate object). Each action script had the same temporal structure that involved three phases: (i) the target is alone (8 sec), (ii) the agent enters the scene and interacts with the patient (14 sec),(iii) the patient is alone again (8 sec). In the human-harming action script, (i) the human agent is dancing and smiling while displaying other happy body language. (ii) The agent walks in, threatens the human patient while walking towards her, pushes her down to the floor, simulates kicking her, and leaves. (iii) The human patient is then lying on the ground and displays distress cues (crying). In the human-comforting action script, (i) the human patient is lying on the floor, displaying distress cues (crying). (ii) The agent walks in, raises the target up, comforts her (caressing her), smiles, and leaves. (iii) The human patient is executing a little dance with happy face and positive body language. Note that stage (i) of the human harming action script is the same as stage (iii) of the human comforting action and vice-versa. The object-harming and object-comforting action scripts are exactly the same as their counterparts with a human patient, with identical timing, action and emotions of the agent: he walks in, threatens while walking towards the inanimate object, pushes it down to the floor, simulates kicking it, and leaves vs. he walks in, raises the inanimate object up, comforts it -caressing it -, smiles, and leaves. Therefore, the only difference is that the human patient has been replaced by an inanimate object. The object, of course, does not display any emotions; it is in one of two states: either standing upright (the equivalent of the girl dancing) or lying on the ground (the equivalent of the girl lying and crying).

Each of the four action scripts was cast twice, using two different male adults as actors (actors A and B), resulting in eight 30-seconds movie clips. In all of the movie clips, the human patient was a female 12-year-old actor and the inanimate object was a backpack resting on a stool, whose size approximately matched the size of the human patient. The movie clips were silent, and were cast in a studio with a uniform blue background.

The movie clips were then mounted into sequences of two consecutive actions separated by a blank screen of two seconds. These sequences involved the same actor but different patients (human patient or inanimate object) and actions (harming or comforting). For instance, in an 'anti-social' sequence, actor A harms the little girl and then comforts the backpack. In a 'pro-social' sequence, actor B hits the object and then comforts the little girl. Eight such sequences were generated by crossing the two actors (A and B), the two roles (pro-social and anti-social), and two orders of presentation of actions (harming first or comforting first). Note that movies are available upon request to the main authors.

Procedure

Before the experiments, the toddlers were familiarized to the puppet character (animated by the experimenter) that will be used subsequently. The puppet played with them and asked them to name and point to various animals in a picture book (what is this animal? Where is the elephant? etc.). The toddlers were then placed two meters away from of a 2×1.5 m projection screen, in front of a table, on their parent's lap. The parents were blindfolded during the entire experiment. The experimenter was seated on the ground facing away from the screen and was, therefore, blind to the movies being played.

The experiment consisted of three parts. In the first part, the toddlers were presented with one of the eight sequences (involving, for instance, actor A in the anti-social role, with the harming action first) played twice, with a 2-second blank screen interval between each repetition. This was followed by a photograph of the actor facing the camera, at which point the toddler was introduced to an experimenter blind to the film, who used the puppet to interact verbally with him/her and asked social/ moral evaluation questions regarding the actor appearing in the photograph: Do you like him? Is he a good guy or a bad guy? Is he nice looking or ugly? Is he scary or nice? Do you want to play with him or not?

In the second part, toddlers were presented twice with a sequence involving the other actor playing the opposite role (here, actor B in the pro-social role, with the harming action first). As in the first part, the sequence was followed by a presentation of actor B's photograph, and the same questions were used again. In the third part, the two sequences with actor A and actor B were shown once and the two actors appeared side by side on the screen. When faced with the two actors, the child was asked one question for each agent "Is he a good guy or a bad guy?" while the puppet pointed first to the actor on the left, then to the actor on the right. Then, they were asked three questions using a contrastive construction: "which one is the nice guy?", "which one is the bad guy?", "which one would you like to play with?" For the contrastive questions, toddlers were requested to point to one of the two sides of the screen. In total, the children were therefore asked 6 individual questions for each of the two actors, plus 3 contrastive questions.

If the child failed to answer a question after 10 seconds of silence, the question was repeated. After 10 more seconds of silence, the question was considered as unanswered and thus as a missing data point in the analysis (average: 3.62 questions unanswered per toddler, SE: 0.68). If the child appeared to become agitated, or refused to answer any more, subsequent questions were skipped (average 1.23 questions skipped, SE: 0.41), and the next video sequences were played. On average, toddlers thus missed 4.85 questions (SE = 0.84). Note that we found no effect of the questionnaire (individual vs. contrastive), of the questions asked or of the counterbalanced factors on none of this factor). For a full description of the data obtained in experiment 1, see Table S1.

The choice of the actor playing the pro-social agent (actor A vs. actor B), the order of presentation of the pro-social agent (first vs. second) and the order of presentation of the action-type (harming vs. comforting) were counterbalanced across 8 groups of toddlers. Toddlers' responses were video, tape-recorded and blindly scored by two independent coders (Cronbach's alpha = .94). We used the average between the two coders 'scores for subsequent analyses.

Participants and Ethical Issues

We tested forty-six 29-month-old toddlers (age range = 28 to 32; 23 males, 23 females) recruited in Paris through mailing and telephone calls. Upon recruitment on the phone, the parents were informed about the aims of the study and about the methodology. When parents arrived, these elements were explained again. The parents were then brought to the experimental room without the toddlers and shown clips of the 4 action scripts (with the same agents and same order for all parents). They were then asked whether they thought these clips were appropriate to their toddlers, and if so, were given the informed consent form to sign, and the experiment proceeded. During the experiment, the parent was blindfolded and given the option of stopping the experiment at any point. This study was approved by the Cochin-Tarnier Hospital Ethical Committee (Comité de protection des personnes "Ile-de-France III", decision A01142-51).

Results and Discussion

A total of eighteen toddlers could not be analyzed due to a technical failure in sound recording (N = 15), a complete absence of coherent or understandable responses (N = 2) and parental intervention during the questionnaire (N = 1). The responses of the remaining twenty-eight toddlers (14 males and 14 females) were analyzed.

Because this experiment was designed to analyze toddlers' evaluation of each agent separately as well as their preference for one agent over another, we analyzed the responses obtained from the individual questionnaires and those from the comparative questionnaire separately.

For individual questionnaires, for each agent evaluated, we computed an Absolute Valence Index (AVI): each child's response *in favor* of the agent ("yes, I like him", "He's nice", "I want to play with him", etc.) was coded as +1 while each response in disfavor of the agent ("no, I do not like him", "He is mean", etc.) was coded as −1. A score of 0 was assigned if the child gave no response or a response that was too ambiguous to code one way or the other. Then, we computed an aggregate Absolute Valence Index by averaging the code of the responses to each question.

For the contrastive questionnaire, we computed a Relative Valence Index (RVI) based on toddlers' responses to comparative questions: each child's response was coded as +1 if the child responded in favor of the pro-social agent or in disfavor of the anti-social agent, −1 if he or she gave the opposite responses. A score of 0 was assigned if the child gave no response or a response too ambiguous to code one way or the other. Here again, we computed an aggregate Relative Valence Index by averaging the code of the response to each question. The RVI was between −1 and +1, a positive value indicating that the "pro-social agent" was globally evaluated more positively than the "anti-social agent", and vice-versa for a negative RVI.

The average AVI for each agent (pro-social vs. anti-social) across toddlers is shown in Figure 1.A. To start, we were interested to know if, irrespective of counterbalancing effects, toddlers found the pro-social agent to be positive and the anti-social agent to be more negative. To this end, we constructed a separate linear model for each agent type using the AVI as the dependent variable. Included in the model were the three counterbalancing factors (actor, order of actions and order of patient) and the resultant intercept was tested against zero. There were no effects of counterbalancing factor on either the pro-social or anti-social agents Furthermore, we found that the AVI obtained for the pro-social agent was slightly negative but

not significantly different from zero (AVI = −0.01, SE = 0.09, $F(1,27) < 1$, $p > 0.1$, $\eta p^2 = 0.001$) whereas, the AVI obtained for the anti-social agent was negative and significantly below zero (AVI = −0.19, SE = 0.09, $F(1,27) = 6.29$, $p<.05$, $\eta p^2 = .34$).

We then ran a repeated-measures ANOVA to examine the difference between pro-social and anti-social AVI. This analysis indicated that the AVI differed significantly as a function of the agent, ($F(1,12) = 10.71$, $p < .02$, $\eta p^2 = .47$) such that the anti-social agent is evaluated more negatively than the pro-social one. No effects of counterbalancing factor or of participant sex were found in these analyses.

The average RVI across toddlers is shown in Figure 1.B and was analyzed using a linear model with the three counterbalancing factors (actor, order of actions, and order of patient) as between subject factors. As above, the intercept was tested against zero. This analysis revealed an intercept significantly above zero (RVI = 0.26, SE = 0.09, $F(1,27)$ = 5.14, $p<.05$, $\eta p^2 = .25$) showing that toddlers evaluated the pro-social agent significantly more positively than the anti-social agent. Again, there were no effects of the counterbalancing factors, participant sex or any interactions between these factors ($p > 0.1$).

Sixteen toddlers occasionally produced short comments during the movie clips (30 comments in total), which we analyzed by taking into account the valence of the comments (neutral, positive or negative) and the action script concerned (human harming, object harming, human comforting or object comforting). All comments which were a description of the action (e.g. "he pushes the girl!", "the girl falls") were considered as neutral, those containing positive words (e.g. "he's nice!") as positive comments and those containing negative words ("bad !", "he's not nice") as negative comments. If a toddler repeated the same comment in a same sequence (for example: "he's bad!") twice, we coded it as a single comment.

A four by three contingency table was constructed (see Table 1), by tabulating the three types of comments across the four types of action scripts. There was a significant effect of comment type ($X^2 (2) = 6.2$, $p < .05$), reflecting the fact that toddlers gave mostly negative comments, and very little positive comments. There was a significant effect of action scripts ($X^2 (3) = 17.2$, $p < .001$), reflecting the fact that the human harming sequence generated the most comments. Finally, there was an interaction between these two factors ($X^2 (6) = 13.1$, $p < .05$), reflecting the fact that by far the most frequent comments were negative comments produced during the human harming sequences. This result indicates overall a greater sensitivity to the negative act performed towards the little girl.

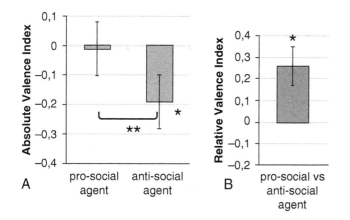

Figure 1   Average indexes for 29 months-olds

A. Average Absolute Valence Index for 29-months-old toddlers computed over the responses to the individual questions regarding the pro-social agent and the anti-social agent separately. *p<.05 (between subjects),**p<.02 (within subjects). A positive score indicates a positive verbal statement toward the agent and vice versa for negative scores. The error bars correspond to one between-subject standard error above and below the mean. B. Average Relative Valence Index computed over the responses to the contrastive questions. A positive score indicates a more positive assessment of pro-social than the anti-social agent, vice-versa for negative scores. The error bars correspond to one between-subject standard error above and below the mean. *p<.05.

https://doi.org/10.1371/journal.pone.0088612.g001

Table 1   Number of Positive, Neutral or Negative Comments During the Four Types of Action Scripts. https://doi.org/10.1371/journal.pone.0088612.t001

| | Action script | | | |
| | Human | | Object | |
Comments	Harming	Comforting	Harming	Comforting
Positive comments	0	2	1	1
Natural comments	5	2	4	0
Negative comments	12	1	1	1
Total	17	5	6	2

doi:10.1371/journal.pone.0088612_t001

Experiment 2
Method

For the 10-month-old infants, we used the same design and stimuli as in Experiment 1, but the movies were recast in order to eliminate the simulated kicking (the negative act was reduced to pushing). Infants were presented with the same set of actions as before, but the questionnaires were removed. Instead, at the end of the entire set of movie clips, the two agents were shown entering the stage from each side, standing still facing the camera, playing with identical toys (teddy bears), and bending towards the camera as if both were simultaneously giving the toy to the infant. Through a mechanical apparatus (see Figure 2.A), the two identical toys then appeared on the table in front of the infant while it disappeared from the agents' hands. Afterwards, the two agents appeared standing still with no toy, looking at the infant. This procedure was repeated four times (with four different teddy bears), with the agents swapping sides from trial to trial. The infants were videotaped and their initial attempts to reach for one of the toys were coded by two independent blind coders.

Ethical Issues

The same procedure as in Experiment 1 was used, and was covered by the same decision from the Cochin Ethical Committee.

Participants

We tested fifty-four 10-month-old infants (age range = 9–10 months; 31 males, 23 females) recruited in Paris through mailing and telephone calls. The parents were fully informed about the protocol and were shown the sequences as in Experiment 1. The babies were seated in the lap of a parent, who was blindfolded during the entire experiment. Among the 10-month-old infants, 4 did not complete the presentation (unrest, technical failure), and 3 did not run the test session, leaving 47 infants to analyze (24 males, 23 females).

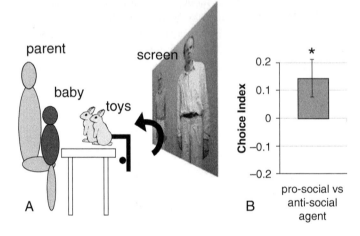

Figure 2   Set up and average preference index for 10-month-olds
A Setup of the experiment for the 10-month-olds. Infants are seated in their parent's lap (who are blindfolded) during the experiment. After the presentation of the sequences described in Figure 1, infants see a novel sequence, where the two actors appear on stage, stare at the camera, play with two identical toys, and present them to the infants. Simultaneously, two real toys appear on the table through a mechanical device. The infants' first attempt to reach one of the toys is coded by two independent scorers. Infants are tested 4 times with different toys, and the actors switching places on the screen. B. Average preference index for 10-month-olds computed over the 4 response trials. A positive score indicates a preference towards the toy of the pro-social agent, a negative score, a preference towards the anti-social agent. The error bars correspond to one between-subject standard error above and below the mean. *p < .05.

https://doi.org/10.1371/journal.pone.0088612.g002

Results and Discussion

Several infants' first attempts at reaching did not succeed either because the infant did not complete his or her gesture, or because they failed to remove the toy from the presentation arm. After an uncompleted reaching attempt, infants tended to reach towards the other object, and even subsequently to alternate between the two objects. Given such behavioral variability, we decided to code the first reaching attempt, towards one of the objects, whether or not the reaching was successful. Coders were instructed to use movements of one or both arms, as well as the orientation of body and head in order to determine the first reaching attempt. It was coded as 1, if directed towards the pro-social agent, and −1, if directed towards the antisocial agent, respectively. No obvious intended action towards one or the other toy after more than one minute was coded as zero The reliability between the two coders was .85 using Cronbach's alpha, and .80 using Cohen's Kappa (see Table S2 for row results). In order to analyze these responses statistically, the scores for the four trials (involving different toys) were averaged across the two coders to produce an average Choice Index (CI) for each infant (between −1 and +1): 57% of the infants had a positive Choice Index, 21% a negative one, and 21% were at zero (see Figure 2.B). An ANOVA of the Choice Index was run, declaring actor, order of the actions, and order of the patients as counterbalancing factors.

The intercept of the Choice Index was significantly above zero (index = 0.138; SE = 0.051, $F(1,37) = 7.9$, $p < .008$, $\eta p^2 = .18$) indicating that infants reached significantly more towards the object of the pro-social agent than the object of the anti-social agent. There was a marginal preference for one of the actors, ($F(1,37) = 3.9$, $p = .06$, $\eta p^2 = .10$) and no other counterbalancing factor introduced a significant effect or interaction ($p > .1$). A separate analysis showed no effect of the sex of the infant on the Choice Index ($F < 1$, $p > .1$).

In order to assess the robustness of the choice index as a measure of preference, we ran separate analyses for each coder separately. We found a significantly positive intercept for both of them (index = 0.165, SE = 0.056, $F(1,37) = 8.9$, $p < .005$, $\eta p^2 = 0.18$ and index = 0.112, SE = 0.053: $F(1, 37) = 4.7$, $p < .035$, $\eta p^2 = .10$, respectively). The Choice Index as a dependent variable was obtained by averaging the results of 4 binary forced choices. As such, it may not respect the normality assumptions for an ANOVA. To check for this possibility, we ran a mixed model logistic regression on the probability of choosing the pro-social agent as opposed to the anti-social agent (1 for a pro-social choice, 0 for an anti-social choice and 0.5 for an indeterminate choice) on each of the four trials separately (the associated probabilities were averaged across the two coders). The logistic model was run with actor, order of the actions, order of the patients and trial number as regressors. We still found a significant intercept ($Z = 2.06$, $p < .04$), while no other factor reached significance.

General Discussion

We investigated infants' responses to the contrast between an anti-social agent and a pro-social agent: while the former pushed down a human patient and comforted an inanimate object, the latter comforted the human patient and pushed the inanimate object. The overall amount of aggressive/threatening cues and comforting/smiling cues displayed by both the pro-social and the anti-social agents were constant, as were the emotional expressions of the human patient. Therefore, the only difference between the actors was the recipient of their respective positive and negative actions. We found that the 10-month-olds chose more often the toy from the pro-social rather than the anti-social agent, while the verbal preferences of the 29-month-olds favored the pro-social agent compared to the anti-social agent.

Low-level Explanation

The preference of toddlers and infants for the pro-social agent cannot be explained by intrinsic features of one actor over the other, as the actors' roles are counterbalanced across subjects, and their overall movements and emotional displays are equated. Note that as pointed by an anonymous reviewer, one may wonder whether our actors displayed exactly the same emotional expressions irrespective of whether their actions were directed toward a little girl or a backpack. The response is that we did ensure that our actors' display of positive and negative emotional expressions were the same whether their target was the little girl or the backpack (see Experiment S1).

Our results can neither be caused by mere associations between one of the agents and the human patient's display of emotional cues, as both agents spent the same amount of time with the object and the human patient. Furthermore, the overall amount of positive and negative affects displayed by the human patient was equated across the pro-social and the anti-social agents' actions. Finally, recency effects can also be discarded because the order between both agents and actions were counterbalanced across our participants.

Thus, what our experiment shows is that toddlers and infants prefer an agent who comforts a human patient and pushes an inanimate object to an agent who caresses an inanimate object and pushes a human patient. If their preferences were primarily based on the valence of the agent's action directed towards the inanimate object, then one would expect them to prefer the agent who caressed the inanimate object over the agent who pushed it. This expectation is contradicted by the results of our experiment. If toddlers and infants' preferences depended on the valence of the agent's action irrespective of the target of this action, one would expect them to express no preference for either agent, which is not what we found in our experiments. Instead, what our data suggest is that toddlers and infants are already evaluating an agent based on how they treat another human. Thus, our results are consistent with the hypothesis that toddlers and infants' preferences primarily reflect the valence of an agent's action directed towards a human patient, not towards an inanimate object.

Our results could be due to the fact that for toddlers and infants, actions directed towards humans are more salient, more memorable, or receive a larger evaluative weight than actions directed towards inanimate objects. This interpretation is compatible with the claim by Premack and Premack [8] that there exists, in early human infancy, a core cognitive ability for the social evaluation of human agents based on their actions towards conspecifics. It is also compatible with several experiments showing that infants express early social preferences toward benevolent agents who performed positive actions toward their conspecifics [9]–[11], [15]. We extended these findings by providing evidence that infants are able to distinguish a benevolent from a malevolent agent whose action impacts a patient's physical integrity.

Thus, in order to account for our results, we need to postulate a combination of at least two psychological components, one of which is sensitive to the nature of the patient and/or to the valence of her emotional states, and the other of which is sensitive to the nature of the agent's action. Importantly, these two components have to be *combined* in a specific way in order to account for the results that we observed in our experiments.

We consider three nonexclusive theoretical possibilities for such combinations, ranging from the least to the most complex. A first simple possibility could be that infants are merely *associating* the identity of the agent of the action with the *emotional change* displayed by the patient, without really attending to the structure or valence of the agent's action. That is, infants would notice that one character is always associated with the patient's changing from happy to sad, and the other with the patient's changing from sad to happy. Such an associative mechanism predicts that infants should prefer the latter to the former, even if the agent performs an action that is not harmful for the patient (i.e., dancing, spinning, etc.).

A second and more complex possibility could be that infants are associating an agent with the positive or negative valence of his or her action (i.e., throwing vs. raising), irrespective of the patient's emotional response. Since, however, the association is stronger when the target of the agent's action is a human patient than an inanimate object, the associative mechanism must further depend on some attentional mechanism geared towards the detection of human beings. Moreover, whether this associative mechanism could bypass the need for a causal analysis of the agent's action is an open question.

A third possibility is that infants track not only the victim's emotional response, but also the causal structure of the agent's action, and that they assign blame for the victim's suffering to the human agent who is causally responsible for the suffering (see [26], [27]). Although we know that infants are sensitive to the causal structure of events [28], [29], we do not know whether they can use this kind of analyses in social evaluation.

On the surface, the three aforementioned mechanisms are quite different in terms of the cognitive resources they require. Unfortunately, they cannot be fully disentangled on the basis of our present findings. Yet, other published results involving older populations suggest possible ways to address this issue. For instance, Leslie et al. [17] tested preschoolers in a situation where the omission of an act (refusing to give a cookie upon request) caused a patient to cry. Preschoolers did not evaluate the agent negatively, even though he was *associated* with the patient's increased distress. This could be taken as evidence that, contrary to the first hypothesis, the nature of the action (i.e., causing physical harm versus omitting to give) matters, and not merely associations with an emotional change (as proposed by the first hypothesis). Vaish, Carpenter and Tomasello [30] presented 18-month-old toddlers with a human patient victimized by an agent through the destruction of his drawing. Despite the fact that the patient did not display an emotional reaction, toddlers were more likely to help the victimized patient than the non-victimized one. This could be taken as evidence that preschoolers are able to track the intrinsic valence of actions, irrespective of the patients' emotional cues, as proposed by the second hypothesis. Buon et al. [31] showed that even when performing a concurrent linguistic task, adults evaluate more negatively an agent who performs an action (swinging) that causes harm to a victim (falling) than an agent who performs the same physical movements but does not cause the victim's suffering (because the victim falls on her own). This suggests that, in adults, complex cognitive/linguistic resources are not necessary to perform blame assignment based on the causal structure of the event, as proposed by the third hypothesis.

These studies show that it is possible, in principle, to dissociate the three hypotheses, although the relevant experimental conditions must be adapted to preverbal infants. Meanwhile, it is important to note that even if 10-month-olds were basing their responses on simple associative mechanisms, the associations should link at least two factors, one of which is the structure of the *action*, and the other is the nature of the *patient* (or her emotional responses). Specifically, infants prefer agents who perform a positive action towards a human patient, and a negative one towards an inanimate object than agents who do the converse. Such a capacity would, in practice, enable infants to detect potentially harmful conspecifics, which, on evolutionary grounds, is useful to their survival. Before closing, we raise four questions for further research: the potential asymmetry between positive and negative actions, the small size of our effects, the role of intentions versus causal role and the link between the Help/Hinder situation and the Comfort/Harm situation.

Positive versus Negative Actions

The first question is: to what extent do respectively the aversion prompted by an agent's negative action and the appeal of an agent's positive action play a symmetrical role in action-based social evaluations by preverbal human infants? Given the evolutionary importance of the detection of potentially harmful and dangerous agents, one would expect that the ability to detect harmful agents plays a stronger role and arises earlier than the ability to track benefactors. However, on the basis of our experimental design, which directly compares positive and negative actions, it is not possible to tease apart the respective contribution of the positive and negative outcomes of an agent's act to infants' evaluation of agents.

There is, however, some independent evidence suggesting that human infants give more weight to negative than to positive emotions. This "negativity bias" appears to emerge within the first year of life and has been documented through several research paradigms. For instance, Mumme and Fernald [32] found that 12-month-old infants display emotional contagion after watching television scenarios conveying negative emotions, but not positive ones. Vaish et al. [33]argue that in social referencing paradigms, negative cues (such as fear and disgust) have a more immediate and greater impact than positive cues. Cacioppo and Gardner [34] argue that negative information serves as a signal to change behavior whereas positive information is more likely to serve as a signal to stay on course. In this context, the negativity bias may serve the crucial evolutionary adaptive function of helping infants to avoid potentially harmful stimuli.

In our experiment, evidence for this hypothetical asymmetry comes from the toddlers' results. When analyzed separately, toddlers' absolute evaluations were significantly negative for the anti-social agent, but neither negative nor positive for the pro-social agent. In addition, toddlers made significantly more comments about negative than positive actions (if performed on humans). This suggests a greater saliency of anti-social actions than pro-social ones. Consistent with this, Hamlin, Wynn & Bloom [10] reported a looking time difference in 3-month-olds between the hinderer and a neutral agent, but not between a helper and a neutral agent. Note that this asymmetry between the processing of positive versus negative interactions was not found at six months [9], since infants were able to distinguish both the helper and the hinderer from the neutral control. This lack of asymmetry at 6-months could, however, be due to a ceiling effect, as in Hamlin et al.'s experimental situations [9], [10], the agents perform only one action (*either* positive *or* negative). In our experiment, each agent performs a pair of actions (one positive and one negative), thereby providing more opportunity for a potential asymmetry to show up. For instance, it could be that the positive action performed towards the human patient by the pro-social agent is partially counterbalanced by the negative action that the same agent performs on the object, which could also be negatively valued by young children and infants [35],

yielding a relatively neutral evaluation of this agent. In contrast, the anti-social agent's negative actions towards a human patient would not be counterbalanced by his positive actions towards objects, yielding a negative aggregate evaluation. More research is needed, using different neutral situations as baselines, to fully test a potential "negativity bias" and the conditions of its expression in the case of the social evaluation of agents based on their actions.

Small Effect Size

Secondly, we have to acknowledge here that our effect size is small compared to those in some others experiments. For example, Hamlin and collaborators showed that infants prefer to interact with an agent who helps over an agent who hinders another to achieve his goal with only 16 participants (only two of them having failed to choose the helper on the test phase). Several hypotheses could account for this large difference in the sample size required. First, as we just noticed, the situations presented to infants and toddlers in our experiments are more complex than the situations presented to infants in Hamlin et al.'s experiment. In Hamlin et al.'s experiment, there are two agents and one patient, each of them performing only one action. In our experiment, there are two agents and two patients. In addition, each animated agent performed two sets of different actions and this could be more costly to process. Moreover, as mentioned above, we counterbalanced all emotional cues associated with both the agents and the victims to ensure that infants' and toddlers' responses were not only based on the emotional cues displayed by different actors. However, while this caution allowed us to explain the nature of our effects, it might also have weakened it. Indeed, while we would attribute a positive evaluation to a character who comforts a little girl, this positive evaluation could be dampened by the threatening cues associated with the action of "hitting a bag".

Intentions to Harm versus Harmful Consequences

The third question is that even though our study controls for low-level effects, it does incorporate a high-level confound: while the anti-social agent has an anti-social intention, he also causes actual harm to a human. Similarly, the pro-social agent has a pro-social intention and also provides comfort to a human. In adults, both intentions and consequences play a role in moral evaluation. However, in case a conflict arises, as in attempted harm, or in unintended harm, intentions are typically assigned a stronger weight than consequences [31], [36], [37]. Here, since intentions and consequences are confounded, we cannot tell whether infants and toddlers were more sensitive to one or the other. Other studies, however, have looked at the role of intentions in early social moral evaluations. For instance, Vaish and collaborators [15]found that preschoolers were more likely to help a neutral agent rather than a malevolent agent even if the latter agent's action failed (attempted malevolent action). Hamlin [38] recently showed that 8-month-olds preferred a puppet who attempted to help a patient to reach its goal over a puppet who attempted to prevent it from achieving its goal, irrespective of whether the attempt succeeded or failed. However, 8-month-olds did not distinguish between two agents that had matched (helpful or harmful) intentions, and differed on the success or failure of their actions. In contrast to these studies suggesting the primacy of intentions over outcomes in infant's social evaluations, others have showed that preschoolers are prone to use information about the consequences of an agent's action rather than information about the agent's intention [21], [39]. Finally, some researchers showed that preschoolers tend to use equally information about consequences and intentions [16], [40]. More research is needed to disentangle the respective roles of intentions and consequences as a function of experimental situations and paradigms during development.

Help/Hinder versus Comfort/Harm Situations

The fourth question emerges from the fact that Premack and Premack [8] seemed to assume that the mechanism underlying social evaluation in preverbal human infants takes as input acts exemplifying either the Help/Hinder contrast or the Comfort/Harm contrast. As already mentioned, from a conceptual standpoint, there is room for drawing a distinction: an agent could not help or hinder someone else unless the latter had a goal; but an agent can harm or comfort a victim, whether or not the victim is pursuing a specific goal. Grasping the distinction between a joint action and an antagonistic action is necessary for understanding the contrast between helping and hindering, not the contrast between comforting and harming. What is required to grasp the contrast between harming and comforting is that the former, not the latter, causes the victim's pain or distress.

It is therefore an open question whether a single cognitive mechanism underlies the responses to these two contrasts (help/hinder and comfort/harm), as hypothesized by Premack and Premack [8].

One possible speculation to be further investigated is that what underlies infants' responses to instances of both the Help/Hinder and the Harm/Comfort contrasts (as well as other malevolent/benevolent contrasts) is a single mechanism for tracking the causation of *physical* and *psychological* distress. Whereas physical aggression causes the former, the frustration caused by either the failure to achieve a goal or the unequal distribution of resources could well induce the latter. It is reasonable to assume that young infants, because of their difficulties in carrying out

planned actions, might have considerable experience with goal frustration, and might come to readily associate such situations with a state of psychological distress. Even though we are not aware of a direct test of this hypothesis, there is evidence that toddlers go to considerable trouble to help perfect strangers who are stuck in a situation where they cannot reach their goals [41]–[43]. If so, then it would follow that they will interpret the hinderer's act in Hamlin et al.'s [9] study as causing the victim's psychological distress (mutatis mutandis for help and psychological relief). An interesting research agenda, therefore, is to study whether the two situations studied by Premack and Premack [8] develop at the same pace in infants, and whether they involve a common mechanism whose function is to track the causation of physical or psychological pain.

Author Contributions

Conceived and designed the experiments: ED PJ. Performed the experiments: MB SM. Analyzed the data: MB ED IB. Contributed reagents/materials/analysis tools: MD DC. Wrote the paper: ED MB PJ.

References

1. Warneken F, Chen F, Tomasello M (2006) Cooperative activities in young children and chimpanzees. Child development 77: 640–663.
2. Warneken F, Tomasello M (2007) Helping and Cooperation at 14 Months of Age. Infancy 11: 271–294
3. Cosmides L (1989) The logic of social exchange: has natural selection shaped how humans reason? Studies with the Wason selection task. Cognition 31: 187–276
4. Keeley LH (1996) War before civilization: the myth of the peaceful savage. Oxford Uni. New York, NY.
5. Behne T, Carpenter M, Call J, Tomasello M (2005) Unwilling versus unable: infants' understanding of intentional action. Developmental psychology 41: 328–337
6. Brandone AC, Wellman HM (2009) You can't always get what you want: infants understand failed goal-directed actions. Psychological science 20: 85–91. doi: 10.1111/j.1467-9280.2008.02246.x7.
7. Onishi KH, Baillargeon R (2005) Do 15-month-old infants understand false beliefs? Science (New York, NY) 308: 255–258. doi: 10.1126/science.1107621.
8. Premack D, Premack AJ (1997) Infants attributed values to goal directed actions of self propelled object. Journal of cognitive neuroscience. 9: 848–56

Friend or Foe? Early Social Evaluation of Human Interactions by Marine Buon et al.

82

9. Hamlin JK, Wynn K, Bloom P (2007) Social evaluation by preverbal infants. Nature 450: 557–559

10. Hamlin JK, Wynn K (2010) Bloom P (2010) *Three-month-olds show a negativity bias in their social evaluations*. Developmental science 13: 923–929

11. Hamlin JK, Wynn K (2011) Young infants prefer prosocial to antisocial others. Cognitive development 26: 30–39. doi: 10.1016/j.cogdev.2010.09.001.

12. Sloane S, Baillargeon R, Premack D (2012) Do infants have a sense of fairness? Psychological science 23: 196–204. doi: 10.1177/0956797611422072.

13. Schmidt MFH, Sommerville JA (2011) Fairness expectations and altruistic sharing in 15-month-old human infants. PLoS ONE 6(10). doi: 10.1371/journal.pone.0023223.

14. Geraci A, Surian L (2011) The developmental roots of fairness: infants' reactions to equal and unequal distributions of resources. Developmental science 5: 1012–1020.

15. Vaish A, Carpenter M, Tomasello M (2010) Young children selectively avoid helping people with harmful intentions. Child development 81: 1661–1669.

16. Nelson SA (1980) Factors Influencing Young Children's Use of Motives and Outcomes as Moral Criteria. Child Development 51: 823. doi: 10.1037/0012-1649.21.2.332.

17. Leslie AM, Mallon R, DiCorcia JA (2006) Transgressors, victims, and cry babies: is basic moral judgment spared in autism? Social neuroscience 1: 270–283. doi: 10.1080/17470910600992197.

18. Weisberg DS, Leslie AM (2012) The Role of Victims' Emotions in Preschoolers' Moral Judgments. Review of Philosophy and Psychology

19. Haidt J (2007) The new synthesis in moral psychology. Science (New York, NY) 316: 998–1002. doi: 10.1126/science.1137651.

20. Smetana JG (1981) Preschool Children's Conceptions of Moral and Social Rules. Child Development 52: 1333. doi: 10.2307/1129527.

21. Zelazo PD, Helwig CC, Lau A (1996) Intention, act, and outcome in behavioral prediction and moral judgment. Child Development 67: 2478–2492. doi: 10.2307/1131635.

22. Walker-Andrews AS (1997) Infants' perception of expressive behaviors: differentiation of multimodal information. Psychological bulletin 121: 437–456. doi: 10.1037/a0024435.

23. Walle EA, Campos JJ (2012) Interpersonal Responding to Discrete Emotions: A Functionalist Approach to the Development of Affect Specificity. Emotion Review 4: 413–422

24. D'Entremont B, Muir D (1999) Infant responses to adult happy and sad vocal and facial expressions during face-to-face interactions. Infant Behavior and Development 22: 527–539

25. Kinzler KD, Dupoux E, Spelke ES (2007) The native language of social cognition. Proceedings of the National Academy of Sciences of the United States of America 104: 12577–12580. doi: 10.1073/pnas.0705345104.

26. Alicke MD (2000) Culpable control and the psychology of blame. Psychological Bulletin 126: 556–574. doi: 10.1037/0033-2909.126.4.556.

27. Mikhail J (2007) Universal moral grammar: theory, evidence and the future. Trends in cognitive sciences 11: 143–152. doi: 10.1016/j.tics.2006.12.007.

28. Leslie AM (1982) The perception of causality in infants. Perception 11: 173–186

29. Leslie AM, Keeble S (1987) Do six-month-old infants perceive causality? Cognition 25: 265–288

30. Vaish A, Carpenter M, Tomasello M (2009) Sympathy through affective perspective taking and its relation to prosocial behavior in toddlers. Developmental psychology 45: 534–543. doi: 10.1037/a0014322.

31. Buon M, Jacob P, Loissel E, Dupoux E (2013) A non-mentalistic cause-based heuristic in human social evaluations. Cognition 126: 149–155

32. Mumme DL, Fernald A (1995) The infant as onlooker: learning from emotional reactions observed in a television scenario. Child development 74: 221–237.

33. Vaish A, Grossmann T, Woodward A (2008) Not all emotions are created equal: the negativity bias in social-emotional development. Psychological bulletin 134: 383–403. doi: 10.1037/0033-2909.134.3.383.

34. Cacioppo JT, Gardner WL (1999) Emotion. Annu Rev Psychol 50: 191–214. doi: 10.1146/annurev.psych.50.1.191.

35. Decety J, Michalska KJ, Kinzler KD (2011) The Contribution of Emotion and Cognition to Moral Sensitivity: A Neurodevelopmental Study. Cerebral cortex. doi: 10.1093/cercor/bhr111.

36. Cushman F (2008) Crime and punishment: distinguishing the roles of causal and intentional analyses in moral judgment. Cognition 108: 353–380. doi: 10.1016/j.cognition.2008.03.006.

37. Piaget J (1997) The moral judgment of the child. Broché. New York: Free Press.

38. Hamlin JK (2013) Failed attempts to help and harm: Intention versus outcome in preverbal infants' social evaluations. Cognition 128: 451–474.

39. Hebble PW (1971) The Development of Elementary School Children's Judgment of Intent. Child Development 42: 1203. doi: 10.1016/j.cognition.2013.04.004.

40. Nelson-le Gall SA (1985) Motive-outcome matching and outcome foreseeability: Effects on attribution of intentionality and moral judgments. Developmental Psychology 21: 332–337. doi: 10.1037/0012-1649.21.2.332.

41. Warneken F, Hare B, Melis AP, Hanus D, Tomasello M (2007) Spontaneous altruism by chimpanzees and young children. PLoS biology. doi: 10.1371/journal.pbio.0050184.

42. Warneken F, Tomasello M (2006) Altruistic helping in human infants and young chimpanzees. Science (New York, NY) 311: 1301–1303. doi: 10.1126/science.1121448.

43. Warneken F, Tomasello M (2009) Varieties of altruism in children and chimpanzees. Trends in cognitive sciences 13: 397–402. doi: 10.1016/j.tics.2009.06.008.

Critical Thinking

1. If infants distinguish between helpful and non-helpful actions, what could the origin of such a skill be?
2. What are some other kinds of measurements or methods to assess young children's judgments of helpfulness of others?
3. Is the ability to discern helpful from non-helpful acts an important social skills? How might the lack of this skill put children at risk in their social relationships?

Internet References

9 Ways for Parents to Promote Prosocial Behavior in Early Childhood
https://psychcentral.com/blog/9-ways-for-parents-to-promote-prosocial-behavior-in-early-childhood/

3 ways Teachers Can Help Children Learn Pro-Social Behaviors
https://choosykids.com/blogs/choosy-blog/3-ways-teachers-can-help-children-learn-pro-social-behaviors

Buon, Marine. et al., "Friend or Foe? Early Social Evaluation of Human Interactions." PLOS One, February 19, 2014.

Is Your Child an Orchid or a Dandelion? Unlocking the Science of Sensitive Kids by Dave Davies

84

Article

Prepared by: Chris J. Boyatzis, *Bucknell University* and
Ellen N. Junn, *California State University, Stanislaus*

Is Your Child an Orchid or a Dandelion? Unlocking the Science of Sensitive Kids

DAVE DAVIES

Learning Outcomes

After reading this article, you will be able to:

- Describe some biological contributions to children's personality and temperament.

- Identify behavioral and temperamental differences that exist between children.

D r. Thomas Boyce, an emeritus professor of pediatrics and psychiatry at the University of California, San Francisco, has treated children who seem to be completely unflappable and unfazed by their surroundings—as well as those who are extremely sensitive to their environments. Over the years, he began to liken these two types of children to two very different flowers: dandelions and orchids.

Broadly speaking, says Boyce—who also has spent nearly 40 years studying the human stress response, especially in children—most kids tend to be like dandelions, fairly resilient and able to cope with stress and adversity in their lives. But a minority of kids, those he calls "orchid children," are more sensitive and biologically reactive to their circumstances, which makes it harder for them to deal with stressful situations.

Like the flower, Boyce says, "the orchid child is the child who shows great sensitivity and susceptibility to both bad and good environments in which he or she finds herself or himself."

Given supportive, nurturing conditions, orchid children can thrive—especially, Boyce says, if they have the comfort of a regular routine.

"Orchid children seem to thrive on having things like dinner every night in the same place at the same time with the same people, having certain kinds of rituals that the family goes through week to week, month to month," he says. "This kind

of routine and sameness of life from day to day, week to week, seems to be something that is helpful to kids with these great susceptibilities."

Interview Highlights

On the lab test he did to determine if a child is an orchid or a dandelion

We made an effort to try to understand these individual differences between children in how they respond biologically to mild, common kinds of challenges and stressors, and the way we did that was we brought them into a laboratory setting. We sat them down in front of an examiner—a research assistant that they had not previously met—and we asked them to go through a series of mildly challenging tasks. These were things like recounting a series of digits that the examiner asked them to say and increasing that from first three to four to five digits; having them just engage in a conversation with this examiner, who might ask them about their birthday or presents or something about their family. That, in itself, is a challenge for a young child. Putting a drop of lemon juice on the tongue was another kind of challenge that was evocative of these changes in biological response. ...

We measured their stress response using the two primary stress response systems in the human brain. [One was] the cortisol system, which is centered in the hypothalamus of the brain. This is the system that releases the stress hormone cortisol, which has profound effects on both immune function and cardiovascular functioning.

And then the second stress response system is the autonomic nervous system, or the "fight-or-flight" system. This is the one that is responsible for the sweaty palms and a little bit of tremulousness, the dilation of the pupils, all of these things that we associate with the fight-or-flight response. So we were monitoring responsivity and both of those systems as the children went through these mildly challenging tasks. ...

We found that there were huge differences [among] children. There were some children at the high end of the spectrum, who had dramatic reactivity in both the cortisol system and the fight-or-flight system, and there were other children who had almost no biological response to the challenges that we presented to them.

On how a child's responsivity to stressors can be connected to physical and emotional behavioral outcomes

We find in our research that the same kinds of patterns of response are found for both physical illnesses, like severe respiratory disease, pneumonia, asthma and so on, as well as or more [in] emotional behavioral outcomes, like anxiety and depression and externalizing kinds of symptoms. So we believe that the same patterns of susceptibility that we find in the orchid child versus the dandelion child work themselves out not only for physical ailments but also for psychosocial and emotional problems. And we believe that the same kinds of underlying biological processes work for both.

We do know, for example, that these two stress response systems ... the cortisol system and the fight-or-flight system, the autonomic nervous system, both of those have powerful effects on the immune system, so they can alter the child's ability to build an immune defense against viruses and bacteria that he or she may be exposed to. And they have also powerful effects on the cardiovascular system, so [they] could eventually, in adult life, predispose to developing hypertension, high blood pressure or other kinds of cardiovascular risk.

On how children's experiences can vary, even within the same family

The experience of children within a given family, the siblings within a family—although they are being reared with the same parents in the same house in the same neighborhood— they actually have quite different kinds of experiences that depend upon the birth order of the child, the gender of the child, to some extent differences in genetic sequence. It is a way of talking about these dramatic differences that kids from different birth orders and different genders have within a given family.

On pushing orchid kids to stretch to do new or difficult things

I think that this is probably the most difficult parenting task in raising an orchid child. The parent of an orchid child needs to walk this very fine line between, on the one hand, not pushing them into circumstances that are really going to overwhelm them and make them greatly fearful, but, on the other hand, not protecting them so much that they don't have experiences of mastery of these kinds of fearful situations.

Critical Thinking

1. In what kinds of environments—school, day-care, peer groups—might orchids and dandelions thrive differently?

2. How could you explain to parents differences between orchid and dandelion children and how parents could determine which type they have?

3. What are some dangers inherent in simple typologies of children, classifying them into broad categories?

Internet References

ChildMind.org
https://childmind.org/article/how-to-help-your-child-get-motivated-in-school/

Psychology Today.com
https://www.psychologytoday.com/us/blog/creative-development/201106/the-highly-sensitive-child

Article

Prepared by: Chris J. Boyatzis, *Bucknell University* and
Ellen N. Junn, *California State University, Stanislaus*

Are Outdoor Preschools the Wave of the Future?

From preschool programs to community-based meetups to weekly nature classes, outdoor programs are increasing in popularity. And it isn't just kids who are reaping the rewards.

SHANTI HODGES

Learning Outcomes

After reading this article, you will be able to:

- Present several benefits of being outdoors for children's development.

- Understand the increasing interest in outdoor preschools given children's current sedentary and indoor lifestyles.

A group of toddlers waddle down a muddy path at Tryon Creek State Natural Area in Portland, Oregon, alternating between moving at a snail's pace and running full-speed ahead. A handful of parents and caregivers are standing back, letting the children lead the way. No one is in a hurry and there's no obvious teaching going on here. For the most part, it just looks like an everyday hike with a few families.

But this is more than a casual outing. This is the Free Forest School, a weekly meetup for families with preschool-age children. It's a community-based version of an outdoor preschool, part of a growing trend to provide children with educational opportunities in the outdoors well before kindergarten.

What Are Outdoor Preschools?

According to the Natural Start Alliance, part of the North American Association for Environmental Education, outdoor preschools share goals with traditional preschools, but achieve those goals by providing children with more time spent in nature. In some outdoor preschools, kids spend four-hour stretches in the fresh air, while in others, children alternate between indoor and outdoor time. Outdoor preschools occur in a range of contexts—from nature centers to botanical gardens to urban green spaces.

The recent interest in nature for children can be attributed to author and journalist Richard Louv, who coined the term nature-deficit disorder to represent the alienation from the outdoors he was observing in American culture in 2005. His book "Last Child in the Woods" called attention to the negative effects of reduced time spent outdoors, especially on children, and ignited a cultural conversation about how children are impacted by technology and long hours spent inside.

David Sobel, a professor emeritus at Antioch University New England, studies the effects of outdoor education on children. Over the past five years, he has seen an increase in the number of outdoor offerings for children, from infants and toddlers to 5-year-olds, as well as increased enthusiasm for studying this phenomenon. "It's only been in the last decade that we've begun to see the effects of 'digitization' and 'indoorization' on toddlers," Sobel said. "I think the growth in these programs comes from the parents' rejection of this trend and the negative impacts of that showing through in their kids."

Between 2016 and 2017, the U.S. saw a 66 percent increase in the number of registered outdoor preschools and kindergartens. Here, a group of preschoolers turn a series of boulders into a make-believe world. (Photo Credit: Jessie Emslie)

How Did Outdoor Preschools Get Started?

While outdoor preschools may be relatively new in the United States, they've been around in Europe since the 1950s, when forest schools began popping up in Denmark. Today, a majority of young children attend preschool in Europe, which may help explain some of the schools' popularity there. In Sweden, where in 1985 the first "I Ur och Skur" or "rain or shine school" was founded, eighty percent of children between 1 and 5 attend preschool. By contrast, in 2016, only 42 percent of 3-year-olds attended pre-primary school, according to the Organisation for Economic Co-operation and Development. By age 5, that number jumped to nearly 90 percent.

But things are changing in the United States. According to a study published in November 2017 by the Natural Start Alliance, the U.S. saw a 66 percent increase in the number of registered outdoor preschools and kindergartens between 2016 and 2017.

That rapid increase has inspired researchers like Sobel and Dr. Pooja Tandon, an assistant professor of pediatrics at the University of Washington, who is investigating the connection between time spent in nature and children's health and development. "Outdoor play and nature contact from an early age provide wonderful opportunities [for kids] to explore [their] senses, be active, and learn," she said. "And there are likely benefits to their health and well-being."

The Case for Outdoor Preschools

Angela Hanscom has been touting the importance of nature for children for much of her 15-year career. In 2012, Hanscom, a pediatric occupational therapist in Barrington, New Hampshire, began to observe that children who weren't getting quality time outdoors lacked fundamental skills like coordination, grip strength and balance. She started documenting what she was seeing in 2013.

> "Programs that get children outdoors, moving, playing and connecting with nature—and with each other—offer invaluable foundational skills."—Pediatric Occupational Therapist Angela Hanscom

"We are starting to see the simultaneous effects of less outdoor play and more screen time on children's development," Hanscom said. "In the [occupational] therapy world, we are struggling to keep up with the growing demand of children needing services. Outdoor schools are a solution that will help bridge the gap between education, health care and the developmental needs of children."

In 2014, Hanscom's observations prompted her to found TimberNook, an outdoor play program for children that educators and therapists can attend. Just two years later, in 2016, she wrote an argument for outdoor play called "Barefoot and Balanced: How Unrestricted Outdoor Play Makes for Strong, Confident and Capable Children."

Sobel and Hanscom say children need time outdoors, beginning at birth, for proper brain development. Whether it's crawling through grass as an infant, or balancing while walking across a fallen tree as a child, these explorations can have a big impact on children's growth.

"Programs that get children outdoors, moving, playing and connecting with nature—and with each other—offer invaluable foundational skills. Simply stepping outdoors and listening to bird sounds helps a child orient their body to the space around them," Hanscom said.

> "We find parents go through this transformational process when they join a program like ours. They realize they want their kids to be these creative, free kids, and as a result we end up with this army of folks who will advocate that for their schools when their kids [enter elementary school]"—Founder of Free Forest School Anna Sharratt

At Tryon Creek State Natural Area, the Free Forest School is wrapping up and the toddlers are heading toward the nature center, where they can dip indoors to warm up and dry out after a soggy Oregon walk. Families who attend the Free Forest School often linger long after the hike is over. Caregivers share book recommendations, exchange tips about toddler-friendly trails, and talk about the little things they do to carry on the natural experience for their children at home. The gathering seems to have an impact that reaches beyond their children's education.

The research on how a school day spent outdoors may affect children's intellectual development is still in its infancy. In 2017, a four-year study conducted by Norwegian researchers found a positive correlation between outdoor schools and lower levels of hyperactivity and inattention among preschoolers.

In analyzing data collected from 2016 to 2017, Sobel's group found that 3- to 5-year-olds attending a Michigan outdoor preschool possessed similar early literacy skills when compared with kids in a traditional setting. In two measures of executive function, however, the children attending the outdoor preschool showed lower levels of development.

Sobel notes that assessing young children's progress can be challenging. "We recognize it's hard to get 3- and 4-year-olds to pay attention and do quantitative testing," he said. "Part of the issue now is figuring out the metrics for this age, so we can really understand outdoor schools' impact."

Roadblocks Currently Faced by Outdoor Preschools

One of the biggest challenges faced by outdoor preschools is that licensing requirements vary from state to state, with some states requiring that schools have a physical building in order to be licensed. This puts preschools without a physical structure in a tough spot: Families can be wary about sending their children to schools that aren't state-licensed.

Children who attend outdoor preschools have freedom to roam. But a lack of a physical structure can pose a challenge for schools when it comes to state licensing.

Now, a pilot program being overseen by the Washington State Department of Early Learning is testing what constitutes proper preschool facilities in Washington state. State officials have awarded 12 outdoor preschools conditional licenses to operate full-day preschool programs, without physical buildings. The results will be used to analyze Washington's current licensure model and, potentially, to adapt regulations. The trial could have implications for outdoor programs in other states, too, especially where access to physical facilities can be a major hurdle for founding a school.

Who Gets to Participate?

Outdoor preschools are primarily private and vary widely in terms of cost. In Portland, Oregon, at the Wildwood Nature School, families pay $495 per month for kids to attend four days a week. That quickly adds up to nearly $6,000 per year, and doesn't cover the cost of childcare for the remaining 28 hours of the week that many caregivers spend working. In Chattanooga, Tennessee, the Wauhatchie Forest School costs $345 per month for three hours, three days a week. These high prices and limited offerings can make outdoor preschools inaccessible for many Americans.

That could be why cost-effective, community-powered offerings like Free Forest School and Hike it Baby's meetups have quickly gained popularity amid the outdoor preschool trend. Both groups have weekly offerings in natural settings, and are virtually free (Hike it Baby charges its members $10 per year and some meeting locations charge parking fees). The downside is that these community meetups are volunteer-led, meaning they don't always happen at times that accommodate working families. On the plus side, the gatherings fill a niche for those who can't afford outdoor preschools and families who are still deciding if outdoor education is right for them.

Anna Sharratt, the founder and executive director of Free Forest School, started her program as a way of creating something affordable for all families to do. "I was living in Brooklyn and what I was seeing were these expensive classes where you would go and make mud pies with your kids in the park," Sharratt said. She founded her free program in 2015. Now, Free Forest School is active in more than 100 cities across the United States and has served close to 150,000 children.

Sharratt feels that outdoor programs can help all members of the family to fall in love with the outdoors. "We find parents go through this transformational process when they join a program like ours. They realize they want their kids to be these creative, free kids, and as a result we end up with this army of folks who will advocate that for their schools when their kids [enter elementary school]" she said.

Weekly Nature Programs: An Emerging In-between

While free programming can be an ideal entry point, there's an emerging in-between inspired by nature-based training programs like TimberNook on the East Coast and Cedarsong Nature School in Washington state: weekly nature programs. These structured, one-to three-hour classes provide immersion in nature for both children and their caregivers. Typically more affordable than outdoor preschools, the offerings are also less time-consuming, making them perfect for families still deciding if outdoor preschools are right for them.

Loblolly Adventures in Charleston, South Carolina, is one such program, cofounded by Danielle Loveless, a former Cedarsong teacher. The structure is simple: Families meet once a week in the same park for 10 weeks in a row. The children lead the way and an informal lesson involves kids migrating from one outdoor discovery to another. Loveless thinks this method allows kids to connect more deeply with the environment.

"We've noticed that after a few weeks in class, the parents begin to exhibit their own enthusiasm for learning from and playing in nature."—Loblolly Adventures Cofounder Danielle Loveless

And there's another benefit: "We've noticed that after a few weeks in class, the parents begin to exhibit their own enthusiasm for learning from and playing in nature," Loveless said. "Children see their [caregivers] enjoying themselves while interacting with their natural surroundings and, in turn, a new level of connection emerges. There is less fear, more curiosity, and unlimited potential for taking what they learned in class and utilizing it in their daily life."

Recently, one of Loveless' lessons became derailed by a group of preschoolers who were fixated on building a fort from rocks, moss and sticks. Instead of trying to keep the group on track, Loveless watched as the adults stood back and, for the next two hours, let the kids teach each other everything they knew about construction and the natural objects they were using.

"We have just reached a point when we as parents are reevaluating the American education system. With what's going on in the world globally, there's a new generation of folks who are seeing what could potentially happen, and we want to make sure that our parks and green spaces are still here for our great-grandchildren," Loveless said.

Whether it's a weekly nature program, a community meetup or a more formal outdoor preschool program, those who are involved with early childhood development programs say these offerings spark interest in nature for both families.

"We're excited because we can see that the trend in nature preschools is carrying over and moving into kindergarten through second grade, which means better accessibility for all," says Emilian Geczi, director of the Natural Start Alliance. "We're seeing schools adding nature study to mainstream education because parents are asking for it. In doing this, it just naturally makes environmental education more inclusive for everyone."

Critical Thinking

1. What are your strongest memories of being outside as a child? How did those experiences differ from ones you had indoors?

2. What might the impact be of spending more time outdoors on children's cognitive outcomes (e.g., attention span) and emotional outcomes (e.g., calmness, well-being)?

Internet References

Outside Online
https://www.outsideonline.com/2346611/how-pick-outdoor-preschool

REI COOP
https://www.rei.com/blog/news/are-outdoor-preschools-the-wave-of-the-future

Article

Prepared by: Chris J. Boyatzis, *Bucknell University* and
Ellen N. Junn, *California State University, Stanislaus*

In Britain's Playgrounds, 'Bringing in Risk' to Build Resilience

ELLEN BARRY

Learning Outcomes

After reading this article, you will be able to:

- Describe England's recent trend by educators to introduce risk in a controlled play environment for children.

- Explain some of the outcomes and benefits of these more controlled risk playgrounds for children and their families.

- Explain how the laws in England make implementing this trend easier than in the United States.

SHOEBURYNESS, England—Educators in Britain, after decades spent in a collective effort to minimize risk, are now, cautiously, getting into the business of providing it.

Four years ago, for instance, teachers at the Richmond Avenue Primary and Nursery School looked critically around their campus and set about, as one of them put it, "bringing in risk."

Out went the plastic playhouses and in came the dicey stuff: stacks of two-by-fours, crates and loose bricks. The schoolyard got a mud pit, a tire swing, log stumps and workbenches with hammers and saws.

"We thought, how can we bring that element of risk into your everyday environment?" said Leah Morris, who manages the early years program at the school in Shoeburyness in southeast Britain. "We were looking at, O.K., so we've got a sand pit, what can we add to the sand pit to make it more risky?"

Now, Ms. Morris says proudly, "we have fires, we use knives, saws, different tools," all used under adult supervision. Indoors, scissors abound, and so do sharp-edged tape dispensers ("they normally only cut themselves once," she says).

Limited risks are increasingly cast by experts as an experience essential to childhood development, useful in building resilience and grit.

Outside the Princess Diana Playground in Kensington Gardens in London, which attracts more than a million visitors a year, a placard informs parents that risks have been "intentionally provided, so that your child can develop an appreciation of risk in a controlled play environment rather than taking similar risks in an uncontrolled and unregulated wider world."

This view is tinged with nostalgia for an earlier Britain, in which children were tougher and more self-reliant. It resonates both with right-wing tabloids, which see it as a corrective to the cosseting of a liberal nanny state; and with progressives, drawn to a freer and more natural childhood. It is also supported by a growing list of government officials, among them Amanda Spielman, the chief inspector of Ofsted, the powerful agency that inspects British schools.

Ms. Spielman has poked fun at schools for what she considers excessive risk aversion, describing as "simply barmy" measures like sending schoolchildren out on city field trips in high-visibility jackets. Late last year, she announced that her agency's inspectors would undergo training that will encompass the positive, as well as the negative, side of risk.

"Inspections will creep into being a bit more risk-averse unless we explicitly train them to get a more sophisticated understanding of the balance between benefits and risk, and stand back, and say 'It's O.K. to have some risk of children falling over and bashing into things,'" she said. "That's not the same as being reckless and sending a 2-year-old to walk on the edge of a 200-foot cliff unaccompanied."

Britain is one of a number of countries where educators and regulators say a litigious, protective culture has gone too far, leaching healthy risks out of childhood. Guidelines on play from the government agency that oversees health and safety issues in Britain state that "the goal is not to eliminate risk."

Australia last fall introduced new standards for playground equipment, instructing operators to consider the benefits, not just the risks, of activities that could result in injuries. Cities and school districts in Canada and Sweden are following suit.

(In the United States, a country with far higher litigation costs, government agencies overseeing play safety are not known to have made any such changes.)

The shift to seeing some benefit in risk, advocates say, signals the end of a decades-long drift toward overprotecting children.

Beginning in the late 1970s, parents were buffeted by warnings about hidden dangers on playgrounds and predators lurking in suburban neighborhoods. Behavior changed: In England, the percentage of schoolchildren who went to school unaccompanied dropped from around 85 percent of 9-year-olds in 1971 to around 25 percent in 1990, a team of British researchers found.

Play spaces also changed: Plank swings and steel merry-go-rounds disappeared, while impact-absorbent rubber surfacing spread over so-called drop zones, driving up the cost of new playgrounds. A market appeared for lab-tested, safety-certified fiberglass boulders. The result has been a gradual sterilization of play, said Meghan Talarowski, an American landscape designer who has compared British and American playgrounds.

"It's a rubber floor, a little structure surrounded by a fence, it's like a little play jail," she said of playgrounds in the United States. "As a grown-up, you're sitting there on your phone, waiting for them to be done."

Ms. Talarowski, who was struck by how much more adventurous playgrounds were when she moved to London in 2015, threw herself into gathering data. Using a quantitative tool developed by the RAND Corporation, a research center, she used video to track the behavior of 18,000 visitors to London playgrounds, then compared it with similar data on visitors to American parks.

The findings suggested that exciting equipment had a pronounced effect: The British playgrounds had 55 percent more visitors over all, and children and teenagers were 16 to 18 percent more active. The features that held visitors' attention the longest—sand, grass, high swings and climbing structures—were elements American park managers use sparingly, because of high maintenance costs and the risk of falls, Ms. Talarowski said.

In Britain, though, risk has become something to (carefully) brag about.

"It's about exploring controlled risk, risk that we've carefully designed," said Chris Moran, manager of Queen Elizabeth Olympic Park, as he led guests through Tumbling Bay playground, built in 2014 at a cost of more than $1.5 million. "We've got the gorse bushes, which are quite spiky," he said. "The child will touch it and learn it is a spiky bush."

Aspects of Tumbling Bay, with its tall tree houses and wobbly bridges, would make an American park manager blanch. Its 20-foot climbing towers, with natural, gnarled boughs lashed together with willow wands, were made by hand, not in a factory (which would share legal liability in case of an accident). Waving prairie grasses stand higher than the head of an adult (which could block sight lines). There are expanses of sand (could contain animal feces or sharp objects) and boulders (no manufacturer, no shared legal liability).

The park requires an intensive safety inspection regime—half of it has been barricaded off since November so that rotten boughs can be replaced—but, so far, any injuries have been minor ones, Mr. Moran said. "We've always won the argument," he said.

Underlying the difference in play is a difference in law. The United States uses the jury system for personal injury cases, and liability costs, as a percentage of gross domestic product, are more than double those of most eurozone economies.

In addition, American families must "find someone to blame to cover the cost" of medical care, unlike their counterparts in European countries, which have socialized health care, said Ellen Beate Hansen Sanseter, a Norwegian professor of education.

"In Norway, the society has already paid for it," she said.

Support for freer, riskier play in Britain has built to the point where even prominent safety advocates endorse the idea. But change on the ground is patchy.

Tim Gill, whose 2007 book "No Fear: Growing Up in a Risk Averse Society" became a handbook for the movement, ascribes this to bureaucratic inertia, and to a sharp drop-off in government investment in play that occurred in 2010, when the Conservative government introduced austerity measures.

And society recoils every time a child is seriously hurt on a playground. Playground deaths are extremely rare—they occur once every three or four years in the Britain—but they tap into a parent's worst fear, and are amplified by widespread reporting.

In 2015, Vida Kwotuah was sitting on a bench in a park in London a few yards away when a tree trunk supporting a swing toppled and crushed her 5-year-old daughter, Alexia. Ms. Kwotuah ran to Alexia, but the child's body had already begun to swell. A few seconds later, she said, "it was like every single blood from her system came out." The base of the tree trunk, she observed, was "powdery."

More than two years later, investigators reported that back in 2011 a contractor, known in the transcript as "Individual A," had unwittingly purchased the trunk of a poplar, which decays rapidly when placed in the ground, mistaking it for oak, a harder wood. Ms. Kwotuah received a financial settlement from her borough council, and parks throughout Tower Hamlets, her neighborhood in East London, underwent strict safety audits.

One such audit found that a popular climbing structure, open since the early 1980s, presented "a medium to high risk potential for severe to fatal injuries," leading to its closure, said Andy Bate, a spokesman for Tower Hamlets, which manages the playgrounds.

Such re-evaluations occur regularly after playground tragedies, even if they are statistically insignificant, said David Yearley, of the Royal Society for the Prevention of Accidents. "As a society, it's difficult to say, 'We need to accept a one in 60 million chance of death,'" he said.

Ask the teachers at the Richmond Avenue Primary School, though, and they will tell you that exposing children to limited risks now, while they are young, will help them survive.

In 1903, when the school opened, its purpose was straightforward: to provide the children of fishermen and farmers with basic literacy and math, enough to take over their parents' vocation, said Debbie Hughes, the school's head teacher.

"There used to be very traditional jobs—blue-collar worker, white-collar worker, you're going to be the electricians and plumbers, you're going to the typist pool," she said. Schools of that era, she said, were designed to turn out rule followers.

"We're very proper, aren't we?" she said. "We have always done as we were told."

But rule followers are unlikely to be rewarded in the future, said Ms. Hughes, whose twin 19-year-old children have just entered the work force. As she thought through these changes, a towheaded kindergartner nearby had fashioned a catapult, stacking seven bricks on one end of a wooden plank and jumping solidly onto the other end, sending the bricks flying into the air, over the heads of his playmates.

"You've got to get out there and find your position in the world," Ms. Hughes said. "If you don't give those children those creative skills, that risk, that take a chance. If they don't have all that risk out there when the child is four, the adult isn't going to do that."

Critical Thinking

1. What are your personal feelings about educators installing more risk in British children's controlled playgrounds? Do the costs outweigh the benefits?

2. Do you think the United States also should consider creating more playgrounds that have riskier features? Why or why not?

3. Would you like your children to have riskier playgrounds at their school? If your school did install such a playground, would you pull your child out of that school? Explain.

Internet References

London Study of Playgrounds
https://static1.squarespace.com/static/562e1f86e4b0b8640584b757/t/5a4cdf2f0d929722a0ed3085/1514987350174/LondonFullStudyReport.pdf

The Overprotected Kid
https://www.theatlantic.com/magazine/archive/2014/04/hey-parents-leave-those-kids-alone/358631/

Playgrounds that rip up the safety rules
https://rethinkingchildhood.com/2012/03/07/playground-safety/

Welcome to British Adventure Play
http://www.adventureplay.org.uk/index.htm

Article   Prepared by: Chris J. Boyatzis, *Bucknell University* and
Ellen N. Junn, *California State University, Stanislaus*

The Upside of Vulnerability

How "bad genes" may actually make us stronger.

Elitsa Dermendzhiyska

Learning Outcomes

After reading this article, you will be able to:

- Describe some contributions of nature and nurture to children's vulnerability and resilience.

- Identify reasons for individual differences in children's personalities and responses to challenging environments.

Not long ago in rural Maryland, a mere 50 miles from the bustle of downtown D.C., there was a lab in which a scientist and a few hundred rhesus macaque monkeys, over five decades, turned out gobs and gobs of data to decode what, ultimately, makes us who we are. The monkeys are gone now but their legacy lives on in some of the most remarkable science behind genes and mothering, evolution, and mental health.

Two things make rhesus macaques particularly suited for the job of studying humans: they share 95 percent of our DNA and exhibit personalities, just like we do. Steve Suomi was the lab's last chief scientist until it closed down in 2008. During his time, he saw generation after generation of monkeys whizz through life, buffeted by biology and circumstance. Suomi had a special interest in a type of macaques he called uptight: shy and fearful as infants, they'd grow into something rather similar to depressed human adults. Suomi wanted to know why. Was it nature or nurture? And what did that mean for us humans? Are some of us wired for suffering? Or is it life that twists us one way or another?

Over the past century, our mental deviances have been blamed on rogue genes or unfeeling parents (also known as refrigerator moms), or some combination of the two. The prevailing view in psychiatry—called the diathesis–stress model—holds that some people have an underlying, usually genetic, predisposition to mental illnesses. On its own, though, being prone isn't enough. Vulnerability tips into disorder once a certain stress threshold has been passed. For illness to ensue, you need a sufficiently harsh environment—a difficult childhood or adversity later in life—to trigger your vulnerability genes.

But something about the monkeys didn't quite fit this story. Thanks to advanced gene sequencing technology that became available in the '90s, Suomi analyzed the DNA of all macaques in his colony and found that some of them carried a genetic mutation, which in humans, has been linked to depression. He looked for the same mutation in the genomes of other primates but found none that had it.

This was odd. "What is it about humans and rhesus monkeys", Suomi wondered, "that differs from these other primate species?" He mulled it over and then it jumped out at him: It's our remarkable adaptability. While most chimps and monkeys perish out of their natural habitat, humans and rhesus macaques have spread, survived, and even flourished across an astonishing range of environments, all over the planet. Could it be that the two things that separated us and rhesus monkeys from all other primates were somehow connected? In other words, is it possible that we owe our extraordinary resilience as a species… to our vulnerability genes? The data suggests that the genes that put us most at risk of mental illness may also be the same genes that help to make us healthier, happier, more resilient, and successful, both as individuals and as a species.

That seemed absurd. It defied both common sense and science canon. But around the same time, a professor of human development at the University of California, Davis, called Jay Belsky, uncovered a curious pattern in the human research that suddenly made Suomi's speculation entirely plausible. Belsky was poring over studies of gene-environment interaction when he found that, in many cases, subjects with a genetic risk of developing mental disorder had not only the worst outcomes but also the best ones.

Separately from Belsky, other researchers were seeing the same puzzling thing in studies across genetics, personality psychology, and child development. Since then, evidence for the upside of vulnerability genes has only been growing. The data suggests that the genes that put us most at risk of mental illness may also be the same genes that help to make us healthier, happier, more resilient, and successful, both as individuals and as a species. The research, though still new, holds out the beguiling possibility that Leonard Cohen had it right, after all: that sometimes the cracks in us are also how the light gets in.

Reviewing the existing research, Belsky found that people with a genetic vulnerability who came from a harsh early environment were at a higher risk of developing mental disorders, just like the diathesis-stress model in psychiatry would predict. But similarly vulnerable people from a nurturing early environment turned out normal—indeed, sometimes better-off than their good-gene peers. Contrary to what you'd expect, the combination bad genes/good environment often produced greater health and superior psychological functioning than good genes/good environment.

In study after study, this pattern appeared with remarkable consistency, yet somehow researchers had completely missed it. A focus on illness, though well-justified in most cases, had blinded them to the silver linings in their own data. But once Belsky and others pointed out the good side of bad genes, it started cropping up everywhere, in old and new studies alike.

In 2004, for example, researchers from the Netherlands set out to study how genes, and moms, affect kids' antisocial behavior. Marian Bakermans-Kranenburg and her colleagues screened over 2,000 families, picking out for further study those with children who scored highest on aggression. The researchers found that kids with insensitive mothers were more aggressive and ran a higher risk of disturbed mental development—but only if they also carried a specific variant of a gene called DRD4. Known as the ADHD gene, the bully gene, and the slut gene, DRD4 helps to process dopamine in the brain and one of its mutations has been linked to violence, hyperactivity, and novelty-seeking. It was kids with this mutation, raised by harsh or aloof mothers, that turned out the most antisocial of all kids in the study.

So far, this is standard diathesis-stress theory: risky gene plus bad environment equals disorder. The surprise came in the second part of the experiment, when Bakermans-Kranenburg and her team split the families into two groups. The first group were followed around by camera-wearing researchers, who then used the video clips to teach the moms how to read their children's behavior and use empathy to quell tantrums. The second group of moms served as a control and received no video feedback or parenting advice.

The kids in the two groups started out similarly aggressive but ended up dramatically different. Two years after the experiment, the research team followed up with the families to measure the impact of the video intervention. Here's what they found: The kids in the intervention group who carried the risky variant of the DRD4 gene, and whose moms had improved their parenting skills, were 37 percent less aggressive. Meanwhile, the kids in the control group, who carried no genetic risk, had reduced their problem behaviors by a mere 8 percent—and that's when their moms, too, had become more sensitive and empathetic (only without the intervention). And even this paltry improvement, the researchers suggest, may have happened anyway simply as a result of growing up.

In another oft-cited study, Ariel Knafo, a psychologist at Hebrew University, brought 167 three-year-olds to his lab. There the youngsters met a female researcher disguised as a sort of damsel in distress: she "accidentally" dropped her pen, then "accidentally" hurt her knee, then, "accidentally" again, lost her finger doll. This was, of course, a ruse designed to test what psychologists call pro-social behavior, meaning the children's willingness to help. As you may expect by now, the kids who carried the risky variant of the DRD4 gene turned out the least pro-social of all, provided that they were also raised by strict, insensitive mothers. And the most pro-social kids? They, too, carried the genetic risk for aggression but had, instead, nurturing mothers. The positive parenting had somehow tipped these kids' antisocial predisposition into its polar opposite—kindness.

But it's not only at-risk kids who seem to respond so strongly to nurturing environments. Shelley Taylor, a psychologist at UCLA, looked at 118 young men and women to see if they would react differently to stress based on which variant of the 5-HTTLPR gene they carried. The 5-HTTLPR gene regulates serotonin levels in the brain and comes it three variants—or alleles, in genetics speak. There's the long/long, the long/short and the short/short allele, the latter of which, research suggests, poses the highest risk of depression and the former protects against it.

Here's what happened. Young adults with the short/short allele and frequent high stress over the previous six months had, indeed, the most depressive symptoms. On the other hand, young adults with the same risky allele but low amounts of recent stress had the fewest depressive symptoms—two times fewer, in fact, compared to their genetically protected peers. Just like in Knafo's experiment, where the kindest kids carried aggressive genes, here, too, the most resilient young adults were those with the depressive genes. Something about their environment—be it loving parents or low stress—seemed to turn their genetic vulnerability into protection against the very disorders it made them susceptible to.

This striking conclusion and the growing evidence behind it has spurred a new theory that is forcing us to profoundly rethink mental health and illness. Spanning evolutionary psychology, child development, neuroscience, and genetics, this theory goes under different names, among them Biological Sensitivity to Context and Differential Susceptibility Theory. I prefer the more poetic rendition coined by science journalist David Dobbs: the Orchid Hypothesis.

The name was inspired by the pioneering work of Bruce Ellis and Thomas Boyce, who, in 1995, proposed that some children are like dandelions and others are like orchids. Dandelions, the innocuous weeds that crop up everywhere, can feel at home in all terrain and climate—from the side of pavements to waste dumps, from mountain slopes to burned forests. Not orchids. Take them out of their native rainforests and they perish. But plant them in the right soil, give them proper care, and you'll have a thing of unutterable, mesmerizing beauty. So irresistible is their appeal, in fact, that over the centuries orchids have fueled an obsession among collectors called orchidelirium. Lives have been risked, blood spilled and billions of dollars squandered on the rarest of species.

Just like dandelions, some children turn out fine no matter what circumstances they find themselves in. In the Bakermans-Kranenburg study, kids who didn't carry the risky variant of the DRD4 gene were all but unaffected by the quality of parenting they received. There was little difference between those with good moms and those with bad moms: their good genes seemed to protect them from the negative aspects of their environment.

We might call these kids normal or well-adjusted. But according to the Orchid Hypothesis, that's not quite accurate. Dandelion kids are simply more impervious, more insensitive, and unresponsive to their environment and, it turns out, not just to its negative effects but to the positive ones, too.

By contrast, Orchid children are extremely susceptible in both directions. They respond to good and bad environments alike, suffering the most in the latter but also making the most out of the former. Theirs, according to Dobbs, is not so much vulnerability to negative experience as sensitivity to "all experience." Where dandelions are hardy, orchids are malleable; while dandelions resist the influence of the outside world, orchids yield to it. Their genes, in this sense, are not vulnerable but extremely plastic, responding to the environment and amplifying its effects—"for better and for worse", as Jay Belsky likes to put it.

One interesting implication of this new research is what Belsky calls "the dark side of resilience." Resilient people, we think, have this highly honed ability to bounce back from setbacks which is key to their health and happiness. And so we scramble to build resilient classrooms and resilient companies that will thrive in an uncertain world. But what if resilience is not a mental superpower that anyone can develop? What if, instead, it is more like insensitivity to adversity, a case of

Dandelionism? The danger, according to Jay Belsky, is that resilience training won't work for the Orchids, who can't override a hardwired propensity to feel stress more intensely just by picking up a few emotional regulation techniques. And if we see resilience as a learnable skill, we are also bound to see its failure to work for some as a personal flaw: they simply didn't put in the effort.

On the other hand, Orchids' very sensitivity may present unexpected treatment advantages and suggest interventions that will actually work for them. It's not hard to imagine that, being more susceptible to good environments, people most at risk of suffering mental distress will also most respond to therapy. Indeed, a 2012 study of Romanian orphanages found that it was only kids with the risky variant of the 5-HTTLPR gene—the short/short allele—that benefited when placed in high quality foster care. Although the research on positive interventions is still in its early stages, the initial evidence seems promising. If it gets confirmed, it can profoundly change things for many people who won't even seek help fearing a verdict that they may be well beyond repair.

Besides illuminating the bright side of vulnerability, the Orchid Hypothesis calls into question our very notion of normalcy, of mental health. Here's a paradox about "bad" genes that mainstream science has trouble explaining: If all these genes do is put us at risk, how have they survived evolution? Why, as Jay Belsky and his colleague Michael Pluess asked in a recent paper, "why would natural selection craft an organism to respond to adversity by becoming disordered or dysregulated?"

Mulling over this question, Belsky proposed that our genetic diversity—the combination of Orchid and Dandelion genes—is not an evolutionary glitch but rather nature's ingenious investment strategy. Far from hindering our normal development, Orchid genes, says Belsky, have actually played a key role in our evolution and dominion over the animal kingdom. Here's how the thinking goes: Because the world is unpredictable, it's impossible to know in advance which traits will aid survival and which ones will not. The best thing for nature to do, then, is to hedge its bets. How? By making some of us more responsive to the external world and others less so—essentially diversifying its risk.

It's this mismatch between our evolutionary programming and reality that can turn a behavior which helped us in one context into something that harms us in another context.

If the future turns out similar to the past, Orchids, being more responsive to their early experiences, will adapt better to it. With a Mom that's never around, for example, they will grow up vigilant, anxious, always on edge—a clear advantage in a dangerous world. But what if the world turns out different—friendly? Then past experience won't help. Indeed it may even hurt if, say, your anxiety keeps you from going out and building valuable relationships. In this case, being insensitive to your early environment becomes an asset. We can thus look at Orchids and Dandelions as employing two different strategies to adapt to an uncertain world. Taken together, these two strategies enable the species as a whole to survive and thrive in the widest range of environments.

It works on the individual level, too. According to Belsky, many behaviors that seem dysfunctional and even outright destructive actually make sense in the context that gave rise to them. In a world of stalking lions, poisonous snakes, and other lurking threats, for instance, anxiety and aggression can be seen as optimal strategies designed to keep you alive. Optimal not in the sense that they maximize your well-being, but rather that they allow you to make "the best of a bad situation." From this vantage point, depression could be seen as an optimal response to chronic stress: in the face of unrelenting battering, your body braces itself and shuts down, holding on to every drop of energy it can spare just to last a little longer. This is not to glamorize or justify depression. Depression is ineffable misery; it whittles you to a shell of a human self. But evolution doesn't care. It would gladly sacrifice your well-being in the service of keeping you alive long enough to procreate.

Of course, whatever threat to your survival you see doesn't always materialize. It's this mismatch between our evolutionary programming and reality that can turn a behavior which helped us in one context into something that harms us in another context. Physiologically, we still live in a world of snakes and lions and other lurking threats—all potentially lethal but also short-lived. Our survival mechanisms haven't yet caught up to the chronic stresses of modern society, which we never encountered during thousands of years of roaming the planet. Nature could not have anticipated and equipped us for a world of broken families, social isolation, rampant unemployment, abject inequality. It's no wonder that once adaptive behaviors often get us in trouble today. But to call them glitches, errors, weaknesses, dysfunctions, disorders, aberrations, and abnormalities is to ignore their inner logic and evolutionary purpose.

This may seem like nitpicking the point but for Belsky and Pluess it carries serious practical implications. The two psychologists compare our treatment of mental disorders to the attempts of early aviators to fly while ignoring gravity. "Some intervention efforts", they say, "reflect little more than attaching wings to the arms and jumping off cliffs." Enshrined in our current practices is a model of mental health that all too often pretzels people into what we think is an optimal shape while paying no regard to the hidden mechanics of their struggles. What we need instead is a deeper understanding of the kind of

beings that we are and the type of traits and feelings, genes, and behaviors that each one of us carries "for better and for worse." And then we need to think: how to mitigate the for worse parts and enhance the for better ones?

Perhaps the most powerful implication of this new research, however, is its immediate, highly personal message to the millions of people who wake up every day to the sounds of shame and stigma, and the stings of well-intended pity. To these people, the Orchid Hypothesis offers hope baked in science: that they are not weak but plastic, not so much vulnerable as responsive, not faultily wired but purposely crafted. Not damaged, just different.

Some time ago, while he was investigating the Orchid Hypothesis, science journalist David Dobbs discovered that he carried the short form of the 5-HTTLPR gene. It confirmed what he had long suspected to be true: he bore depression deep in his biology. His reaction to the news, however, was not the one he had expected:

That new way of thinking changed things. I felt no sense that I carried a handicap that would render my efforts futile should I again face deep trouble. In fact, I felt a heightened sense of agency. Anything and everything I did to improve my own environment and experience—every intervention I ran on myself, as it were—would have a magnified effect. In that light, my short/short allele now seems to me less like a trapdoor through which I might fall than like a springboard—slippery and somewhat fragile, perhaps, but a springboard all the same.

Critical Thinking

1. Think of some intense stressors or challenges in your own childhood or more recent life. How did they affect you, and how do your responses reflect some major points in the article?

2. Did this article help you better appreciate individual differences between children and the underlying biological factors that can contribute to them?

Internet References

Brown University Center for the Study of Children at Risk
https://www.brown.edu/research/projects/children-at-risk/
Children at Risk
https://childrenatrisk.org/

Article   Prepared by: Chris J. Boyatzis, *Bucknell University* and
                                         Ellen N. Junn, *California State University, Stanislaus*

Maximizing Children's Resilience

KIRSTEN WEIR

Learning Outcomes

After reading this article, you will be able to:

- Understand and describe the most influential factors contributing to developing a child's resilience.

- Explain specific parenting practices that build resilience in children, as well as parenting behaviors that put children at risk.

- Describe specific schooling interventions or programs that can strengthen children's resilience.

- Based on the study of Kauai children, identify a set of key protective factors that were common among resilient children who experienced extremely impoverished, stressful and chronic family conditions.

They call them "the formative years" for a reason. A wealth of research has shown that stress and hardship in childhood—such as that caused by abuse, neglect, exposure to violence and mental illness in caregivers—can alter the brain architecture of a developing child. Those physiological changes, in turn, raise the risk of cognitive and developmental delays, physical health problems such as diabetes and heart disease, and behavioral and mental health problems such as substance abuse and depression.

Yet some people flourish despite those long odds, and psychologists are homing in on the factors that boost resilience.

Early on, resilience researchers focused on traits of resilient individuals, says University of Minnesota psychologist Ann S. Masten, PhD, who has studied the subject for 40 years and directs the Project Competence program of research on risk and resilience. More recently, the field has shifted toward looking at resilience from a systems perspective, she says. "The resilience of an individual depends on drawing resources from many other systems."

To be sure, some resilience factors are drawn from within, involving abilities such as problem solving, self-control, emotion regulation, motivation to succeed and self-efficacy. But external factors are important, too. Some of those influences are related to the attachment system, including having supportive parents or primary caregivers, close relationships with other caring adults and close peer relationships. Still others exist in systems beyond the family, such as effective schools and neighborhoods and the qualities of faith and hope embedded in spiritual and cultural beliefs.

"A child is embedded in interactions with friends, family, community. The way those other systems are functioning plays a huge role in the capacity of that child to overcome adversity," Masten says.

Those same resilience factors show up in research again and again, in many different populations. And that short list of protective systems also serves as a checklist of places to intervene to aim a child down a promising path.

Relationships Foster Resilience

Researchers agree that, of all the factors that boost resilience, good parenting is often the most significant. "The thing that makes the biggest difference, over and above one's genetic blueprint, is the relationship a child has with a primary caregiver," says Philip Fisher, PhD, a professor of psychology at the University of Oregon who studies early childhood interventions to improve the functioning of children from disadvantaged backgrounds. "The presence of a supportive, consistent and protective primary caregiver—especially when the underlying stress systems are activated—is the factor that makes the biggest difference in healthy development."

Many of the problems that stem from childhood adversity involve inadequate self-regulation, which has been linked to parents' behaviors and the home environment. As described in a detailed report from the U.S. Department of Health and

Human Services Office of Planning, Research and Evaluation, children who have experienced maltreatment, harsh parenting and challenges such as poverty and food insecurity show poorer self-regulation in cognitive, emotional and behavioral domains. Yet parental warmth, responsiveness, and sensitivity foster the development of self-regulation, and can buffer the effects of other stressors (Self-Regulation and Toxic Stress, OPRE Report #2015-30, 2015).

"Resilience rests, fundamentally, on relationships," says Suniya Luthar, PhD, a professor of psychology at Arizona State University who has studied vulnerability and resilience for more than three decades.

This year, she and her colleague Nancy Eisenberg, PhD, published a special section in the journal *Child Development* to highlight evidence-based interventions demonstrated to maximize resilience in families and children (*Child Development*, Vol. 88, No. 2, 2017). Among those articles addressing diverse vulnerable populations, many highlight programs that support parents. "If you want a child to be functioning well, tend to the person who's tending the child," Luthar says.

In one paper, Amanda Sheffield Morris, PhD, and colleagues reviewed several programs designed to strengthen social support for parents and increase positive parent-child interactions to improve well-being for children living in poverty. In one brief home-visit program, for instance, parents were helped to develop skills for becoming more positive and effective in their parenting, and were referred for additional family-based interventions as needed. Parents who participated in the program showed more positive parenting behaviors and fewer depressive symptoms. Their children showed fewer internalizing and externalizing problems.

Another program for mothers promoted their responsivity to their children, maternal feelings of support from their communities and maternal self-efficacy. The mothers attended weekly group sessions led by trained supervisors at early childhood agencies or pediatric primary-care sites. Compared with the control group, children whose mothers participated had fewer behavioral and socioemotional problems.

Increasing access to such programs could have a significant effect on public health by improving health and well-being in childhood and beyond, Morris and her co-authors conclude. By partnering with community sites—such as pediatric clinics and Head Start centers—the programs could be scaled up to reach large numbers of at-risk families, they say (*Child Development*, Vol. 88, No. 2, 2017).

Better Parenting

Other papers in the special section focus on specific subsets of parents. In one, Sherryl Goodman, PhD, and Judy Garber,

PhD, explored evidence-based interventions for mothers with depression—a significant risk factor for maladjustment in young children. Depression can negatively affect parenting behaviors: Depressed mothers are more likely to be disengaged, harsh or critical with their kids.

But a variety of research has shown that treating maternal depression can trickle down to improve mental health in kids. Goodman and Garber reviewed programs that involved interpersonal therapy or cognitive-behavioral therapy (CBT) strategies to manage maternal depression and improve parenting, and found both in-home programs and those administered through sites such as child-care or community health centers improved parenting skills and reduced depression in mothers and their children (*Child Development*, Vol. 88, No. 2, 2017).

In another example, Zoe E. Taylor, PhD, and Rand Conger, PhD, reviewed the evidence for enhancing the strength of single mothers. Several factors boost well-being and positive parenting behaviors for these mothers, including perceived social support from friends and family, as well as internal traits such as high optimism, self-efficacy and self-esteem, the authors say.

After reviewing the research, Taylor and Conger concluded that interventions that combine peer support for mothers and CBT are likely to improve single mothers' coping skills, increasing their well-being and that of their children. Group-based interventions are likely to be particularly effective, because they are both cost-effective and they encourage participants to form meaningful and lasting connections with one another, strengthening their social support networks (*Child Development*, Vol. 88, No. 2, 2017).

When it comes to the role of fathers in a child's well-being, numerous studies have found associations between fathers' positive parenting and children's cognitive, social and emotional development and mental health, as Marsha Kline Pruett, PhD, and colleagues describe in another review in the special section. Unfortunately, interventions to increase fathers' involvement in low-income families have had mostly disappointing results, Pruett and her colleagues note. But their research suggests that focusing on couples, rather than fathers alone, can have positive effects. Through their Supporting Father Involvement project, Pruett and colleagues held weekly group sessions for low-income families that covered such topics as strengthening the couple's relationship, paternal involvement and finding help to deal with external stresses. Families who participated in the program reported increases in father involvement and decreased parenting stress. And while families in the control group reported increasing problem behaviors in their children, those who participated in the intervention reported no such increase (*Child Development*, Vol. 88, No. 2, 2017).

Social-emotional Schooling

Investing in children's development early pays off exponentially, Masten says. "The skills you need at one age are the platform for building future skills. If you establish a sound foundation early, you can build forward."

Yet research has shown that children raised in poverty are more likely to start school with fewer social-emotional skills. And such skills matter, says Roger Weissberg, PhD, a professor of psychology and education at the University of Illinois at Chicago, and board vice chair and chief knowledge officer at the Collaborative for Academic, Social, and Emotional Learning (CASEL), a national organization working to incorporate evidence-based social and emotional learning into education.

In a meta-analysis of more than 200 studies, Weissberg and colleagues found that children who participated in evidence-based social-emotional learning (SEL) programs had better social skills, behavior and attitudes, as well as academic achievement gains of 11 percentile points, compared with children who did not participate (*Child Development*, Vol. 82, No. 1, 2011).

The earlier children develop those skills, the better, researchers agree. "Early adolescence is a period of rapid change in the brain, and it might be a good window to recover some functioning and recover to a good trajectory," Masten says.

Luthar agrees that adolescence is a critical period. But it's more than just an opportunity to correct for early adversities, she says. It's also a period when new developmental issues arise—and there's a need for more programs targeting adolescents and their parents. "The onset of adolescence presents its own set of unique challenges that must be directly addressed among at-risk populations," she says. "The needs, dilemmas and parenting challenges are entirely different for parents of at-risk adolescents as compared to at-risk toddlers—and so much is at stake as kids start to explore things like sex, drugs and delinquency."

The good news is that support for school programs that emphasize social and emotional learning is growing as educators and administers realize that such programs benefit all children, whether they're at risk of maladjustment or not. "Teachers and principals see these as critical strategies to enhance children's development," Weissberg says.

Social-emotional learning programs target many of the same skills that predict resilience: self-awareness, self-management, responsible decision-making, social awareness and relationship skills. Through CASEL, Weissberg and his colleagues review social-emotional learning interventions nationwide and help districts implement effective programs in their schools. So far, they've worked with 20 large urban districts, reaching about 2.5 million kids, he says. "If you have kids who have experienced trauma and they're at risk, I think it's critical for them to have schooling that promotes their social, emotional and academic competencies. If you don't do that, you're not going to be able to meet their needs," Weissberg says.

Still, for some children whose brain development was derailed by hardship, school-based programs might not go far enough. They may need more tailored interventions—but to customize those interventions, it helps to know what's missing. New advances in neuroscience are helping to uncover those mechanisms and point toward interventions, says Fisher (*New Directions for Child and Adolescent Development*, Vol. 2016, No. 153, 2016).

Children from high-adversity backgrounds often have trouble learning from their mistakes, for instance. Using neuroimaging, he and his colleagues showed that such children don't show normal patterns of brain activity after receiving corrective feedback when they make a mistake during a computer task. "It's not that the kids don't care. The information isn't getting through," he says.

But in a pilot study of foster children from high-adversity backgrounds, he and his colleagues demonstrated that those brain patterns could be changed through a family-based intervention that provided regular services from behavioral specialists, therapeutic playgroups and extensive support for foster parents.

With the right support, in other words, at-risk children can learn to make use of the information that can help them thrive. "Neuroscience measures allow us to understand more precisely the things that have been impacted [by adversity], and can help us tailor our interventions," he says. Emerging findings from neuroscience can help researchers zero in on strategies that can help struggling children succeed. Yet, in the recent *Child Development* special section, the co-authors caution that for interventions intended for use on a large scale, it will be impractical to use biological measures to personalize interventions. Furthermore, when programs are known to be generally beneficial, it could be ethically questionable to plan to exclude some kids based on aspects of their biological or genetic profiles.

Following Up on the Kauai Study

Some of the brain changes resulting from early-life hardships are likely to persist, Fisher says. Still, research shows it is possible to continue to develop skills related to resilience, even into adulthood. For proof, look to Hawaii.

In 1955, psychologists Emmy Werner, PhD, and Ruth Smith, PhD, launched the Kauai Longitudinal Study, which has followed all the children born on Kauai that year from birth into adulthood. Nearly a third of those children lived in impoverished or stressful conditions, such as in families with mental illness or alcoholism.

Many children developed mental health or behavioral problems in childhood, but about a third seemed to thrive despite those setbacks. They showed no signs of behavioral or learning problems and developed into competent, well-adjusted adults.

Werner and Smith identified common protective factors among those standouts. Resilient participants tended to have a well-developed sense of their own self-efficacy, and supportive relationships with at least one reliable family member and other caring adults such as teachers and community elders.

What was intriguing about the Kauai study, however, wasn't that a third of the kids thrived despite adversity. It was that among the two-thirds of at-risk children who did show signs of problem behavior in childhood and adolescence, the majority had turned things around by age 40, as Werner described in a report for Portland State University (*Focal Point: Research, Policy, and Practice in Children's Mental Health*, Vol. 19, No. 1, 2005).

When she surveyed participants at 40, Werner found that the turning point usually came from forces that presented the participants with new opportunities: continuing education in adult high school or community college, joining the armed forces, marrying a stable partner, participating in a religious community, recovering from serious illness or accident, and in some cases, psychotherapy.

"There isn't a formula that dooms or blesses a child with success," says Laurie "Lali" McCubbin, PhD, a psychology professor at the University of Louisville who has since taken over as principal investigator of the Kauai study. "There are many pathways of resilience."

McCubbin recently followed up with the participants, now in their 60s. Many of those who have created stable, happy lives have drawn support from their cultural heritage, she says. One man, who had been abandoned by his mother as a child, drew purpose from his Hawaiian culture and his island, becoming involved in local conservation efforts and spending time on the water when something was troubling him. Another, who as a child had a difficult relationship with his father, took pride in caring for his dad in old age.

That experience of drawing meaning from adversity is something that clinical and counseling psychologists can help facilitate, McCubbin adds.

"What I love most about resilience is the creativity involved. It's wonderful as a clinician to help clients negotiate that experience in therapy," she says. "Resilience is a process, and we can help clients change at any point in the lifespan."

Additional Reading

Ordinary Magic: Resilience in Development, Masten, A. S., 2014
Special Section: Developmental Research and Translational Science: Evidence-Based Interventions for At-Risk Youth and Families, Luthar, S. S., & Eisenberg, N. (Eds.), *Child Development*, 2017

Critical Thinking

1. Do you know of any friends or acquaintances who have experienced extremely difficult childhood circumstances and yet seemed to transcend this to become successful adults? Did this person share characteristics and factors described in this article?

2. Based on this article, if you are an educator and learned of a child experiencing trauma, what could you do to help intervene to help them build resiliency?

3. Do you think to be a foster parent, that laws should be changed to educate and help foster parents learn to parent more effectively for their foster children who may have been traumatized in their former homes? Justify your answer.

Internet References

Building Resilience in Children – 20 Practical, Powerful Strategies (Backed by Science)
https://www.heysigmund.com/building-resilience-children/
Resilience
https://developingchild.harvard.edu/science/key-concepts/resilience/
Resilience Guide for Parents & Teachers
https://www.apa.org/helpcenter/resilience
Resilience in Children: Strategies to Strengthen Your Kids
https://www.psycom.net/build-resilience-children

Parenting and Family Issues

UNIT

Prepared by: Chris J. Boyatzis, *Bucknell University* and
Ellen N. Junn, *California State University, Stanislaus*

Parenting and Family Issues

Few people today realize that the potential freedom to choose parenthood, deciding whether to become a parent, deciding when to have children, or deciding how many children to have is a relatively recent historical development due to the advent of reliable methods of contraception and other recent sociocultural changes. Moreover, unlike any other significant adult job to which we may aspire, few, if any, of us will receive any formal training or research-based information about the lifelong responsibility of parenting.

For most of us, our behavior is generally based on our own conscious and subconscious recollections of how we were parented, as well as on our observations of the parenting practices of others around us. In fact, our society often behaves as if the mere act of producing a baby automatically confers upon the parents an innate parenting ability, and furthermore, that a family's parenting practices should remain private and not be subjected to scrutiny or criticism by outsiders, government officials, or institutions. Given this climate, it is not surprising that misconceptions about many parenting practices persist. Only within the last 70 years or so have researchers turned their lenses on the scientific study of the family. Many challenging social, historical, cultural, and economic forces also have dramatically changed the face of the American family today. In fact, the vast majority

of parents today never take courses or learn of the research on parenting.

This unit helps present some of the research on the many complex factors related to successful parenting. Interestingly, societal and economic conditions are putting greater pressure on parents today in interesting ways compared to prior years, and today, an ever-increasing number of parents are opting to become even more intensely involved and overprotective of their children, even to the extent that some parents are relinquishing their parental role over to their children. This unit seeks to provide readers with the newest research on parenting trends and the concomitant positive and potentially negative outcomes associate with differences in parenting styles to shed more light to parents and educators.

Similarly, most parents express interest and concerns about how best to discipline and set limits for their children. "Spare the rod or spoil the child" is an oft-heard retort used to justify spanking children for misbehaving. Even today, a majority of parents in the United States admit to relying on spanking as a form of discipline, and many do not view spanking as inappropriate or effective. Researchers are beginning to accumulate evidence of the negative consequences and effects of spanking for children and advocating the use of other more effective forms of discipline.

Article

Prepared by: Chris J. Boyatzis, *Bucknell University* and
Ellen N. Junn, *California State University, Stanislaus*

Psychological Biases Play a Part in Vaccination Decisions

TANIA LOMBROZO

Learning Outcomes

After reading this article, you will be able to:

*   Describe the controversy and reasons surrounding parents' fears of vaccinating their child.

*   Evaluate and assess the research supporting the pros and cons for childhood vaccinations.

*   Reflect upon your own psychological biases either for or against childhood vaccinations. Based on this article, explain how and why your biases have changed or not.

With the recent outbreak of measles originating from Disneyland, there's been no shortage of speculation, accusation and recrimination concerning why some people won't vaccinate their children. There's also been some—but only some—more historically and psychologically informed discussion.

Some people's motivation for skipping vaccines likely comes from persistent misinformation and, in particular, the unfounded belief that there's a link between vaccines and autism. And, as Adam Frank pointed out in a post last week, vaccinations also play into a larger cultural conversation about science and its place in society.

What's received less attention is how vaccination plays into subtle psychological biases that can contribute to parents' unwillingness to "intervene" on their kids. The particular bias I have in mind is sometimes called "omission bias," and it has to do with the difference between bringing about some outcome by *acting* versus by *failing to act*. For example, *lying* about whether one is married (an action) seems worse than failing to correct an invalid assumption (an omission), even if the outcome—in terms of what the other person believes about one's marital status—is the same in each case.

With vaccination, choosing to vaccinate is an action—it involves a deliberate intervention on your child. In contrast, having a child fall prey to an illness that could have been prevented results from an omission, the failure to vaccinate.

The action/omission distinction is subtle, and it might seem irrelevant here: Surely, the relevant question to ask, in choosing to vaccinate, is whether the risk of the vaccine (typically very, very low) is higher or lower than the risk of the disease (typically much higher). It's not surprising that people with different beliefs about the risks might make decisions differently and, in fact, at least one study has found that parents who objected to vaccinating their children (in this case, with the DPT vaccine) were more likely than others to think that vaccinating was more dangerous than not vaccinating.

But people also vary in the extent to which they exhibit omission bias, and this bias may influence parents' decisions above and beyond the straight calculation of relative risk.

To illustrate, consider a vignette used in the same study. Participants were asked to imagine the following vaccination decision: There's been a flu epidemic in your state, and the kind of flu in question can be fatal to children under 3. In fact, out of 10,000 children under 3 who are not vaccinated, 10 will die from the flu. A vaccine is available, and while it completely eliminates the chance of contracting the flu, it leads to fatal side effects in 5 out of 10,000 children under 3. Would you vaccinate your child under 3?

Based on a straight calculation of risk, parents should have said they would vaccinate: A risk of 5 in 10,000 is lower than a risk of 10 in 10,000. But that's not what the researchers found. Parents who objected to the DPT vaccine for their children showed a stronger omission bias than those who did not object to the vaccine, in the sense that the mean "tolerable risk" was higher for this group: They would only vaccinate when the risk from the hypothetical flu vaccine corresponded to an average of 2.4 deaths per 10,000 (versus 10 per 10,000 deaths from the flu), whereas those who had vaccinated or intended to vaccinate their kids with the DPT vaccine accepted a mean tolerable risk corresponding to 5.4 deaths per 10,000 (versus 10 per 10,000 deaths from the flu). Both groups, on average, needed a higher risk from the disease than from the vaccine to favor vaccination, but the gap was much greater for nonvaccinators.

Why might this be?

One factor could be some people's preference for what they perceive to be "natural." For instance, those parents who objected to the DPT vaccine were more likely than vaccinating parents to endorse the claim, "I do not want to interfere with nature by giving the DPT vaccine." Another study found that university employees who didn't take advantage of a free flu vaccine were more likely than those who did to exhibit a "naturalness bias," as reflected in their preference for a medication extracted from an herb rather than a chemically identical one that was synthesized in a laboratory.

Another factor seems to be people's feelings of causal responsibility for actions versus omissions. For example, one study that had participants decide whether to opt for a hypothetical flu vaccine for their child found that those who exhibited omission bias explained that they would feel more responsible for a death caused by their decision to vaccinate than for a death caused by the decision not to vaccinate.

A final and related factor may be anticipated regret. If some parents feel they would be more causally responsible for the negative consequences of a decision to vaccinate (as opposed to a decision to abstain), they may also anticipate that they would experience greater regret were the vaccine to lead to negative outcomes. And that, in turn, could make them hesitant to pursue a course with this risk: The fear of anticipated regret could push them away from vaccination.

In fact, other studies suggest that it is anticipated regret *per se*—and not omission bias—that drives attitudes toward vaccination, and that greater anticipated regret can go either way. That is, some parents worry more about the regret they would feel if vaccination led to a negative outcome, but others worry more about the regret they would feel if their *failure to vaccinate* led to a negative outcome.

Studying these issues is difficult, in part, because what we construe as an "act" versus an "omission" could itself depend to some extent on the personal and social context of our decisions.

In an environment in which vaccination is the norm—and in which *withholding* vaccination requires applying for a rare exemption—that application for exemption could be construed as the act and not the omission. There's also evidence that how a behavior is construed—as *doing* harm versus merely *allowing* harm—depends on whether the behavior itself is regarded as morally good (doing one's duty for herd immunity, say) versus morally bad (free-riding on others' immunization, or putting one's child at unnecessary risk).

There's more than one lesson to draw from this body of research, but let me end with some bad news and some good news.

The bad news is that educating people about the relative risks of vaccination versus the diseases they prevent is almost certainly insufficient to change attitudes toward vaccination. There's a lot more in play here, including a host of psychological biases that don't always lead to optimal decision-making.

The good news is that relatively simple measures—such as communicating pro-vaccination community norms and focusing on exemptions from vaccination (rather than vaccination itself) as the deliberative *act* could potentially have some positive effects.

Critical Thinking

1. Recent research finds no significant correlation between childhood vaccinations and increases in conditions such as autism. Explain why there appears to be public and parental fear of vaccinating children?

2. Design an education program that might address parental fear of childhood vaccinations.

3. Examine the research on childhood vaccinations worldwide and evaluate the consequences for childhood diseases. How does this global data add to the debate in America?

Internet References

Autism Science Foundation
http://www.autismsciencefoundation.org/autismandvaccines.html

Centers for Disease Control and Prevention, CDC
http://www.cdc.gov/vaccinesafety/concerns/autism/

Mayo Clinic
http://www.mayoclinic.org/healthy-lifestyle/infant-and-toddler-health/in-depth/vaccines/art-20048334

National Center for Biotechnology Information, NCBI, NIH
http://www.ncbi.nlm.nih.gov/pmc/articles/PMC3096324/
http://www.ncbi.nlm.nih.gov/pubmed/23444591

Princeton University Study
http://www.princeton.edu/main/news/archive/S43/10/03O18/index.xml?section=topstories

Article   Prepared by: Chris J. Boyatzis, *Bucknell University* and
Ellen N. Junn, *California State University, Stanislaus*

The Relentlessness of Modern Parenting

Raising children has become significantly more time-consuming and expensive, amid a sense that opportunity has grown more elusive.

CLAIRE CAIN MILLER

Learning Outcomes

After reading this article, you will be able to:

- Define what the difference is between "intensive" and "free-range parenting" and describe how social and economic class levels are influencing recent changes in parent involvement and spending for their children.

- Identify what at which age range parents today spend the most money on their children and how has this spending pattern changed over the last several decades.

- Discuss gender and recent historical differences in parental involvement with their children for mothers and fathers in the United States.

Parenthood in the United States has become much more demanding than it used to be.

Over just a couple of generations, parents have greatly increased the amount of time, attention and money they put into raising children. Mothers who juggle jobs outside the home spend just as much time tending their children as stay-at-home mothers did in the 1970s.

The amount of money parents spend on children, which used to peak when they were in high school, is now highest when they are under 6 and over 18 and into their mid-20s.

Renée Sentilles enrolled her son Isaac in lessons beginning when he was an infant. Even now that he's 12, she rarely has him out of sight when he is home.

"I read all the child-care books," said Ms. Sentilles, a professor in Cleveland Heights, Ohio. "I enrolled him in piano at 5. I took him to soccer practices at 4. We tried track; we did all the swimming lessons, martial arts. I did everything. Of course I did."

While this kind of intensive parenting—constantly teaching and monitoring children—has been the norm for upper-middle-class parents since the 1990s, new research shows that people across class divides now consider it the best way to raise children, even if they don't have the resources to enact it.

There are signs of a backlash, led by so-called free-range parents, but social scientists say the relentlessness of modern-day parenting has a powerful motivation: economic anxiety. For the first time, it's as likely as not that American children will be less prosperous than their parents. For parents, giving children the best start in life has come to mean doing everything they can to ensure that their children can climb to a higher class, or at least not fall out of the one they were born into.

"As the gap between rich and poor increases, the cost of screwing up increases," said Philip Cohen, a sociologist at the University of Maryland who studies families and inequality. "The fear is they'll end up on the other side of the divide."

But it also stokes economic anxiety, because even as more parents say they want to raise children this way, it's the richest ones who are most able to do so.

"Intensive parenting is a way for especially affluent white mothers to make sure their children are maintaining their advantaged position in society," said Jessica Calarco, a sociologist at Indiana University and author of "Negotiating Opportunities: How the Middle Class Secures Advantages in School."

Stacey Jones raised her two sons, now in their 20s, as a single mother in a working-class, mostly black neighborhood in Stone Mountain, GA. She said she and other parents tried hard to give their children opportunities by finding affordable options: municipal sports leagues instead of traveling club teams and school band instead of private music lessons.

"I think most people have this craving for their children to do better and know more than they do," said Ms. Jones, who works in university communications. "But a lot of these opportunities were closed off because they do cost money."

'Child-centered, Expert-guided, Emotionally Absorbing'

"Parent" as a verb gained widespread use in the 1970s, which is also when parenting books exploded. The 1980s brought helicopter parenting, a movement to keep children safe from physical harm, spurred by high-profile child assaults and abductions (despite the fact that they were, and are, exceedingly rare). Intensive parenting was first described in the 1990s and 2000s by social scientists including Sharon Hays and Annette Lareau. It grew from a major shift in how people saw children. They began to be considered vulnerable and moldable—shaped by their early childhood experiences—an idea bolstered by advances in child development research.

The result was a parenting style that was "child-centered, expert-guided, emotionally absorbing, labor intensive and financially expensive," Ms. Hays wrote in her 1998 book, "The Cultural Contradictions of Motherhood." And mothers were the ones expected to be doing the constant cultivation.

The time parents spend in the presence of their children has not changed much, but parents today spend more of it doing hands-on child care. Time spent on activities like reading to children; doing crafts; taking them to lessons; attending recitals and games; and helping with homework has increased the most. Today, mothers spend nearly five hours a week on that, compared with 1 hour 45 minutes hours in 1975—and they worry it's not enough. Parents' leisure time, like exercising or socializing, is much more likely to be spent with their children than it used to be. While fathers have recently increased their time spent with children, mothers still spend significantly more.

Ms. Sentilles's mother, Claire Tassin, described a very different way of parenting when her two children were young, in the 1970s. "My job was not to entertain them," said Ms. Tassin, who lives in Vacherie, LA. "My job was to love them and discipline them."

Of her grandchildren, Isaac and his three cousins, she said: "Their life is much more enriched than mine was, but it definitely has been directed. I'm not saying it doesn't work. They're amazing. But I know I felt free, so free as a child. I put on my jeans and my cowboy boots and I played outside all day long."

In a new paper, Patrick Ishizuka surveyed a nationally representative group of 3,642 parents about parenting. Regardless of their education, income or race, they said the most hands-on and expensive choices were best. For example, they said children who were bored after school should be enrolled in extracurricular activities, and that parents who were busy should stop their task and draw with their children if asked.

"Intensive parenting has really become the dominant cultural model for how children should be raised," said Mr. Ishizuka, a postdoctoral fellow studying gender and inequality at Cornell.

Americans are having fewer children, so they have more time and money to invest in each one. But investment gaps between parents of differing incomes were not always so large. As a college degree became increasingly necessary to earn a middle-class wage and as admissions grew more competitive, parents began spending significantly more time on child care, found Valerie Ramey and Garey Ramey, economists at the University of California, San Diego.

Parents also began spending more money on their children for things like preschools and enrichment activities, Sabino Kornrich, a sociologist at Emory, showed in two recent papers. Rich parents have more to spend, but the share of income that poor parents spend on their children has also grown.

In states with the largest gaps between the rich and the poor, rich parents spend an even larger share of their incomes on things like lessons and private school, found Danny Schneider, a sociologist at the University of California, Berkeley, and colleagues in a May paper. Parents in the middle 50 percent of incomes have also increased their spending. "Lower socioeconomic status parents haven't been able to keep up," he said.

Besides having less money, they have less access to the informal conversations in which parents exchange information with other parents like them. Ms. Jones recalled that one of her sons liked swimming, but it wasn't until he was in high school that she learned about swim teams on which he could have competed.

"I didn't know because I don't live in a swim tennis community," she said. "Unfortunately colleges and universities tend to look at these things as a marker of achievement, and I feel like a lot of kids who have working-class backgrounds don't benefit from the knowledge."

Race influences parents' concerns, too. Ms. Jones said that as a parent of black boys, she decided to raise them in a mostly black neighborhood so they would face less racism, even though it meant driving farther to many activities.

This is common for middle-class black mothers, found Dawn Dow, a sociologist at the University of Maryland whose book, "Mothering While Black: Boundaries and Burdens of Middle-Class Parenthood," comes out in February. "They're making decisions to protect their kids from early experiences of racism," Ms. Dow said. "It's a different host of concerns that are equally intensive."

The Growing Backlash

Experts agree that investing in children is a positive thing— they benefit from time with their parents, stimulating activities and supportive parenting styles. As low-income parents have increased the time they spend teaching and reading to their children, the readiness gap between kindergarten students from rich and poor families has shrunk. As parental supervision has increased, most serious crimes against children have declined significantly.

But it's also unclear how much of children's success is actually determined by parenting.

"It's still an open question whether it's the parenting practices themselves that are making the difference, or is it simply growing up with college-educated parents in an environment that's richer in many dimensions?" said Liana Sayer, a sociologist at the University of Maryland and director of the Time Use Laboratory there. "I don't think any of these studies so far have been able to answer whether these kids would be doing well as adults regardless, simply because of resources."

There has been a growing movement against the relentlessness of modern-day parenting. Utah passed a free-range parenting law, exempting parents from accusations of neglect if they let their children play or commute unattended.

Psychologists and others have raised alarms about children's high levels of stress and dependence on their parents, and the need to develop independence, self-reliance and grit. Research has shown that children with hyper-involved parents have more anxiety and less satisfaction with life, and that when children play unsupervised, they build social skills, emotional maturity and executive function.

Parents, particularly mothers, feel stress, exhaustion and guilt at the demands of parenting this way, especially while holding a job. American time use diaries show that the time women spend parenting comes at the expense of sleep, time alone with their partners and friends, leisure time and housework. Some pause their careers or choose not to have children. Others, like Ms. Sentilles, live in a state of anxiety. She doesn't want to hover, she said. But trying to oversee homework, limit screen time and attend to Isaac's needs, she feels no choice.

"At any given moment, everything could just fall apart," she said.

"On the one hand, I love my work," she said. "But the way it's structured in this country, where there's not really child care and there's this sense that something is wrong with you if you aren't with your children every second when you're not at work? It isn't what I think feminists thought they were signing up for."

Critical Thinking

1. Think back to your childhood. Reflect and assess the levels of involvement of your father versus your mother at different points in your childhood. How important do you think their involvement was in shaping your attitudes?

2. What are your views on how much you have been or hope to be involved with your children? Will you also try to influence your spouse's or partner's involvement with your children? Why or why not?

3. What advice might you give to someone who is an over-involved helicopter parent?

Internet References

Helicopter Parenting: From Good Intentions to Poor Outcomes
https://www.google.com/search?q=helicopter+parenta&rlz=1C1GCEA_enUS808US808&oq=helicopter+parenta&aqs=chrome..69i57j0l5.6178j0j7&sourceid=chrome&ie=UTF-8

How Parents Are Robbing Their Children of Adulthood
https://www.nytimes.com/2019/03/16/style/snowplow-parenting-scandal.html

Snowflake Children and Helicopter Parents
http://www.parentingsuccesscoaching.com/2016/09/snowflake-children-and-helicopter-parents/

Snowplow parenting: What to know about the controversial technique
https://www.todaysparent.com/blogs/snowplow-parenting-the-latest-controversial-technique/

What Is Helicopter Parenting?
https://www.parents.com/parenting/better-parenting/what-is-helicopter-parenting/

Article Prepared by: Chris J. Boyatzis, *Bucknell University* and Ellen N. Junn, *California State University, Stanislaus*

The Collapse of Parenting: Why It's Time for Parents to Grow Up

If anyone can be called the boss in modern, anti-hierarchical parenthood, it's the children.

Cathy Gulli

Learning Outcomes

After reading this article, you will be able to:

- Summarize the author's views that parents today are now catering and overindulging their children and relinquishing their control over to their children.

- Understand that ceding significant parental control over to children does have unintended consequences that may have negative impact on children's development.

For modern families, the adage "food is love" might well be more true put another way: food is power. Not long ago, Dr. Leonard Sax was at a restaurant and overheard a father say to his daughter, "Honey, could you please do me a favour? Could you please just try one bite of your green peas?" To many people, this would have sounded like decent or maybe even sophisticated parenting—gentle coaxing formed as a question to get the child to co-operate without threatening her autonomy or creating a scene.

To Sax, a Pennsylvania family physician and psychologist famous for writing about children's development, the situation epitomized something much worse: the recent collapse of parenting, which he says is at least partly to blame for kids becoming overweight, overmedicated, anxious and disrespectful of themselves and those around them.

The restaurant scene is a prime example of how all too often adults defer to kids because they have relinquished parental authority and lost confidence in themselves. They're motivated by a desire to raise their children thoughtfully and respectfully. In theory, their intentions are good and their

efforts impressive—moms and dads today are trying to build up their kids by giving them influence; they also want to please them and avoid conflict. In reality, parents are at risk of losing primacy over their children.

The dinner table is ground zero. "When parents begin to cede control to their kids, food choices are often the first thing to slide," Sax writes in his new book, *The Collapse of Parenting: How We Hurt Our Kids When We Treat Them Like Grown-Ups*. A rule such as "No dessert until you eat your broccoli" has recently morphed into "How about three bites of broccoli, and then you can have dessert?" The command has become a question capped with a bribe, as Sax puts it. Dinner at home requires polling kids on what they're willing to eat; the options might include roast chicken and potatoes or chicken fingers and fries. You can bet which they choose. So parents renegotiate: *How about sweet potato fries?*

Parents in North America have become prone to asking their children rather than telling them. "It's natural," says Gordon Neufeld, a prominent Vancouver psychologist cited in Sax's book. "Intuitively, we know that if we're coercive, we're going to get resistance." For trivial choices such as which colour of pants to wear, this approach is fine, he says. But "when we consult our children about issues that symbolize nurturance like food, we put them in the lead." That triggers an innate psychological response, and their survival instincts activate: "They don't feel taken care of and they start taking the alpha role."

So if the girl served green peas does eat one bite as her dad asked, Sax says, "she is likely to believe that she has done her father a favour and that now he owes her a favour in return." Food may be the first manifestation of the collapse of parenting, but many of the problems within families are a result of this type of role confusion. In this way, what happens over a meal is a metaphor for how uncomfortable parents have become in their position as the "alpha" or "pack leader" or "decider" of the family—the boss, the person in charge. The grown-up.

That discomfort comes from a loving place, of course. Many parents strive to raise their kids differently from how they grew up. They say, "I can't do the stuff I was raised with, it doesn't feel right. I don't want to yell, I don't want to spank," says Andrea Nair, a psychotherapist and parenting educator in London, Ont. "There's a massive parenting shift between our generation and the one before. We've come a long way from when you called your dad 'sir' and when he walked in the house you would jump out of 'his' chair."

The evolution hasn't been easy, though. "We're trying to pull off the emotion coaching but we haven't received the training," says Nair. "It's like teaching your kids to speak French while you're learning it in the textbook." Parents have made it a top priority that their kids feel heard and respected from a young age. They want to be emotionally available to them, and for their children to be able to express their own emotions. "Kids have permission to have tantrums now because [they're] learning how to manage feelings," says Nair. "Someone said to me, 'Are we seeing more tantrums now than we used to?' And I wonder."

Parents also want a democratic household where each family member has a say about what happens—*Should we go outside now? Are we ready to have a bath? Would you like to have the party here?*—and they cultivate independence and freedom of thought in their children. Strict obedience used to be praised; now it is seen as outdated and potentially dangerous. Compliance might mean your kid is a pushover, which no parent wants, especially as bullying has spread from the schoolyard to cyberspace.

There are broader influences shifting the parent–child dynamic as well. Over the past half-century or more, the public has come to scorn power imbalances based on gender, race, religion and sexual orientation, and historic gains have been achieved in the pursuit of equality. Even corporations are now replacing pyramidal management with "flat organization." In Western society, where equality for everyone has become a cultural objective and a constitutional right, children are treated like they are one more minority group to honour and empower. "Empower has come to seem virtuous," Sax says. "Empower everyone, why not?"

But many kids are actually overpowering their parents. That's the problem, say those working in child development. A functional family unit hinges on the one social construct that contemporary society has been working hard to dismantle: hierarchy. "You need a strong alpha presentation to inspire a child to trust you and depend upon you," says Neufeld of parents. "If we don't have enough natural power then we're hard-pressed to [make] the demand or [set] the limit" for children. "The

parent always has to be honoured as the ultimate person," he continues. "We need to put parents back in the driver's seat."

If not, the consequences can be far-reaching, starting with children's eating habits, which might contribute to them becoming overweight and obese. Like the father in the restaurant, many parents can't convince their kids to eat well. It doesn't help that junk food is sometimes a reward for acing a test or scoring a goal. The message: healthy food is for losers. On-demand snacking—in the car, at the mall, while out for a walk—appears to disrupt metabolism and circadian rhythms, as well as hormonal balance. That many parents carry with them a canteen of water and a stash of goodies wherever their kids go is further proof of how much they want to satisfy their children, literally and figuratively. "I don't want them to get hypoglycemic," one mom told Sax while lugging a cooler of snacks to her car for a 30-minute drive.

Contributing to the extraordinary weight gain among North American children in recent years is a dramatic decline in fitness. There is even a medical term for it, "deconditioning," which is described in the *Collapse of Parenting* as a euphemism for "out of shape." It has landed kids as young as 11 and 12 in the cardiologist's office complaining of heart-disease symptoms including chest tightness and shortness of breath. In fact, some hospitals in the U.S. have even opened pediatric preventive cardiology clinics.

While children are less active than ever, they do not, ironically, get enough rest. A common question Sax asks students is, "What's your favourite thing to do in your spare time, when you are by yourself with no one watching?" The most common answer in recent years: sleep. That's because children are too busy with school assignments and extracurricular activities to go to bed at a good hour, or because when they get to bed, they are on their cellphone or computer, or playing video games.

This chronic fatigue may be associated with the rise of attention-deficit hyperactivity disorder and prescription drug use among children. "Sleep deprivation mimics ADHD almost perfectly," writes Sax. In his experience as a doctor, insufficient sleep is one reason why kids are more likely to be diagnosed with the disorder. In general, "It is now easier to administer a pill prescribed by a board-certified physician, than to firmly instruct a child and impose consequences for bad behaviour." Stephen Camarata, a professor of hearing and speech sciences and psychiatry at Vanderbilt University in Nashville, echoes that point: "Parents say, 'My child can't do this particular exercise, they're not paying attention,' therefore I have to identify them as having a clinical condition." A medical diagnosis might negate parental shortcomings or a child's misbehaviour. "It displaces that failure," he says.

Camarata worries that parents are asking too much of kids too soon, as he outlines in his latest book, *The Intuitive Parent: Why the Best Thing For Your Child Is You*. He points to the surge of books, toys and software marketed to parents of young children promising to accelerate learning. The ubiquitous metaphor that kids are information sponges has parents saturating them with educational exercises. "We're treating them like little hard drives," says Camarata, but "this idea of pushing children to the absolute max of their developmental norm doesn't give them time to reason and problem-solve. It actually undermines both self-confidence and fluid reasoning, or the ability to think."

Schools, too, have been focusing more on academic achievement than socialization. Sax documents how, 30 years ago, American students in kindergarten and Grade 1 learned "Fulghum's rules," which include tenets such as "Don't take things that aren't yours" and "Clean up your own mess" as well as "Share everything" and "Don't hit people." But since the 1980s, as other nations pulled ahead of the U.S. in scholastic performance, the primary objective of educators has become literacy and numeracy. In Canada too, says Neufeld, "we have lost our culture. Our society is far more concerned that you perform. Schools will always drift to outcome-based things."

That's partly why a "culture of disrespect" has sprouted in North America. As kids have become less attached to and influenced by the adults in their lives, same-age peers have come to matter more to them. It's a theme in Neufeld's book, *Hold On to Your Kids: Why Parents Need to Matter More Than Peers*, co-authored by Dr. Gabor Maté. Young children "are not rational beings," says Neufeld. Part of growing up is testing boundaries; little ones, by their very nature, can't be relied on to hold each other accountable—nor should they.

"Kids are not born knowing right from wrong," says Sax, pointing to longitudinal studies showing that children who are left to discover right from wrong on their own are more likely to have negative outcomes in the future: "That child in their late 20s is much more likely to be anxious, depressed, less likely to be gainfully employed, less likely to be healthy, more likely to be addicted to drugs or alcohol. We now know this," he says. "Parents who are authoritative have better outcomes, and it's a larger effect than the effect of race, ethnicity, household income or IQ."

With stakes so high, authoritative parenting would seem imperative. But there is a psychological hurdle that people will have to overcome first, says Nair: "How to respect their child but also be the decider" of the family. Part of the challenge lies in the fact that parents don't want to fail—at nurturing and governing *simultaneously*—and they certainly don't want their children to fail in their personal development, in school and at social networking. These worries feed off each other in the minds of parents; that's why parents second-guess the way they speak to their kids, what they feed them, how they discipline them and what activities they permit.

This is all the more true for the growing number of parents who delayed having children until they were "ready" with a secure job, a good home and a dependable partner. "People purposely wait so they can nail it," says Bria Shantz, a 35-year-old mother of two in Vancouver. "That creates even more pressure. They want to get this perfect." Shantz is, in fact, the daughter of Neufeld, and she has called upon him for advice or reassurance. That Shantz, who has a leading child psychologist in her family, one who helped raise her, can still occasionally succumb to parental insecurity, says everything about its potency: "There's this slight panic. You want to do everything right," she says. "Nothing prepares you for how much you want it to go well."

So as soon as parents conceive, they begin amassing a library of books on how to deal with the fantastic chaos about to enter their lives in the form of a baby; the collection grows with each developmental stage. They subscribe to online newsletters and smartphone apps that alert them on milestones their children should reach by a certain age. From the outset, parents are tracking how quickly their child is growing, how much they are achieving. For every expert a parent consults by phone or in person, they're also checking in with the virtual wise man, Google. That almost never helps.

There is no parental concern too obscure not to have an online group devoted to it. Shantz is part of one focused on "baby-wearing" because she's trying to decide whether a "wrap" or a "ring sling" would be better for her nine-month-old. "It's the weirdest site to be on. You see posts and you feel guilty because [parents] are carrying their babies everywhere, doing all these things, having this connection." And yet Shantz hasn't been able to delete herself from the group, even though she keeps meaning to; nor has she been able to pick between a wrap or sling.

That pull and push moms and dads feel—between caring about how other parents are raising their kids while rejecting the constant comparisons—defines this generation of parents for better and worse. Katie Hurley, a psychotherapist in Los Angeles and author of *The Happy Kid Handbook: How to Raise Joyful Children in a Stressful World*, says, "We've been conditioned to question ourselves—to constantly look for information to make sure we're doing it right. Because of that, parents are in a state of learned helplessness."

So what are people supposed to do? The answer is so basic that at first it might seem unsatisfying: For starters, says Hurley, realize that "nobody knows what they're doing when they leave the hospital with an infant. Every parent learns by trial and error"—every year of their child's life, and with every child they raise. That's as true today as it ever was, and parents who recognize this will shed some guilt and anxiety. Building on this idea, Nair says that parents must "have a higher tolerance for things not going well." How they recover from their own occasional mistake, outburst, loss of patience or bad call may say more to a child than how they are in happy times. "We're missing that opportunity, which is how learning works," she says. "That's how we become more confident."

A significant portion of Sax's book is devoted to the importance of parents modelling traits they want to encourage in their children. Chief among them, he says, should be humility and conscientiousness—which run counter to inflating a child's self-esteem and sense of entitlement. To that end, he encourages parents to fortify their adult relationships so they are not overly concerned with pleasing their kids as a way of satisfying their own need for affection. Neufeld also urges parents, including his own adult children, to establish a network of surrogate caregivers—relatives, neighbours, daycare workers—who will not undermine their authority but back them up when they need help.

And invariably, they will. "Parenting is awfully frustrating and often a lonely place," says Neufeld, especially when a child misbehaves. In those moments, he recommends parents reassure kids that their relationship isn't broken. "When parents realize that they are their children's best bet, it challenges them to their own maturity." It gives them the confidence that they know what's good for their kids, and that they should stand up to them—this is, in fact, an act of love required of parents. They become, in effect, the grown-ups their children need.

Critical Thinking

1. Based on this article, do you think parents today are over-catering to their children? Why do you think more parents are doing this today as opposed to the past?

2. How did your parents control you and your family when you were growing up? Do you use similar standards in your own parenting or future parenting? Why or why not?

3. Did the author of this article provide research evidence on this perspective and did it convince you to think about changing your philosophy of parenting? Explain why or why not.

Internet References

Authoritative Versus Authoritarian Parenting Style
https://www.psychologytoday.com/us/blog/thinking-about-kids/201409/authoritative-versus-authoritarian-parenting-style

The authoritative parenting style
https://www.parentingscience.com/authoritative-parenting-style.html

Overindulgent Parents, Narcissistic Children?
https://www.webmd.com/parenting/news/20150309/overindulgent-parents-may-breed-narcissistic-children#1

Overindulgent Parenting? That's So Ten Years Ago
https://www.huffpost.com/entry/overindulgent-parenting_n_1344591

What Is Childhood Overindulgence?
https://www.psychologytoday.com/us/blog/the-age-overindulgence/201809/what-is-childhood-overindulgence

Article   Prepared by: Chris J. Boyatzis, *Bucknell University* and
                                   Ellen N. Junn, *California State University, Stanislaus*

'Intensive' Parenting Is Now the Norm in America

The style of child-rearing that most aspire to takes a lot of time and money, and many families can't pull it off.

JOE PINSKER

Learning Outcomes

After reading this article, you will be able to:

- Describe what "intensive parenting" is and summarize the research and historical changes in parenting styles in America.

- Explain some of the factors that have contributed in making the practice of intensive parenting more common among parents today.

- Describe another opposing practice of "free range" parenting that has now surfaced.

Supervised, enriching playtime. Frequent conversations about thoughts and feelings. Patient, well-reasoned explanations of household rules. And extracurriculars. Lots and lots of extracurriculars.

These are the oft-stereotyped hallmarks of a parenting style that has been common in upper-middle-class households for at least a generation. But according to a recent survey, this child-rearing philosophy now has a much broader appeal, one that holds across race and class. The survey, which polled roughly 3,600 parents of children ages 8 to 10 who were demographically and economically representative of the national population, found evidence that hands-on parenting is not just what the well-off practice—it's what everyone aspires to.

Intensive is the adjective that researchers, including Patrick Ishizuka, a postdoctoral fellow at Cornell University who published the survey results late last year, use to describe this model of raising kids. It's difficult to nail down precisely when it became the standard that so many American parents hold themselves to, but its approach seems built for an era of widening economic inequality, in which the downsides of a child falling behind economically are the largest they've been in generations.

Intensive parenting was first identified as a middle-class phenomenon, most notably by the sociologists Sharon Hays and Annette Lareau in the 1990s and 2000s, respectively. Lareau in particular called the approach "concerted cultivation" and contrasted it with a vision of parenting she labeled "the accomplishment of natural growth," which entails much less parental involvement and which she found to be more common among working-class and poorer parents. A big lingering question since then has been why these class differences exist: Did poorer families have different notions of what makes for good parenting, or did they simply lack the resources to practice the parenting styles they believed would be better?

What's useful about Ishizuka's survey data is they suggest that even if parenting style differs by class, parenting attitudes—what parents think they *should* do—currently don't. Jessica McCrory Calarco, a sociologist at Indiana University who studies parenting and has written about it for *The Atlantic*, explained in an email why she thinks this new study (which she was not involved in) is significant: "If parents from different social class backgrounds are engaging in different parenting practices . . . it's not because those parents value different parenting practices," she wrote. "Instead, there must be some other reason."

Because intensive parenting requires an abundance of time and money, the reason is likely that some families have more resources than others. "Poverty not only limits parents' ability to pay for music lessons, for example, but is also a major source of stress that can influence parents' energy, attention, and patience when interacting with children," Ishizuka told me.

Academic researchers have traced the origins of intensive parenting to the mid-20th century. But the timing of how it spread is somewhat uncertain: Ishizuka said there unfortunately aren't historical survey data showing "how pervasive cultural norms of intensive parenting were among parents of different social classes and when they may have diffused."

A plausible history of the past couple decades of American parenting, though, is that a critical mass of families with sufficient means started engaging in intensive parenting, and then everyone else followed. "That would be consistent with prior research on cultural shifts, which have shown that elite culture gradually becomes mass culture," Calarco explained.

Intensive parenting is a style of child-rearing fit for an age of inequality, indicative of a stratified past, present, and future. The past: As some social scientists have theorized, the tilt toward intensive parenting originated at least in part from parents' anxieties about their children competing for education and jobs. (The more extracurriculars, the logic of intensive parenting goes, the better the odds of getting into an excellent college and of securing one of the high-paying jobs that America cordons off for the best-credentialed.) The present: As Ishizuka described, intensive parenting is an ideal that's currently out of reach for many families. And the future: Practiced as it is by some families but not others, it might replicate—or even widen—inequities in future generations. Many children surely benefit from being raised like this—concerted cultivation can serve them well later in life, teaching them how to manage their time and assert their individuality. But heavily involved parenting can at the same time stunt kids' sense of self-reliance, and overcommitted after-school schedules can leave them exhausted. Also, there is some evidence that parents who overdo it increase the risk that their children will grow up to be depressed and less satisfied with life. And on the parents' side, the intensive ideal can lead parents—particularly mothers—to fear that they aren't doing enough to give their child the best future possible.

In part because of the strain that intensive child-rearing puts on parents and kids, some parents have started moving away from the practice and toward free-range parenting, a hands-off child-rearing philosophy that recommends against constant monitoring (and that isn't unlike "the accomplishment of natural growth").

But as Calarco has pointed out, free-range parenting comes with a double standard: When whiter, more affluent parents practice it, it's welcomed as a corrective to more overbearing approaches, but when poorer parents and parents of color practice it, it can be viewed as neglectful. Which means free-range parenting might be rooted in inequality, just like the philosophy that it's a reaction to.

Critical Thinking

1. Given the debate between intensive versus free-range parenting, which style of parenting did your parents use? Reflect on your feelings about how your parents raised you and how it has influenced you as an adult and influenced your attitudes about parenting.

2. Since parenting is not a skill that is taught in schools, how should parents know what style of parenting is most effective? Do you think parenting is something that should be formally taught? Explain.

3. Different cultures do show differences in parenting practices. What is your opinion about these new trends in American parenting styles in comparison to other cultures or countries.

Internet References

How Parent-Child Relations Have Changed
 https://www.psychologytoday.com/us/blog/the-prime-life/201504/how-parent-child-relations-have-changed

Intensive Parenting: Everything You Need to Know About the New Helicopter Parenting: Parenting Styles
 https://www.parents.com/parenting/better-parenting/style/intensive-parenting-everything-you-need-to-know-about-the-new/

Parenting Styles
 https://www.apa.org/act/resources/fact-sheets/parenting-styles

Parenting Styles and Child Behavior
 https://www.psychologyinaction.org/psychology-in-action-1/2018/4/23/k17ziyfqt1vy9tlytr9l9k48epdnur

Parenting through History: A Look at Childrearing in Five Historic Societies
 https://www.neatorama.com/neatobambino/2010/07/26/parenting-through-history-a-look-at-childrearing-in-five-historic-societies/

Article

Prepared by: Chris J. Boyatzis, *Bucknell University* and
Ellen N. Junn, *California State University, Stanislaus*

Spanking Is Ineffective and Harmful to Children, Pediatricians' Group Says

The American Academy of Pediatrics ... issued its most strongly worded policy statement against spanking children.

CHRISTINA CARON

Learning Outcomes

After reading this article, you will be able to:

- Why pediatricians' current opposition to corporal punishment of children is now stronger than it was in the past.

- Describe a number of undesirable outcomes in children linked to being spanked.

Parents should not spank their children, the American Academy of Pediatrics said on Monday in its most strongly worded policy statement warning against the harmful effects of corporal punishment in the home.

The group, which represents about 67,000 doctors, also recommended that pediatricians advise parents against the use of spanking, which it defined as "noninjurious, openhanded hitting with the intention of modifying child behavior," and said to avoid using nonphysical punishment that is humiliating, scary or threatening.

"One of the most important relationships we all have is the relationship between ourselves and our parents, and it makes sense to eliminate or limit fear and violence in that loving relationship," said Dr. Robert D. Sege, a pediatrician at Tufts Medical Center and the Floating Hospital for Children in Boston, and one of the authors of the statement.

The academy's new policy, which will be published in the December issue of the journal Pediatrics, updates 20-year-old guidance on discipline that recommended parents

be "encouraged" not to spank. The organization's latest statement stems from a body of research that was unavailable two decades ago.

A 2016 analysis of multiple studies, for example, found that children do not benefit from spanking.

"Certainly you can get a child's attention, but it's not an effective strategy to teach right from wrong," Dr. Sege said.

Recent studies have also shown that corporal punishment is associated with increased aggression and makes it more likely that children will be defiant in the future. Spanking alone is associated with outcomes similar to those of children who experience physical abuse, the new academy statement says.

There are potential ramifications to the brain as well: A 2009 study of 23 young adults who had repeated exposure to harsh corporal punishment found reduced gray matter volume in an area of the prefrontal cortex that is believed to play a crucial role in social cognition. Those exposed to harsh punishment also had a lower performance I.Q. than that of a control group.

Although the study was small in scope, it can help provide a biological basis for other observations about corporal punishment, Dr. Sege said.

So what is the best way to discipline children? That largely depends on the age and temperament of the child, experts say.

Effective discipline involves practicing empathy and "understanding how to treat your child in different stages in development to teach them how to cool down when things do get explosive," said Dr. Vincent J. Palusci, a child abuse pediatrician at Hassenfeld Children's Hospital at N.Y.U. Langone.

The academy's parenting website, HealthyChildren.org, offers tips for disciplining younger and older children. Rewarding positive behavior, using timeouts and establishing a clear relationship between behavior and consequences can all be effective strategies.

"We can't just take away spanking," Dr. Palusci said. "We have to give parents something to replace it with."

The number of parents who spank their children has been on the decline. A 2013 Harris Poll of 2,286 adults surveyed online found 67 percent of parents said they had spanked their children and 33 percent had not. In 1995, however, 80 percent of parents said they had spanked their children while 19 percent said they had not.

Attitudes about spanking are also changing. Although seven in 10 adults in the United States agreed a "good, hard spanking is sometimes necessary to discipline a child," according to the 2014 General Social Survey, spanking has become less popular over time.

In 1970, Fitzhugh Dodson, a clinical psychologist and best-selling author of books on parenting, was quoted in The New York Times as saying that many discipline problems could be solved by using his "pow wow approach."

"It's my pow, followed by his wow," he explained, demonstrating how he would swat a child's bottom.

"I know some books say parents shouldn't spank, but I think it's a mistake," he said. "A poor mother is left with nowhere to go. She's mad at the kid, has had it up to the eyebrows with him, and longs to give him a big smack on the behind, but she's been told she shouldn't. She should, and it's good for her, because it releases her tension. And the child definitely prefers it to long parental harangues."

And in the 1945 edition of "Baby and Child Care," Dr. Benjamin Spock said spanking "is less poisonous than lengthy disapproval, because it clears the air, for parents and child." (In the '80s, however, he changed his mind.)

Today, most doctors don't support it.

A recent survey of 1,500 pediatricians in the United States found that 74 percent did not approve of spanking and 78 percent thought spanking never or seldom improved children's behavior.

It's a different situation among legislators and school administrators. Although corporal punishment in public schools is not permitted in 31 states and the District of Columbia, there are 19 states, mainly in the South, that either allow the practice or do not have specific rules prohibiting it.

In 2000, the academy recommended that corporal punishment in schools be abolished in all states. And in 2016, the Centers for Disease Control and Prevention published a tool kit for preventing child abuse and neglect that highlighted a need for legislation to end corporal punishment.

But attempts to do so at the federal level have failed.

"I think people see school discipline and parental discipline very differently," said Elizabeth T. Gershoff, a professor at the University of Texas at Austin who has studied corporal punishment in public schools.

Even so, she added, it's possible the new academy statement could lead to change down the road.

"It shows we are seeing the beginning of a shift away from believing it is O.K. to hit children in the name of discipline," she said.

Children "need to know that you have their best interests at heart," Dr. Gershoff said. "If the kid doesn't trust the parent, then they're never going to want to do what they say."

Critical Thinking

1. What cultural, religious, and legal factors might shape how parents think about punishing their children?

2. Might parents' beliefs about spanking their children reflect an underlying belief that children are parents' "property"?

3. How might pediatricians and other professionals who work with families help parents learn alternatives to corporal punishment?

Internet References

A Fine Parent
https://afineparent.com/be-positive/positive-discipline.html

Mother Jones
https://www.motherjones.com/politics/2018/04/new-research-on-disciplining-children-will-make-you-better-parent-and-spouse/

Psychology Today
https://www.psychologytoday.com/us/blog/compassion-matters/201411/six-rules-live-when-you-discipline-your-child

Prepared by: Chris J. Boyatzis, *Bucknell University* and
Ellen N. Junn, *California State University, Stanislaus*

Article

Responding to Defiance in the Moment

EDUCATION DIGEST

Learning Outcomes

After reading this article, you will be able to:

- Discuss the reasons why children defy authority.

- Explain how fear of failure, lack of attention or toxic stress contribute to defiance.

- Identify response options to de-escalate a situation with a defiant child.

Why Do Children Defy Authority?

At certain ages, children are more likely to defy us and take active steps to test limits. At other ages, children are tuned in to issues of fairness and may push back when they sense an adult is being unjust. Picture Amelia, a sixth grader. Whenever presented with an assignment that she found less than engaging, she'd say, "I'm not going to do that. It's a waste of my time." One day, when a teacher asked her to go to the back of the line as a consequence for a rulebreaking behavior, Amelia sat down and refused to move.

With students like Amelia, it's easy to get enmeshed in a power struggle. We may think that students use defiant behavior to annoy us or ruin our day. But their acts of defiance rarely have much to do with us. The main reasons why students act defiantly include:

Unmet physical needs—When students are hungry or tired, they have less energy and it's harder for them to regulate their behavior.

Academic challenges—Some students refuse to do assignments to hide their fear or inability to do what's being asked, such as solving a math problem. They would rather be seen as defiant than incapable, especially in front of their peers.

A sense of belonging and significance—Children who struggle academically or socially may believe that they're "bad" students and thus are not valued. They may use defiance as a way to gain a sense of personal importance.

A need for more control—Sometimes what we say and do unintentionally diminishes a child's feelings of significance. If we find ourselves being too controlling with children who defy us, they may rebel even more—starting a frustrating cycle of our trying to impose more control and receiving back more defiance.

A need for more attention—Some children have learned that defiance can bring them extra attention from teachers and classmates—even if that attention is negative.

Testing limits—Testing limits is a natural part of childhood; some children may thoroughly test adults to find out where the limits are and whether we will keep our word.

Experiencing toxic stress—Children who experience toxic stress come to school on high alert. (In brief, toxic stress is when a child experiences strong, frequent, and/or prolonged adversity, such as physical or emotional abuse or chronic neglect.) These children quickly react when they sense that trouble is coming; they may talk back to teachers, fight, and argue with peers.

The more we can focus on the underlying reasons students engage in defiance, the more we'll be able to maintain our cool in the moment when students act defiantly.

Early Signs of Distress

Children who are defiant usually give clues that they're feeling distressed. If you can watch for these early signs, you can often tell when they may be headed toward a confrontation. Here are some typical warning signs:

- Shifting in seat,
- Opening and closing fists,
- Drumming on desk with fists,
- Slumping shoulders,
- Crossing arms against chest, and
- Trouble making eye contact.

De-escalating Defiance in the Moment

The key to responding effectively to a child who's being defiant is straightforward: Keep the child (and classmates) safe while giving the defiant child a chance to cool down. When a child is behaving defiantly, avoid responses that will heighten stress and invite more resistance. Don't expect that you can reason with the child or make an emotional appeal to get them to behave.

In the moment:

Avoid public confrontations: When you publicly give redirections or consequences to a student who's challenging you, the stakes become higher for both of you. Public disagreements between you and the student can also harm a student's relationship with peers; classmates may label them as "bad" and avoid them as a result. Whenever possible, give reminders, redirections, and consequences privately. Doing so will help preserve your relationship with the student and their relationship with classmates.

Stay calm: When you notice that a child is getting upset or refusing to do what you asked, first tell yourself to slow down. Don't rush to respond (unless to take immediate action for safety's sake). If you stay calm, you give the child more of an opportunity to calm down, too. Allow yourself a few seconds to pause or take a few deep breaths. This will give you time to assess the situation calmly and objectively.

Respectfully remind or redirect: Students who have difficulty cooperating can be especially sensitive to being "bossed around." Whether you're responding to early warning signs or full-blown defiance, use respectful words and an even tone. For example, to a child who's challenging your directions, you might say, "Morgan, take a seat. You can read or draw for now." Here are some more tips:

- Be brief. Avoid lectures and sarcasm.
- Speak in a calm, matter-of-fact tone.

- Use short, direct statements.
- Don't ask questions (unless you will accept any answer).
- Keep your body language neutral.

Intervene as early as possible: As soon as you notice early warning signs, respond to them with respectful reminders or redirections. If you wait until a student acts defiantly, they will be less capable of responding rationally to your directions.

Offer limited choices when possible: Because children who struggle with defiance are often seeking power, it can help to offer them two options. By offering two options—not one "do this"—the child can hold on to a sense of significance while you remain consistent. This teaches the child (and the class) that he is still being held accountable for his behavior. However, don't expect immediate compliance. The child will likely need a minute or two to decide what to do.

Avoid negotiating in the moment: Negotiating during an incident will invite further testing. It also sends the message that children can avoid a consequence or redirection by resisting. If you find yourself in a power struggle, take a deep breath and disengage. Let the child (and the whole class, if they're watching) know that you're finished talking for now and will address the issue after the child calms down. For instance: "Max, we're done talking for now. Everyone else, get your writing journals and start on your stories."

Give children time and space to cool down: Once children start to refuse directions or speak angrily to adults, they're likely in the "fight-or-flight" mindset and can't think rationally. Whenever possible, avoid any discussion until the child has completely calmed down. Consider ways to help the child regain self-control. For example, gross motor movement, such as taking a walk or getting a drink of water, may help more than having the child sit still.

Reflect on What's Working and What's not

It's worth taking some time after an incident of defiance to take a step back and reflect: Are your expectations for yourself or the child simply too high? Is there another approach you haven't tried that might help?

Remember that your main objective in responding in the moment is to keep the child and other students safe. However, in-the-moment responses play a limited role in helping children develop prosocial skills such as cooperation, empathy, and self-control. Helping a child develop these prosocial skills can go a long way toward reducing acts of defiance. After all, the ultimate goal of discipline is to help a child develop these and other social–emotional skills that are essential to their success in school—and in life.

Note

Condensed, with permission, from a November 7, 2016 article on the Responsive Classroom *website. Read the entire article at* https://www.responsiveclassroom.org/responding-defiance-moment.

Critical Thinking

1. What can parents do differently when raising children to prevent some of the insecurities that lead to defiance from developing?

2. What can we do to encourage the development of prosocial skills in children?

Internet References

8 Strategies for Dealing with a Defiant Child
 http://www.quickanddirtytips.com/parenting/behavior/8-strategies-for-dealing-with-a-defiant-child
Dealing with Defiance
 http://www.parenting.com/article/disobedience-and-defiance
Parent Acts: How to Deal with a Defiant Child
 http://www.cnn.com/2016/08/30/health/parent-acts-defiant-children/index.html
Why Is My Child So Angry and Defiant? An Overview of Oppositional Defiant Disorder
 https://www.additudemag.com/parenting-a-defiant-adhd-child/

Culture and Societal Influences

UNIT

Prepared by: Chris J. Boyatzis, *Bucknell University* and
Ellen N. Junn, *California State University, Stanislaus*

Cultural and Societal Influences

Social scientists and developmental psychologists now advocate the importance of understanding that children are influenced by a multitude of complex social and larger societal and historical forces. In this unit, we present articles to illuminate how children and adolescents are influenced by broad factors such as economics, culture, politics, the media, and technology. These influences in turn also affect the family in substantial ways, which is a major context of child development, and many children are now faced with more complex family challenges than ever.

In addition, understanding more about exceptional or atypical children gives the reader a more comprehensive account of child development. Some children must cope with very challenging psychological, emotional, and cognitive challenges, severe psychological trauma, while other children are exposed to environmental insults such as violence and sexualization. These children are often mistreated and misunderstood and have special challenges to overcome.

The powerful role that siblings, families, morality, educators, and other influences such as media, online influencers, and social media are playing an increasingly prominent role in child growth and development. The groundbreaking use of technology by both parents and children, including the omnipresent usage of smartphones and the Internet, and now the almost ubiquitous pervasiveness and acceptance of social media, blogging, and video vlogging is forever altering and immutably changing the fabric of communications between children, parents, and members of the family unit. Thankfully, the advent of these disruptive and fast-growing technologies is now gaining the attention of researchers, who are collecting data on childhood outcomes and interventions to better inform parents and educators with important information and interventions.

Finally, readers are introduced to articles on how best to support and raise children who are not biased, who appreciate and understand advocacy for equity, and the fair treatment of all children, regardless of ethnicity, non-gender conforming identities, and other dimensions of diversity.

In this final unit, we provide a wide variety of articles that hopefully will shed light on the new research, implications, and practical interventions that parents, educators, and others might utilize to help all children reach their maximum potential in an ever increasingly complex world.

Prepared by: Chris J. Boyatzis, *Bucknell University* and
Ellen N. Junn, *California State University, Stanislaus*

Article

The Gay History of America's Classic Children's Books

From "Frog and Toad" to "Where the Wild Things Are," many of the most enduring 20th-century titles share a secret language of queer compassion.

JESSE GREEN

Learning Outcomes

After reading this article, you will be able to:

- Identify some ways in which a handful of classic children's books present sexuality.

- Discuss the links between authors' personal experiences and childhoods and the kinds of books they write.

IN 1998, WHEN my sons were still too young to read by themselves, my partner and I gave them a picture book called "Lucy Goes to the Country." It's about a cat who lives with two gay men; you can tell by the tchotchkes.

The book, then just published, was evidently meant to help normalize already boringly normal families like ours by using the traditional substitution of animals for people in order to illustrate how much fun having gay dads can be. But the plot rang no bells for us as it built to its crisis: When the "big guys" give a party for colorful friends at their weekend house, a bee-hive ends up in the baba ghanouj, Lucy winds up in a tree and a hunky fireman comes to the rescue.

"The Hunky Fireman" would be a fine title for a very different kind of picture book, but his presence in this one made me wonder about the intended readership. (So did the name of a town en route to the country: Peckerwood.) And if you stopped to think about it, "Lucy" seemed to argue that the gay dads, however full of fun, were inadequate: When the pita chips were down, they needed rescuing, too.

Maybe that's why my boys didn't love it. Among gay-themed children's stories, they preferred "Frog and Toad." No, I know: "Frog and Toad"—a series of four picture books by Arnold

Lobel, originally published between 1970 and 1979—is not gay-themed. But it's not gay-themed either. The title characters are best friends, both male, who essentially spend their lives together. Toad, shorter and wartier, is a worrier. Frog, sleeker and greener, is an ameliorator. They wear tight pants, collarless jackets and no shirts: outfits that would surely look great on the hunky fireman.

But Lobel is careful to make Frog and Toad entirely nonsexual. They sleep apart, and Toad even dons a modest Edwardian bathing suit when he swims. Instead of innate animal passion, they model the elements of love that have to be discovered and cultivated: companionship, compromise, acceptance, good humor. They get into scrapes separately but get out of them together, which is not a bad definition of marriage.

Our boys loved the stories, as did we—but not because Lobel was gay. We didn't even know that at the time; indeed, when he started writing the series, Lobel may not have known it himself. Not until 1974, after "Frog and Toad Are Friends" and "Frog and Toad Together" had been published, did he come out to his wife, the illustrator Anita Lobel, and their children. They continued to make books together for years: a Frog and Toad tale if ever there was one.

Still, Lobel's gayness, when I learned of it much later, seemed like something I should have known all along; it lurked everywhere in his words and pictures. I don't know how any parent, reading the stories aloud, uttering phrases like "Come back, Frog. I will be lonely!" in a heartsick, croaky voice, could avoid being forced into intimate sympathy with the animal and thus the author. Which is not to say Frog and Toad could turn you gay. But in their gentleness, their sensitivity to small gestures and their haze of slowly dispersing sadness, the stories were part of the literature of otherness that had been a central theme of adult fiction forever, if only more recently of children's. They suggested, no less to us as gay parents than to our sons with their polar personalities, how separateness could become solidarity and oddness accommodation. Nor did Lobel neglect to show how much work it takes to achieve those victories, and how tenuous they can be; he died, in 1987, of complications from AIDS.

However coded the books' gay content, it was no surprise once decoded. What *did* surprise me, as I recently began to look back at the classics I loved most as a child in the 1960s and as a father in the 1990s, is that Lobel was not an outlier. Among the foxed hardbacks still standing sentry in my sons' abandoned childhood bedroom are "The Gashlycrumb Tinies" by Edward Gorey (1963), "Strega Nona" by Tomie dePaola (1975), the "George and Martha" series by James Marshall (1972 to 1988) and several by Maurice Sendak, including "Where the Wild Things Are" (1963) and "In the Night Kitchen" (1970). Also still extant is "The Runaway Bunny" (1942) by Margaret Wise Brown; her "Goodnight Moon" (1947) would be there, too, if it hadn't long since disintegrated, from overuse, into a pile of dark green dust.

These books are connected not merely by having found favor in our family—and probably yours; in various configurations and collections, "Frog and Toad" still sells more than 500,000 copies a year. Nor is it just their hushed contemplation of aloneness and connection that links them. It's also that all of their authors were gay. (Tomie dePaola, at 84 the only one living, still is.) This observation comes with caveats, of course. Brown was apparently bisexual; she had opposite-sex relationships but spent most of her last decade in a tempestuous romance with a poet and actress who went by the name Michael Strange. And though Gorey, who never married, refused to be pigeonholed—he told Boston magazine in 1980 that he was "reasonably undersexed" and "neither one thing nor the other"—his stories of spinsters and singletons and waifs are certainly queer in both senses of the word. As if that weren't enough, he referred to the gay community, who took him as one of their own whether he liked it or not, as "les boys."

In any case, the more you look, the more pronounced the pattern gets. Louise Fitzhugh, whose immensely popular "Harriet the Spy" books of the 1960s and 1970s kicked Nancy Drew's Junior League butt, was openly (if not publicly) lesbian. Remy Charlip's "Fortunately" (1964), John Steptoe's "Stevie" (1969) and Sandra Scoppettone's "Bang, Bang, You're Dead" (1969), written with Fitzhugh, all bear the stamp, however obscure, of their authors' sexuality. I don't mean to suggest that the upper echelon of children's lit was a restricted club: E.B. White, Dr. Seuss and Shel Silverstein were presumably heterosexual, no matter that Silverstein glowered from the photos on his book jackets like a hot Scruff daddy.

But it remains the case that the authors of many of the most successful and influential works of children's literature in the middle years of the last century—works that were formative for baby boomers, Gen-Xers, millennials and beyond—were gay. At a time when those writers wouldn't dare (as dePaola recently told me) walk hand in hand with a lover, when only a straight children's author like Silverstein could get away with publishing a story in Playboy about life in the homophile Eden that is Fire Island Pines, they won Caldecott and Newbery Medals for books that, without ever directly speaking their truth, sent it out in a secret language that was somehow accessible to those who needed to receive it. And not just to them. These works comforted the proto-gay but also tenderized the proto-straight in a way no other literature could.

THINK ABOUT WHAT was happening under the cover of children's literature. In illustrated series like Lobel's "Frog and Toad" and Marshall's "George and Martha," authors who could not marry as they liked were showing children what marriage should look like. (The ideal: a dependency of independents, preferably with separate bedrooms.) Failing that, they might do better avoiding marriage entirely, at least as traditionally practiced. The observant 11-year-old heroine of Fitzhugh's "Harriet the Spy" (1964) eyes her own parents' marriage caustically, eventually learning, with relief, that there are "as many ways to live as there are people on the earth." Just a year later, in the sequel "The Long Secret," Harriet has been radicalized, telling her conventional friend Beth Ellen that a husband and babies will make her "very boring." "I won't have *time* for that nonsense," she screams.

Elsewhere, especially in Sendak's work, childless authors were showing children—and thus their mothers and fathers—what proper parenting should look like. In "Where the Wild Things Are," a mother who sends a roughhousing son to bed without supper becomes, in his dream, a monster to be subjugated. In "In the Night Kitchen," parents barely exist; the child in a state of nature is self-created and, eventually, self-modulated. The message: Leave me alone with my imagination and I'll be fine.

It must have delighted Sendak to know that, despite the occasional censorship kerfuffle, an America terrified of gay influence on children was devouring his oeuvre as fast as he could whip it up. (His books have sold more than 30 million copies.) While the Save Our Children crusader Anita Bryant and the Focus on the Family attack dog James Dobson were hunting down homosexual propaganda in schools and statehouses, Sendak and the others were hiding it in the one place no one bothered to look: on their children's night stands.

If this wasn't a deliberate strategy of subversion, it wasn't a coincidence either. Consider that they were all talented writers with a deep autobiographical concern for children whose alienation from society was somehow connected to a longing they had no words for. This was not a theme to be addressed openly in stories meant for adults; even if it were possible, it would be useless, already too late. The children's book editor

Ursula Nordstrom, who published much of Sendak, plus some of Brown, Lobel and Fitzhugh and dozens of others who tested the nerve of even liberal librarians, thought grown-ups were a lost cause anyway. "Thank god for anyone under 12 years of age," she wrote in a 1966 letter to Fitzhugh included in "Dear Genius," a collection of Nordstrom's correspondence published in 1998. After that, "everyone goes to pieces."

But writing from a gay perspective for the under-12 set was tricky. The first young adult novel to depict a homosexual encounter—John Donovan's "I'll Get There. It Better Be Worth the Trip"—did not come out until 1969; the first picture book to get near the word "gay" was dePaola's "Oliver Button Is a Sissy," in 1979. Roughly encompassing the first 10 years of the modern gay rights movement, these books (and their authors) could only dream of a world in which "Lucy Goes to the Country," by a male couple who announce themselves as such on the flap, would seem commonplace, or in which a picture book called "Stonewall: A Building. An Uprising. A Revolution" could be published, as it will be by Random House in April, for children 5 through 8.

Before Stonewall, though, authors including Brown and Gorey, like Lobel later, had to find a way to express their own vulnerabilities and their quest for belonging in terms that would not startle the horses or set the pedophile canard a-quacking. ("If it became known you were gay, you'd have a big red 'G' on your chest," dePaola recalls, "and schools wouldn't buy your books anymore.") The traditions of children's literature, in which toddlers are presexual and often not even human, provided the camouflage they needed to write about real things without offense. Brown's two most famous tales, both illustrated by Clement Hurd, are powerful evocations of parental attachment and separation—as experienced by bunnies. Gorey doesn't use animals but rather the conventions of the macabre to represent the terrible loneliness of his youthful characters. Indeed, it's the contrast between horror and doggerel that produces his characteristic deadpan humor: In "The Gashlycrumb Tinies," an abecedary of solo children who meet bad ends, "E is for Ernest who choked on a peach." Take that, T.S. Eliot!

Happier variations on the theme of connection and alienation (with its undercurrent of life and death) inform much of the work by these gay authors. Oliver Button is a multi-enthusiast who doesn't understand why his oversize talent (he's a tap dancer) makes him a target for bullies. (He is rescued, as dePaola says he himself once was, by an unknown benefactor who crosses out the word "sissy" scrawled on a wall and replaces it with "star.") And in Marshall's "George and Martha" series, a loving pair, not unlike Frog and Toad, works through a number of wry adventures that turn their conflicts into companionship. But George and Martha, being hippopotamuses instead of amphibians, are huge; they sometimes threaten the edges of the frame. Rereading the books now I see how their size stands in for the problem of personality; Marshall named them for

the main characters in "Who's Afraid of Virginia Woolf?" His loving, light line, encompassing but also dignifying their volume, suggests the delicacy it takes to be large in the world.

That delicacy, for Marshall as for many of the others, was a stopgap solution to the existential problem of the closet: How do you grow up when you cannot fully and genuinely present yourself as an adult? (In deference to his mother, Marshall's 1992 obituary omitted his longtime partner—and listed a brain tumor as the cause of death instead of complications from AIDS.) Even the gloomy Jeremiah of children's literature whom Marshall lovingly called Morose Sendak was too cowed by his parents to come out publicly until long after both were dead. You can feel the crosscutting energies of that conflict at the wild heart of his greatest works, which are full of rage at punitive elders but also a grudging respect, because their restrictiveness is what forces the child's imagination to flower. Nor is that imagination asexual; Mickey, the stark naked hero of "In the Night Kitchen," is baked into a cake batter by three adult men. Sendak presses right up against the taboo, allowing him to write about sexuality and to access its energies and disappointments safely. Otherwise he would never have dared to publish such a story or, for that matter, needed to write it.

CLOSETS TEND TO be small, lonely places—a fine fit for children playing hide-and-seek, if not always comfortable for adults. Yet they are also, it seems, conducive to literature, in the way almost any constraint is. Today, Mickey would just go to Bennington and wind up marrying that hunky fireman.

Back then, though, if Sendak and the others got any pleasure from their secret identities, they suffered for them as well. How often did they have to put masks on in public, then take them off to live and write? Masks were, in fact, the main motif of Marshall's "Miss Nelson" series, written with Harry Allard between 1977 and 1985, about a grade school teacher's increasingly unorthodox methods of maintaining order and morale. In the first book, "Miss Nelson Is Missing!," she decides to teach her ungovernable class a lesson by vanishing—only to reappear, the next day, disguised as the worst substitute ever. This Miss Viola Swamp is a "real witch," complete with fright wig, honker and wart: "If you misbehave," she warns, "you'll be sorry." At the end, once the class is tamed, Miss Nelson retires her Swamp costume, hanging it in her closet and saying, with a smile, "I'll never tell."

Not many descriptions of gay "passing" get deeper than that: There's the delicious victory and, unspoken, the realization that maintaining the victory means maintaining the ruse. Yet because these authors were out to entertain children—it's no accident the books remain popular—they never tip into the maudlin; if anything, they lean into camp. By the end of the "Miss Nelson" series, even the school principal is in drag.

Such winks may be useful in distracting adults. While studying the Easter eggs in Mickey's night kitchen (Sendak has even hidden the Brooklyn address of his childhood home in the gutter between two pages), a parent may not focus so much on the weirdness of what's going on. But children aren't distracted by such things. Instead, they track the jokes and the emotions, which in the hands of these authors are much the same thing. Another of Lobel's characters, the bachelor owl of "Owl at Home" (1975), is almost a caricature of loneliness: His only friend, the moon, is inconstant; he makes tea from his own tears.

That he's not in fact a caricature is the result of Lobel's careful modulation of tone, which turns the pathos inside out. As someone who had experienced the forced deprivations of the closet, he was perfectly suited to meet sensitive children on their own ground of powerlessness and unbelonging, and to show them how such feelings can be mastered. Owl is lonely, yes, but jovial, natural, staunch, a survivor. He and George and Martha and Max and Mickey and Frog and Toad and Oliver and Harriet are like celebrities in an It Gets Better public service announcement, armed with wit instead of condescension. They whisper from the other side of the struggle for authenticity, saying, "*You* are not wrong, dear one. Everyone else is."

But if the creators of these characters were thus the ideal people to speak to, and for, children, they did so at a cost. The world they imagined had not yet come to pass; if it had, they wouldn't have had to imagine it. No wonder Nordstrom, without whom the golden age of children's literature would not have happened, spent so much time in her letters carefully nursing her authors' neuroses. ("Thanks for your card telling me you are having a nervous breakdown," she wrote in 1972 to Gorey, who was late with a manuscript. "Welcome to the club.") She needed them calm enough to create, but not so calm as to have nothing to say.

It was their power as outcasts she sought to harness, even at the expense of their comfort. (Perhaps jokingly, she encouraged writers to stay single lest they lose their focus.) She seemed drawn to the intensity of feeling that the closet aroused, especially when it produced a kind of vengeful chaos. Her motto as the head of juvenile books at Harper & Brothers (later Harper & Row) from 1940 through 1973 was "Good books for bad children." This was partly a matter of temperament; she was a tough broad. After flipping the pages of dePaola's portfolio while talking on the phone and dragging nonstop on a chain of cigarettes, she told him to come back when he'd learned how to draw. But dePaola was already well established, and besides, Nordstrom preferred to birth new talent. For her favored gay children, she was a sheltering mother, and also, as a lesbian, a comrade. That she was able to live openly with her companion, Mary Griffith, may have something to do with the anonymity of being an editor, not an author—and yet she did write and publish one book.

Called "The Secret Language," it concerns Victoria, a lonely 8-year-old in her first year at boarding school. There she befriends a butch girl named Martha—not quite Harriet-level butch (she wears no tool belt), but tough, antiauthoritarian and, in Mary Chalmers's illustrations, the possessor of a fine set of bowl-cut bangs. It is Martha who has invented the titular language, in which "ick-en-spick" means silly and "ankendosh" disgusting. Amazingly, the word to use "when something is just lovely" is (I'm not making this up) "leebossa," which is dying to be an anagram of "lesbian."

I guess readers in 1960 didn't notice that, nor that at the climax of the story the two girls build a hut. Even now, though the book is weirdly mesmerizing, it's difficult to guess what Nordstrom was after—and she burned the only copy of its sequel, "The Secret Choice," just shy of completing it. (In a way, Fitzhugh took over the job with Harriet.) But it's hard to miss at least one message Nordstrom is sending, in code of course, when the kindly housemother tells Victoria and Martha that "the world will always need those who do not try to be just like everyone else."

It's the same message so many of the other authors of the classic children's books of the era were sending to readers, of whatever eventual sexuality—readers on whom it would someday fall to change the world. Whether frog or toad or hippo or human, you could only genuinely engage with others by first becoming fully and openly yourself.

In short, these books were blueprints for blowing up the closet. But what if the closet is the only place you are safe? When Frog is scared, that's where he hides; Toad likewise jumps under the covers. ("They stayed there for a long time, just feeling very brave together.") How strange Lobel and the others would have found the world their works ushered in: strange and necessary. And maybe even leebossa.

Critical Thinking

1. What are some benefits of using books that indirectly depict aspects of sexual orientation and sexuality?

2. Were you surprised by this article's claims about and analyses of sexual orientation in classic children's books?

3. Why might some schools or families either want to expose their children to these books more or less?

Internet References

Book Riot
https://bookriot.com/2018/09/19/childrens-books-about-diversity/
Bustle
https://www.bustle.com/articles/87976-30-lgbtqia-positive-childrens-books-thatll-teach-kids-how-beautifully-diverse-the-world-is
The National Children's Book and Literary Alliance
https://thencbla.org/advocacy/why-do-kids-need-books/

Article

Prepared by: Chris J. Boyatzis, *Bucknell University* and
Ellen N. Junn, *California State University, Stanislaus*

The Problem with Separate Toys for Girls and Boys

What started our obsession with assigning gender to playthings, and how can parents combat it?

REBECCA HAINS

"Boys and girls stop playing together at a much younger age than was developmentally typical until this recent gender segmentation," says psychologist Lori Day.

Learning Outcomes

After reading this article, you will be able to:

- Describe changes in how toys have been marketed and packaged to boys and girls from earlier times when many classic toys were for "children," not one sex or the other.

- Discuss some potential problems with toy companies and marketers emphasizing that a given toy is "for" boys or girls but not both.

- Share some ways that parents or educators could discuss gender-themed toys with children so that children may be able to believe that any toy could be appropriate for them.

Girls' toys. Boys' toys. To many parents, the ubiquity of separate color-coded shopping aisles feels natural, reflecting a belief in innate gender differences and discrete interests. Recently, however, campaigns such as Let Toys Be Toys and No Gender December have made international headlines for championing desegregated toy aisles, recommending reorganization by theme or interest instead. Rather than believing dolls and crafts are for girls while trucks and science kits are for boys, "we think all toys are for all children,"

explains Let Toys Be Toys campaigner Jo Jowers, who lives in England.

President Obama waded into the matter in December, when at a Toys for Tots event he suggested a T-ball set was an ideal gift for girls. "I'm just trying to break down these gender stereotypes," he said at the time.

Continue reading below

"Children use toys to try on new roles, experiment, and explore interests," explains Susan Linn, executive director of the Boston-based Campaign for a Commercial-Free Childhood and a psychologist at Harvard Medical School. "Rigidly gendered toy marketing tells kids who they should be, how they should behave, and what they should be interested in"—an unhealthily prescriptive situation.

Recent research demonstrates today's toys are divided by gender at historically unprecedented levels. "There are now far fewer non-gendered items available for children than in any prior era," says Elizabeth Sweet, a postdoctoral scholar at the University of California at Davis—even fewer than 50 years ago, when gender discrimination was socially acceptable.

How can this be? The answer lies in significant media industry changes during the 1980s, when the Federal Communications Commission's television deregulation removed longstanding limitations on children's advertising and widespread consumer adoption of cable allowed media owners to target more narrowly segmented audiences than ever before. As a result, marketers suddenly viewed children as a segmentable, highly lucrative demographic after largely ignoring them for 50 years.

Traditionally gender-neutral toys like building blocks now come in "boy" and "girl" versions.

Perhaps it is unsurprising, then, that two of today's most successful companies—Disney, whose Princess brand is the No. 2 licensed property in the United States and Canada, and LEGO, which recently surpassed Mattel as the world's largest toy maker—were early adopters of the trend to meticulously segment the child market by gender in the late 1980s. The licensing success of Disney's *The Little Mermaid* in 1989 prompted several additional princess film releases in quick succession, positioning Disney as a formidable power in the girl market. Likewise, in 1988, LEGO debuted its "Zack the LEGO Maniac" campaign, squarely positioning itself as a boy brand. A year later, LEGO began tailoring its minifigs' historically gender-neutral faces to include lipstick and facial hair—clear gender markers.

The ripple effects of these monumental 1980s-era marketing changes are evident today. Now, once classically gender-neutral toys are produced in "boy" and "girl" versions: Radio Flyer wagons, Tinkertoys, Mega Bloks, Fisher-Price stacking rings, and everything in between come in "pinkwashed" varieties, in hopes that families with children of each sex will buy twice the toys. Meanwhile, Disney Princess's record-breaking profits prompted a proliferation of princess items from competitors, and Disney bought Marvel and Lucasfilm, the *Star Wars* creator, to compete for the boy market. Similarly, LEGO competes for girls' purchasing power not through inclusivity but by offering separate, stereotypically girlish themes, like Disney Princess and LEGO Friends.

What does this mean for today's families? Lori Day, an educational consultant and psychologist in Newburyport and author of *Her Next Chapter: How Mother-Daughter Book Clubs Can Help Girls Navigate Malicious Media, Risky Relationships, Girl Gossip, and So Much More,* argues that children's play has been altered, with long-term consequences. "Boys and girls stop playing together at a much younger age than was developmentally typical until this recent gender segmentation," she says. "The resulting rigidly stereotyped gender roles are unhealthy for both males and females, who are actually more alike than different." Sweet concurs: "This kind of marketing has normalized the idea that boys and girls are fundamentally and markedly different from one another, and this very idea lies at the core of many of our social processes of inequality."

LEGO's Friends line has been criticized for featuring hair salons and shopping malls.

Parents can push back against these problems, however, by raising critically aware children. Jennifer Shewmaker, a psychology professor at Abilene Christian University in Abilene, Texas, and author of *Sexualized Media Messages and Our Children: Teaching Kids to Be Smart Critics and Consumers,* suggests: "When you see stereotyped advertisements, ask the child, 'What do you think about the way that depicts girls and boys? Is that how the boys and girls in your life act?'" Carolyn Danckaert, cofounder of Washington, D.C.-based empowerment resource site A Mighty Girl, adds, "When parents explain that some people think only girls or only boys are good at something but their family disagrees, children can recognize stereotypes for what they are."

Not all parents share such concerns, of course. Jo Paoletti, an American studies professor at the University of Maryland in College Park and author of *Pink and Blue: Telling the Boys From the Girls in America,* attributes differing opinions to ongoing culture wars. "Adults who subscribe to more traditional, conservative gender roles see children's preferences for stereotypical clothing and toys as natural expressions of innate differences," Paoletti says. As such, Erin McNeill, founder and president of Watertown-based Media Literacy Now, advocates for integrating media literacy into the K-12 curriculum. "Some parents won't notice or be concerned about the gendering of products. It's important that all children have the opportunity to gain the critical thinking skills to understand how and why gendered ads target them," she says.

Critical Thinking

1. Why do you think marketing and packaging of toys has become more "gendered" in recent years?
2. Is there something wrong with "separate" toys for boys and girls, or are the authors of the article exaggerating a problem?
3. If you were a parent, how would you talk with your children about toys that seem marketed for one sex only?

Internet References

Girl toys, boy toys, and parenting
https://www.parentingscience.com/girl-toys-and-parenting.html
What the research says: Gender-typed toys
https://www.naeyc.org/resources/topics/play/gender-typed-toys

Article

Prepared by: Chris J. Boyatzis, *Bucknell University* and
Ellen N. Junn, *California State University, Stanislaus*

Boys and Girls on the Playground: Sex Differences in Social Development Are Not Stable across Early Childhood

STÉPHANIE BARBU, GUÉNAËL CABANES, AND GAÏD LE MANER-IDRISSI

Learning Outcomes

After reading this article, you will be able to:

- Describe sex differences in social behavior in early childhood.

- Discuss how the emergence of boys' and girls' social play behaviors seem to follow different trajectories across early childhood.

- Consider how sex differences interact with age differences in boys and girls.

Introduction

Human sex differences are a perennially hot topic that not only grips the public interest, but that has triggered a great deal of scientific focus from biological to social sciences. One of the many, and perhaps most striking, paradoxes of gender studies is that, despite decades of concerted efforts, the very existence of sex differences remains debated [1]–[3]. Discrepancies between studies undoubtedly feed the continuing debate. Some studies found no sex differences whereas others reported differences that were either congruent or not with gender stereotypes. Such discrepancies are especially marked in childhood. Here, we present evidence that sex differences are not stable over time. Between-sex differences appear during a limited window of development and even change direction with age. Our findings contribute to resolve the puzzling null or contradictory conclusions drawn from limited age-range samples or collapsed age-groups and raise important methodological issues such as the representativeness of samples in studies. Developmental studies are thus especially needed in order to go beyond the current debate.

One pervasive stereotype about sex-related differences is that girls and women are more socially oriented and skilful than boys and men [4]–[6]. There is some evidence in support of this view. From birth to the first year, infant females show stronger social orientation responses than infant males, with a stronger interest in human faces [7]–[8], a greater amount of eye contact [9]–[11], and more accurate imitative abilities [12]. Throughout childhood and adulthood, girls and women continue to be more socially expressive and responsive than age-matched males. Females display more emotional expression and are more skilled at decoding others' emotions [13], [14] and understanding others' thoughts [15]–[17]. They are also more prone to behave prosocially [18]. In childhood, these abilities are related to general social competence, especially in dealing with peers [17], [19], and to different interaction and communication styles that prefigure differences in women's and men's interpersonal goals [20], [21]. Finally, a variety of clinical conditions with marked social deficits, such as autism, occurs more often in males than in females, and has been described as an extreme manifestation of some male-typical traits, suggesting a continuum between typical and atypical social development [22].

Although the literature provides some empirical evidence, the picture is not as simple and univocal as described. Beyond a great heterogeneity in methodologies, whether studies found differences or not seems dependent on children's ages. Moreover, the differences reported are not especially large or consistent throughout childhood [6]. Yet the developmental dynamics of sex differences has been rarely investigated, with one notable exception, but that focused on within-sex variation rather than between-sex differences [23]. Thus, the magnitude, consistency and stability across time of between-sex differences remain questioned [5], [6], [18]. As play is at least to some extent a universal activity of childhood [24] and provides an excellent window into children's social development [25], [26] and psychosocial adjustment [27], we investigated sex-and age-related trends in social play development throughout early childhood.

Both the amount and the quality of children's play are associated with measures of social motivation and competence, in particular with peers [28]–[30]. It is well documented that with increasing age, children are more likely to engage in social play, proceeding from less to more mature forms of social interactions [25], [26], [29], [31]. However, there are also marked individual differences in the degree to which children are willing to participate in peer play [27]. Among available peer play scales, we adapted the seminal Parten's [32] framework which covers the social spectrum of children's participation in peer play, with non-social activities: unoccupied behavior (absence of focus or intent) and solitary play (playing alone or independently); semi-social activities: onlooker behavior (observing others' activity, but without entering into the activity) and parallel play (playing beside, but not with); and social play: associative play (playing with other children, but with no role assignment or organization of activity) and cooperative play (playing in organized and coordinated activities). To cover all children's social activities, we also recorded social interactions with peers when children are not playing, but are involved in sustained social exchanges (mostly conversations, which are more frequent in older children [26]), and social interactions with adults, as adults were present on playgrounds. We investigated whether girls show consistently more socially oriented and skilful forms of peer play and interactions than same-age boys from 2 to 6 years old, when most children begin to experience peer social interactions, or whether the sex difference changes as children grow older. To this end, children's play behavior was observed under naturalistic conditions at nursery schools during self-selected activities and spontaneous peer-groups.

Results
Developmental Trends Over the Preschool Years

Children's social play showed important changes during the preschool period, becoming more peer-oriented and structured with age (Fig. 1; see also Table S1). We found significant effects of age for all the social categories: interactions with adults, unoccupied and onlooker behavior, solitary and parallel play decreased, while associative play, cooperative play and interactions with peers increased over the preschool years (two-way

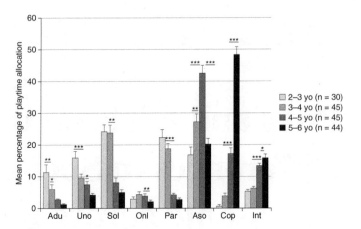

Figure 1 Developmental trends of children's social play from 2 to 6 years

https://doi.org/10.1371/journal.pone.0195456.g003

Interactions with adults (Adu), unoccupied behavior (Uno), solitary play (Sol), onlooker behavior (Onl) and parallel play (Par) decreased significantly over the pre-school years while associative play (Aso), cooperative play (Cop) and interactions with peers (Int) increased, notably with an abrupt change at 4–5 years with the predominance of associative play, and thereafter of cooperative play at 5–6 years. Bars and error bars represent mean + standard error of the percentages of children's playtime allocation within social participation categories. *$P < 0.05$, **$P < 0.01$, ***$P < 0.001$ by Fisher's PLSD post hoc comparisons among age groups (see also Table S1 for complete descriptive statistics and S2 for true P values).

https://doi.org/10.1371/journal.pone.0016407.g001

ANOVAs, all $F3,156 > 5.2$, all $P < 0.002$; see Table S2). Thus, age groups were characterized by distinct social participation profiles (Fig. 1, see also Table S3). 2–3 years old children were observed more frequently playing alone or beside other peers or even unoccupied, although associative play occupied a not negligible part of their activities. They were also observed more frequently interacting with adults than older children for whom this proximity became rare. The social profile of 3–4 year olds remained quite similar to that of 2–3 year olds, except that associative play became as frequent as solitary play and more frequent than parallel play. From the age of 4–5 years, children's sociality changed abruptly, notably associative play predominated at 4–5 years and cooperative play predominated at 5–6 years.

Sex Differences Over the Preschool Years

We evidenced important sex differences in children's social play, differences that stress a developmental gap between girls and boys (Fig. 2; see also Table S1). Solitary play was influenced by sex (two-way ANOVA, sex: $F1,156 = 14.30$, $P = 0.0002$; agex-sex: $F3,156 = 2.02$, $P = 0.11$): preschool boys played alone more frequently than preschool girls (Fig. 2e, top right). This difference was especially marked at 3–4 years (Fisher's PLSD, 3–4 years: $P = 0.0001$; 2–3 years: $P = 0.08$; 4–5 years: $P = 0.15$; 5–6 years:

$P = 0.59$). Moreover, we found significant interactions between age and sex for associative play (age×sex: $F3,156 = 4.22$, $P = 0.005$; sex: $F1,156 = 0.03$, $P = 0.85$), cooperative play ($F3,156 = 10.20$, $P < 0.0001$; $F1,156 = 0.45$, $P = 0.50$), and interactions with peers ($F3,156 = 4.13$, $P = 0.008$; $F1,156 = 8.36$, $P = 0.004$), indicating that differences between sexes changed over time. At 3–4 years, girls were involved in associative play more frequently than boys (Fig. 2f) (Fisher's PLSD, $P = 0.05$), but at 4–5 years, boys were involved in associative play more frequently than girls ($P = 0.02$). No significant differences were found in the youngest or the oldest children (2–3 years: $P = 0.34$; 5–6 years: $P = 0.06$). Sex differences in cooperative play (Fig. 2g) appeared a year later than in associative play. They appeared again first in favour of girls at 4–5 years ($P = 0.005$), but afterwards in favour of boys at 5–6 years ($P < 0.0001$). No significant differences were found before these ages (2–3 years: $P = 0.99$; 3–4 years: $P = 0.61$). Thus, for both associative and cooperative play, sex differences first in favour of girls were reversed the following year. Sex differences in interactions with peers (Fig. 2h) appeared only during the final preschool year (5–6 years: $P < 0.0001$; 2–3 years: $P = 0.66$; 3–4 years: $P = 0.11$; 4–5 years: $P = 0.56$), when this form of social involvement was observed gradually more frequently in girls than in boys. Finally, we evidenced neither effects of sex nor age×sex interactions for interactions with adults ($F1,156 = 1.49$, $P = 0.22$; $F3,156 = 1.86$, $P = 0.14$), unoccupied behavior ($F1,156 = 1.41$, $P = 0.24$; $F3,156 = 0.36$, $P = 0.79$), onlooker behavior ($F1,156 = 0.72$, $P = 0.40$; $F3,156 = 1.48$, $P = 0.22$), and parallel play ($F1,156 = 2.42$, $P = 0.12$; $F3,156 = 0.27$, $P = 0.85$) (Fig. 2a–d, left column).

Girls' and Boys' Social Profiles

To get an overall picture of sex differences, the relative frequencies of the different forms of social play at each age for both sexes must be taken into consideration (Fig. 2, see also Tables S1 and S4). At 2–3 years, the profiles of girls and boys were quite similar: children of both sexes were observed either in solitary, parallel and associative play or unoccupied in significantly similar proportions (pairewise t-tests, all $P > 0.08$; except solitary vs. unoccupied for boys: $P = 0.0003$). Interactions with adults by boys were less frequent than the above activities (all $P < 0.04$), but this was not so for girls (all $P > 0.20$). At 3–4 years, associative play, which was more frequent in girls than in boys, was also the main form of girls' social activity (all $P < 0.04$), whereas associative play was still as frequent as solitary play ($P = 0.27$) and parallel play ($P = 0.17$) for boys. At 4–5 years, although cooperative play was more frequent in girls than in boys and associative play more frequent in boys than in girls, associative play was however the main form of social activity for both sexes, ahead of the other activities (all $P < 0.001$). Similarly, at 5–6 years, although girls interacted with

peers more frequently than boys did, whereas cooperative play was more frequent in boys, cooperative play became the main form of play for both sexes (all $P < 0.01$). Thus from 3–4 years old, girls were actually more associative than same-age boys, but in the later stages, both girls' and boys' play was mostly associative at 4–5 years and mostly cooperative at 5–6 years.

Discussion

Our study highlights that although all children progress towards more socially oriented and skilful forms of play during early childhood, girls develop social and structured forms of play at younger ages than boys. Preschool boys also display more

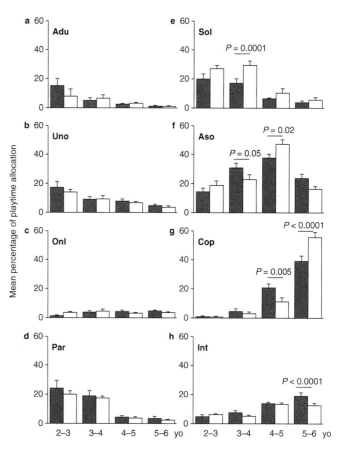

Figure 2   Girls develop social and complex forms of play earlier than boys, but boys catch up

Bars and error bars represent percentages (mean + s.e.m.) of children's playtime allocation within social participation categories (girls: dark bars, boys: white bars). No sex differences are found for interactions with adults (a, Adu), unoccupied behavior (b, Uno), onlooker behavior (c, Onl) or parallel play (d, Par). Sex differences appear at some ages successively in solitary play (e, Sol), associative play (f, Aso), cooperative play (g, Cop), and interactions with peers (h, Int). Significant P values are given for Fisher's PLSD post hoc comparisons between girls and boys within age groups. (See also Table S1 for complete descriptive statistics.)

https://doi.org/10.1371/journal.pone.0016407.g002

solitary play than preschool girls. However, boys catch up at the following developmental stages. Sex differences are not stable throughout social development, but they rather reflect a developmental gap between girls and boys. While boys catch up and same-age girls move on towards more complex social play and interactions, a sex difference recorded in favour of girls in a particular social play pattern at a given age can be reversed the following year, as we evidenced for associative and cooperative play. Therefore, it is not surprising that some studies based upon limited age-range samples or collapsed age-groups failed to find significant results or found results that were not congruent with gender stereotypes [6], making the case for more developmental studies to capture the dynamics of sex differences.

Moreover, discrepancies between studies can also be related to differences in the operationalization of sex differences and comparisons [5]. There are two ways to measure sex differences, which can provide quite different pictures of sex differences and conclusions: asking whether the behavior is more frequent in one sex than in the other or asking whether the behavior is the main form expressed by one sex compared to the other. Here, we show that, despite the advance of girls, both girls' and boys' play is associative at 4–5 years and cooperative at 5–6 years. Therefore, girls' advantage appears systematically the year before that the play activity becomes the predominant one for both sexes.

As play involves communication, role taking and cooperation, sex differences in social play may be a by-product of sex differences in socio-cognitive skills, as girls develop language [6], [33] and theory-of-mind [15]–[17] skills earlier than boys do. These sex differences may also appear during a limited window of development (during the preschool years in particular) and disappear in later ages. It is clear that there is a linkage between children's socio-cognitive skills and some aspects of social play [34], [35]. However, the relation between social play, skills and cognition must be further explored as more mature forms of play may also promote children's social and socio-cognitive skills. Play and associated interactions with peers is considered to both reflect children's social competence and to provide children with a unique environment where they can acquire important social and socio-cognitive skills [27], [28], [36]. Although there are a number of correlational studies, there is very little relevant experimental evidence, remaining open the question of cause-and-effect between play and children's skills.

Sex differences in social play patterns may also result in children's sex-typed toys and activities. Sex differences in toys and activities represent one of the largest non-reproductive physical or psychological sex differences that have been widely observed across cultures and taxa [37], [38]. Children's preferences for sex-typed toys are apparent as early as infancy [39] and increase over the preschool years [5], [6]. The context of play (e.g., play areas and materials) has significant effects on the quantity and quality of play and attendant social interactions [40]. Both girls and boys show the greatest play complexity when playing with female stereotyped toys than with neutral or male stereotyped toys [41]. Therefore, early sex differences in interests may impact upon the evaluation of children's play quality and related social and socio-cognitive skills.

The contribution of the socio-cultural and biological factors in human sex social differences is not yet known given their complex interplay [3], [38]. Many of these differences may to some extent be the result of socialization. Differences in styles of parenting towards the sexes [6] and in peer cultures within sex-segregated peer groups [42] may enhance the development of different interests and skills in boys and girls. Nevertheless, sex differences were also reported despite seemingly similar social environment and experiences suggesting a differential effect of the early environment. In particular, boys are more vulnerable to disruptive events and adverse home environments than girls [43], [44]. Sex differences at birth [7], [12] and correlations with prenatal testosterone in normally developing children (such as in eye contact [11], vocabulary size [45], and sex-typed play [46]) strongly suggest that biological factors play a role as well, at least in early sex differences. During atypical social development, foetal testosterone is also associated with the severity of autistic traits [47]. Prenatal hormonal exposure may shape the neural mechanisms underlying early social development during both typical and atypical development [22].

The questions why girls are more socially precocious than boys, and how boys eventually catch up in normally developing children, but not in children with some social developmental deficits must be studied in much depth. Understanding the developmental dynamics of relationships between social competence, social cognition and sex should provide new insights on how the nature and the weight of underlying biological and social processes change over time [48] and even between sexes [49], [50] during both typical and atypical development [22].

Materials and Methods
Ethics Statement
The study consisted in non-invasive and unconstrained behavioral observations of children at nursery schools during daily activities. According to the current French laws on the protection of persons in biomedical research (law No 88-1138, so-called Huriet-Sérusclat law of the 20th December 1988, amended in 2004 -law of the 9th August 2004), such protocol does not require the approval of an ethics committee. The study

complies with the ethics guidelines given by the National Consultative Ethics Committee of the French Centre National de la Recherche Scientifique (COMETS). Only children, for whom parental written consent was obtained, participated in the study. The observations started after receiving written consent from the local Inspection of French National Education and permission from the schools. The data were analyzed anonymously.

Subjects and Setting

Children were selected from 16 classes in two nursery schools from urban surrounding (Rennes, France). The selection criteria were (1) that the parents provided a written consent, (2) that the child attended school fulltime, and (3) that the child age pertained to the second half of the year in order to reduce age range within age-groups and to avoid overlap between age-groups. Following a cross-sectional design, the children (n = 164: 82 boys), ranging in age from 29 to 74 months, were divided into four age groups corresponding to the four French school grades: 2–3 year olds, 3–4 year olds, 4–5 year olds, and 5–6 year olds (see Table 1 for age and sex composition of the sample). Age groups differed significantly in age (two-way ANOVA, $F_{3,156} = 1080.93$, $P < 0.0001$) and contained equal numbers of children, except the youngest group as only 20% of the 2-year-old children attend school in France whereas near all children do while they are 3 years old. In each group, girls and boys (in roughly equal numbers) did not differ in age (sex: $F_{1,156} = 0.64$, $P = 0.42$; age×sex: $F_{3,156} = 0.99$, $P = 0.40$), nor they did in family backgrounds. The children were from diverse socioeconomic backgrounds (20.1% upper-class, 37.8% middle-class, 25.6% lower-class, 7.3% unemployed and 9.2% no reply).

Children were observed during outdoor playtimes that occurred twice a day (morning and afternoon). Playgrounds were large outdoor areas fully equipped for children (e.g., slides, sandbox, tricycles, balls). Numbers of children in the playground varied with the size of the school (2 to 3 classes in one school and 5 to 6 classes in the other). Peer groups were mixed-aged, generally including classes from two successive grades. The adult-children ratio was approximately the same in all playgrounds and schools as teachers accompanied their classes. The teachers were in sight of the children in order to help settle any problems that might arise, but they never directed the children's activities.

Observational Procedure

The observations were made from March to May 2005 and 2006. We used scan sampling for data collection [51]. The children's activities were recorded every 2 minutes during playtime that lasted on average 30 minutes. As it was not possible to observe all the children who were present on the playground at the same time, the observer followed a same-age group of fifteen children during a session. The same number of observations was conducted for each child (i.e. 120 scans that is 4 hours of observation per child). On average, 10 free-play sessions over two weeks were needed to collect data for a group. Observation sessions were counterbalanced daily (morning and afternoon) and for a school term (beginning and end) among age groups. The daily observation order of the children was also randomized within a group. Two trained observers (both male), one in each school, collected data. They were unaware of the purpose of the study (i.e. investigation of sex differences). The observer remained visible to the children during observation sessions and adopted an integrative non-participant attitude. After a preliminary habituation period of two weeks, the observer recorded children's activities on a check sheet, using a stopwatch.

Coding and Reliability

Coding was derived from Parten's [32] peer play categories: (1) unoccupied behavior (wandering around aimlessly, watching anything of passing interest or staring off into space) (k = 0.67); (2) solitary play (playing apart from other children or playing independently without acknowledging peers playing in close proximity) (k = 0.71); (3) onlooker behavior (observing the activity of other children, within speaking distance, making eventually some comments on the activity, but with no entry into the activity) (k = 0.72); (4) parallel play (playing beside – within 3 feet, with materials that are similar to those being used by others in close proximity, but independently without substantial interaction) – in order to introduce a more clear-cut distinction between

Table 1 Age and Sex Composition of the Sample

	2–3 years old			3–4 years old			4–5 years old			5–6 years old		
	M	s.d	n	M	s.d	n	M	s.d	n	M	s.d	n
Boys	35.6	2.8	17	44.9	3.0	22	55.6	2.0	20	69.8	3.1	23
Girls	34.1	2.3	13	44.9	2.8	23	56.2	2.4	25	69.2	3.4	21
Overall	34.9	2.7	20	44.9	2.9	45	56.0	2.3	45	69.5	3.2	44

(M: Mean age in months, s.d.: standard deviation, n: number of children). doi:10.1371/journal.pone.0016407.t001

parallel and solitary play, we relied on parallel aware play [29] that is accompanied with eye-contacts and/or a few brief social exchanges (e.g., vocalization, smile) (k = 0.93); (5) associative play (being involved in similar playful activities accompanied with sustained social exchanges and following a common plan, but with a mild control of group membership and no role assignment or organization of activity) (k = 0.90); (6) cooperative play (playing in organized and coordinated activities, that is showing group membership control, division of labour and differentiation of roles, mostly enacting complementary roles within social pretend play or games with rules) (k = 0.99). We added two categories: (7) social interactions with peers when children are not playing, but are involved in sustained social exchanges (e.g., mostly conversations) (k = 0.75); (8) social interactions with adults as teachers were present on playgrounds (k = 0.95). Finally, when the target child was engaged in an activity that did not fall into the categories, mostly when he/she performed maintenance behaviors (e.g., eating a snack, going to restroom…), these scans were discarded and replaced by supplementary scans so as to have the same number of observations for each child. Before observations and coding, the two observers were previously trained on videotapes of children's outdoor free-play until they reached satisfactory inter-coder reliability. Inter-coder reliability was then established on 12 videotapes selected randomly. Cohen's kappa statistics for each social category ranged from 0.67 to 0.99 (global kappa = 0.84).

Statistical Analyses

A proportion score was calculated for each child for each of the eight social categories based on the proportion of time intervals spent in each category (relative to total number of time intervals). Two-way ANOVAs were carried out on proportion scores to test the effects of age, sex and their interaction. When an effect was significant, Fisher's PLSD post hoc tests compared age groups or boys and girls within age groups. To assess children's social participation profiles, pairwise t-tests were used to compare the proportions of social categories. All tests were two-tailed and $\alpha = 0.05$.

Author Contributions

Conceived and designed the experiments: SB. Performed the experiments: GC. Analyzed the data: SB GC. Wrote the paper: SB GLMI.

References

1. Mehl MR, Vazire S, Ramirez-Esparza N, Slatcher RB, Pennebaker JW (2007) Are women really more talkative than men? Science 317: 82.
2. Wallentin M (2009) Putative sex differences in verbal abilities and language cortex: A critical review. Brain Lang 108: 175–183.
3. Lippa RA (2005) Gender, nature, and nurture. New York: Taylor & Francis Group.As the 335 p.
4. Maccoby EE, Jacklin CN (1974) The psychology of sex differences. Stanford, CA: Stanford University Press. 634 p.
5. Ruble DN, Martin CL, Berenbaum SA (2006) Gender development. In: Eisenberg N, editor. Social, emotional, and personality development. Hoboken, NJ: Wiley. pp. 858–932.
6. Blakemore JEO, Berenbaum SA, Liben LS (2009) Gender development. New York: Psychology Press. 519 p.
7. Connellan J, Baron-Cohen S, Wheelwright S, Batki A, Ahluwalia J (2000) Sex differences in human neonatal social perception. Infant Behav Dev 23: 113–118.
8. Lutchmaya S, Baron-Cohen S (2002) Human sex differences in social and non-social looking preferences, at 12 months of age. Infant Behav Dev 25: 319–325.
9. Hittelman JH, Dickes R (1979) Sex differences in neonatal eye contact time. Merrill Palmer Q 25: 171–184.
10. Leeb RT, Rejskind FG (2004) Here's looking at you, kid! A longitudinal study of perceived gender differences in mutual gaze behavior in young infants. Sex Roles 50: 1–5.
11. Lutchmaya S, Baron-Cohen S, Ragatt P (2002) Foetal testosterone and eye contact in 12-month-old human infants. Infant Behav Dev 25: 327–335.
12. Nagy E, Kompagne H, Orvos H, Pal A (2007) Gender-related differences in neonatal imitation. Inf Child Dev 16: 267–276.
13. Hall JA, Carter JD, Horgan TG (2000) Gender differences in nonverbal communication of emotion. In: Fischer AH, editor. Gender and emotion: Social psychological perspectives. New York: Cambridge University Press. pp. 97–117.
14. McClure EB (2000) A meta-analytic review of sex differences in facial expression processing and their development in infants, children, and adolescents. Psychol Bull 126: 424–453.
15. Happé FGE (1995) The role of age and verbal ability in the theory of mind task performance of subjects with autism. Child Dev 66: 843–855.
16. Charman T, Ruffman T, Clements W (2002) Is there a gender difference in false belief development? Soc Dev 11: 1–10.
17. Walker S (2005) Gender differences in the relationship between young children's peer-related social competence and individual differences in theory of mind. J Genet Psychol 166: 297–312.

18. Eisenberg N, Fabes RA, Spinrad TL (2006) Prosocial development. In: Eisenberg N, editor. Social, emotional, and personality development. Hoboken, NJ: Wiley. pp. 646–718.

19. Walker S, Irving K, Berthelsen D (2002) Gender influences on preschool children's social problem-solving strategies. J Genet Psychol 163: 197–210.

20. Maccoby EE (1990) Gender and relationships. A developmental account. Am Psychol 45: 513–520.

21. Leaper C, Smith TE (2004) A meta-analytic review of gender variations in children's language use: Talkativeness, affiliative speech, and assertive speech. Dev Psychol 40: 993–1027.

22. Knickmeyer RC, Baron-Cohen S (2006) Fetal testosterone and sex differences in typical social development and in autism. J Child Neurol 21: 825–845.

23. Golombok S, Rust J, Zervoulis K, Croudace T, Golding J, et al. (2008) Developmental trajectories of sex-typed behavior in boys and girls: A longitudinal general population study of children aged 2.5–8 years. Child Dev 79: 1583–1593.

24. Göncü A, Gaskins S (2007) Play and development: Evolutionary, sociocultural, and functional perspectives. Mahwah, NJ: Lawrence Erlbaum. 328 p.

25. Fromberg DP, Bergen D (2006) Play from birth to twelve: Contexts, perspectives, and meanings. New York: Routledge. 455 p.

26. Rubin KH, Bukowski WM, Parker JG (2006) Peer interactions, relationships, and groups. In: Eisenberg N, editor. Social, emotional, and personality development. Hoboken, NJ: Wiley. pp. 571–645.

27. Coplan RJ, Rubin KH, Findley LC (2006) Social and nonsocial play. In: Fromberg DP, Bergen D, editors. Play from birth to twelve: Contexts, perspectives, and meanings. New York: Routledge. pp. 75–86.

28. Coplan RJ, Arbeau K (2008) Peer interactions and play in early childhood. In: Rubin KH, Bukowski W, Laursen B, editors. Handbook of peer interactions, relationships, and groups. New York: Guilford Press. pp. 143–161.

29. Howes C, Matheson CC (1992) Sequences in the development of competent play with peers: Social and social pretend play. Dev Psychol 28: 961–974.

30. Colwell MJ, Lindsey EW (2005) Preschool children's pretend and physical play and sex of play partner: Connections to peer competence. Sex Roles 52: 497–509.

31. Robinson CC, Anderson GT, Porter CL, Hart CH, Wouden-Miller M (2003) Sequential transition patterns of preschoolers' social interactions during child-initiated play: Is parallel-aware play a bidirectional bridge to other play states? Early Child Res Q 18: 3–21.

32. Parten MB (1932) Social participation among preschool children. J Abnorm Soc Psychol 27: 243–269.

33. Bornstein MH, Hahn CS, Haynes OM (2004) Specific and general language performance across early childhood: Stability and gender considerations. First Lang 24: 267–304.

34. Harris PL (2006) Social cognition. In: Kuhn D, Siegler R, editors. Cognition, perception, and language. Hoboken, NJ: Wiley. pp. 811–858.

35. Smith PK (2007) Evolutionary foundations and functions of play: An overview. In: Göncü A, Gaskins S, editors. Play and development: Evolutionary, sociocultural, and functional perspectives. Mahwah, NJ: Lawrence Erlbaum. pp. 21–49.

36. Pellegrini AD, Smith PK (1998) The development of play during childhood: Forms and possible functions. Child Psycho Psychiatry Review 3: 51–57.

37. Berenbaum SA, Martin CL, Hanish LD, Briggs PT, Fabes RA (2008) Sex differences in children's play. In: Becker JB, Geary KJ, Hampson E, Herman JP, Young EA, editors. Sex differences in the brain: From genes to behavior. New York: Oxford University Press. pp. 275–290.

38. Hines M (2004) Brain gender. New York: Oxford University Press. 307 p.

39. Jadva V, Hines M, Golombok S (2010) Infants' preferences for toys, colors, and shapes: Sex differences and similarities. Arch Sex Behav. DOI 10.1007/s10508-010-9618-z.

40. Brenner M, Omark DR (1979) The effects of sex, structure and social interaction on preschoolers' play behaviors in naturalistic setting. Instr Sci 8: 91–105.

41. Cherney ID, Kelly-Vance L, Glover KG, Ruane A, Ryalls BO (2003) The effects of stereotyped toys and gender on play assessment in children aged 18–47 months. Educational Psychology 23: 95–106.

42. Martin CL, Fabes RA (2001) The stability and consequences of young children's same-sex peer interactions. Dev Psychol 37: 431–446.

43. Murray L, Fiori-Cowley A, Hooper R, Cooper P (1996) The impact of postnatal depression and associated adversity on early mother-infant interactions and later infant outcome. Child Dev 67: 2512–2526.

44. Morisset CE, Barnard KE, Booth CL (1995) Toddlers' language development: Sex differences within social risk. Dev Psychol 31: 851–865.

45. Lutchmaya S, Baron-Cohen S, Ragatt P (2002) Foetal testosterone and vocabulary size in 18-and 24-month-old infants. Infant Behav Dev 24: 418–424.

46. Auyeung B, Baron-Cohen S, Ashwin E, Knickmeyer R, Taylor K, et al. (2009) Fetal testosterone predicts sexually differentiated childhood behavior in girls and in boys. Psychol Sci 20: 144–148.

47. Auyeung B, Baron-Cohen S, Ashwin E, Knickmeyer R, Taylor K, et al. (2009) Foetal testosterone and autistic traits. Br J Psychol 100: 1–22.

48. Huttenlocher J, Haight W, Bryk A, Seltzer M, Lyons T (1991) Early vocabulary growth: Relation to language input and gender. Dev Psychol 27: 236–248.

49. Galsworthy MJ, Dionne G, Dale PS, Plomin R (2000) Sex differences in early verbal and non-verbal cognitive development. Dev Sci 3: 206–215.

50. Iervolino AC, Hines M, Golombok SE, Rust J, Plomin R (2005) Genetic and environmental influences on sex-typed behavior during the preschool years. Child Dev 76: 826–840.

51. Altmann J (1974) Observational study of behavior: Sampling methods. Behaviour 49: 227–267.

Critical Thinking

1. Why might boys and girls of the same age show different types of play behavior?
2. What are some benefits for children of engaging in the different types of play described in the article?
3. Should parents and teachers be worried if children display only solitary play and not group play?

Internet References

At What Age are Children Aware of Gender Differences?

https://www.smh.com.au/lifestyle/at-what-age-are-children-aware-of-gender-differences-20170406-gveptn.html

Children's Ideas about Gender Differences May Surprise You

https://www.psychologytoday.com/us/blog/beyond-pink-and-blue/201404/childrens-ideas-about-gender-differences-may-surprise-you

Barbu, Stéphanie. Cabanes, Guénaël and Maner-Idrissi, Gaïd Le. "Boys and Girls on the Playground: Sex Differences in Social Development Are Not Stable across Early Childhood." PLOS One, January 28, 2011.

Do Girls See Themselves as Less Smart than Boys? Study Says Yes by Lois M. Collins

136

Prepared by: Chris J. Boyatzis, *Bucknell University* and
Ellen N. Junn, *California State University, Stanislaus*

Article

Do Girls See Themselves as Less Smart than Boys? Study Says Yes

Lois M. Collins

Learning Outcomes

After reading this article, you will be able to:

- Discuss the views of girls and boys on intellectual abilities of the sexes.

- Explain some of the cultural dimensions that may affect one's perception of their abilities.

Little girls may stereotype themselves out of education and career options, according to a study.

At age 5, both boys and girls saw themselves as smart. By age 6, when asked who was "brilliant," both boys and girls selected males, researchers found. Asked to choose between work that required brilliance and work that required effort, the girls sorted themselves into the hard-work tasks.

"We found this stereotyping at a very young age and we also found this association has immediate impact on activities boys and girls are interested in," said lead author Lin Bian, from the University of Illinois at Champaign, who co-authored the study with researchers from New York University and Princeton.

Published in the journal Science, the study concluded stereotypes that "associate high-level intellectual ability" with men more than women "discourage women's pursuit of many prestigious careers."

Bian noted some of the high-paying jobs at stake require high-level mental ability, such as physics or engineering. "It's important to know if young women and girls are held back from pursuing these jobs because of the stereotypes they are exposed to," she said. "If they don't learn early that they are capable and smart, then by the time they reach adulthood and are in a position to decide on a career, it could be hard for them to catch up."

Young Stereotypes

For the first part of the research, children were read a story about someone who is "really, really smart," then asked to pick from pictures of two men and two women who they think that person is. At age 5, boys and girls were both inclined to select someone of their own gender. By age 6, both selected a male as the smart person.

Girls said that female students were more likely to get good grades than male students. But instead of associating that with intellectual ability, they credited hard work.

The researchers then offered children two games from which to choose. One, the children were told, is "for children who are really, really smart," while the other is for "children who try really, really hard." The boys most often picked the game for smart children, while girls picked the game for hard-working children—a choice Bian suggests reflects less confidence in intellectual skills.

Research from Brigham Young University last summer noted a similar potential chilling effect from gender stereotypes young children absorb. Little girls who embrace "princess culture" could sell themselves short when it comes to believing in their own capabilities. That study was published in the journal Child Development.

"Feminine behavior can be great on so many dimensions, like being kind and nurturing," lead author Sarah Coyne, an associate professor of human development in BYU's School of Family Life, told the Deseret News. "But girls can be limited by stereotypes in a number of ways. They can think they can't do well in math and science or they don't want a career."

The difference in the responses between age 5 and 6 in the recently published Science study was somewhat startling, but the researchers noted that children at early school ages begin to learn about the social world around them. "Identifying whether it's because of parents, schools, peers, media, or something else—well, there are so many factors and we're failing to figure this out," said Bian.

Very young children have a "wonderful egocentrism," said clinical psychologist Stephanie O'Leary of Mount Kisco, New York, who was not involved in this research. "They see and identify with all this good stuff within themselves." But by first grade, they're more likely to see intellectual good stuff in the boys, not the girls, she added.

Bian said looking into the sources that lead to stereotyping is an important next step for the researchers.

Combatting Stereotypes

Parents, teachers, coaches, and others should be "mindful of the way we talk about intelligence and the way we communicate to our children," said O'Leary.

Parents have many opportunities to call attention to bright females. If a parent is reading a book to young children, he or she can comment on how clever or smart the writer is. It's not pitting men and women against each other, but rather noting that both genders are smart and capable.

People need to pay attention to their own unconscious biases, too, she said. It's not uncommon for folks to assume that a doctor or an attorney they haven't met is a man. It's easy to ask and then get it right when speaking to kids about that person.

Women should examine how they present themselves to children, said O'Leary. It's not about bragging, but it is important that children see women's intellect, reasoning skills, and dedication. "It's bragging when you beat it to death. It's fact-checking when you say, 'I had a great idea and it helped us get everything we needed done.'"

Men also need to point out examples of bright, capable women. "It is very powerful for boys and girls to hear their fathers point out brilliance in women and to hear their fathers discuss why stereotyping is problematic," said O'Leary.

She said she was pleased that young girls identified with being hard workers in the study. That demonstrates their resilience, she said. "In the long haul, that's more protective than being brilliant. When you're choosing to do things (designed) for smart kids, if you fail, you could take it you're not smart. If hard workers fail, it just means they have to keep working. These girls have spitfire and tenacity."

Critical Thinking

1. Provide specific examples of some ways to combat stereotypes.

2. What can parents and teachers do to raise competent and confident children of both sexes?

Internet References

Girls in STEM
http://www.gstemdenver.org/

Girls in Tech
https://girlsintech.org/

Raising a Powerful Girl
http://www.pbs.org/parents/parenting/raising-girls/body-image-identity/raising-a-powerful-girl/

Lois M. Collins is a reporter and columnist for the *Deseret News*.

Collins, Lois M., "Do Girls See Themselves as Less Smart than Boys? Study Says Yes," *Deseret News*, February 15, 2017. Used with permission.

Article

Prepared by: Chris J. Boyatzis, *Bucknell University* and
Ellen N. Junn, *California State University, Stanislaus*

Inequality at School

When Black and White teachers evaluate this student, White teachers are 12 percent less likely to predict that he will finish high school, and 30 percent less likely to predict that he will graduate from college.

KIRSTEN WEIR

Learning Outcomes

After reading this article, you will be able to:

- Name differences in teachers' biased or unconsciously biased behaviors and expectations of African American students as compared to White students in the classroom.

- Discuss the multiple negative impacts of a variety of teacher behaviors on African American students' academic achievement and sense of self.

- Describe a number of intervention programs for educators and teachers that have been shown to significantly improve African American students' academic and personal success in schools.

For decades, black students in the United States have lagged behind their white peers in academic achievement. In 2014, the high school graduation rate for white students was 87 percent, according to the National Center for Education Statistics. For black students, the rate was 73 percent. Test scores show a similar racial gap.

To be sure, many factors contribute to the achievement gap, including home and neighborhood environments and school factors unrelated to teachers' performance. But one dynamic is becoming impossible to ignore: Notable differences in the way black students are treated by teachers and school administrators.

Research shows that compared with white students, black students are more likely to be suspended or expelled, less likely to be placed in gifted programs and subject to lower expectations from their teachers.

The disparities can be tough to discuss, says Anne Gregory, PhD, a professor of psychology at Rutgers University. "There's this idea that if we name the phenomenon, it's teacher blaming."

Yet in many cases, such differences in treatment aren't malicious or intentional. Some disparities arise from cultural misunderstandings or unintentional "implicit biases" that unknowingly affect our thoughts and behaviors.

"Everyone holds biases of one kind or another," says University of Maryland psychologist Melanie Killen, PhD. "Maybe we can't eliminate them, but we can do all we can to avoid acting on them."

Evidence of Disparities

A variety of recent studies help to illustrate the differences in the ways black and white students experience a school day. Teachers might be less likely to spot black students who excel academically, for instance. Using national data from the Early Childhood Longitudinal Study, Sean Nicholson-Crotty, PhD, at Indiana University, and colleagues found black students were 54 percent less likely than white students to be recommended for gifted-education programs, after adjusting for factors such as students' standardized test scores. But black students were three times more likely to be referred for the programs if their teacher was black rather than white (*Journal of Public Administration Research and Theory*, 2016).

Such disparities might have something to do with teachers' expectations for students. Seth Gershenson, PhD, at American University, and colleagues reported that when black and white teachers evaluate the same black student, white teachers are 12 percent less likely to predict the student will finish high school, and 30 percent less likely to predict the student will graduate from college (*Economics of Education Review*, 2016).

Teachers' expectations for themselves also come into play. In a series of studies, Rutgers University psychologist Kent Harber, PhD, studied white middle-school and high-school teachers in mostly white, upper-middle-class districts and more diverse, working-class districts in the northeastern United States. He found that when white teachers give feedback on a poorly written essay, they are more critical if they think the author was a white student rather than a black one (*Journal of Educational Psychology*, 2012).

What's more, Harber can essentially turn that bias on or off by enhancing or allaying the teachers' concerns that they might appear prejudiced. In other words, white instructors might go easy on their black students in order to avoid appearing racist, if only in their own minds. In their attempts to be egalitarian, however, they might avoid constructive criticism that would benefit black students.

Giving feedback is difficult for teachers in any circumstance, Harber points out. Teachers must strike a balance between being assertive and respectful. "Add the issue of race and teachers might worry they're displaying a lack of racial sensitivity. That can tip the scale and lead to a positive bias," Harber says.

White teachers' implicit prejudices or stereotypes can also make them less effective when teaching black students, suggests a study by Drew Jacoby-Senghor, PhD, at Columbia University, and colleagues. The researchers recruited white college students to prepare and present a history lesson to either a white or a black student.

When the "teachers" had higher levels of implicit racial bias, their black (but not white) students scored more poorly on a history test based on the lesson. Later, the researchers played recordings of the lessons to white students. Those who watched recorded lessons originally presented to black students also did more poorly on the history test, suggesting that the quality of the lesson itself, and not the student's aptitude, was to blame. Teachers who gave lectures to black students appeared more nervous, the researchers found, which seemed to impair the quality of their lesson (*Journal of Experimental Social Psychology*, 2016). Although the study didn't evaluate actual teachers, it does suggest that student performance can be significantly influenced by the way that lessons are taught.

The Discipline Divide

Racial bias doesn't just influence how teachers teach. Bias also affects whether and how they discipline students for misbehavior.

According to 2013–14 data collected by the U.S. Department of Education's Office of Civil Rights, black K–12 students are 3.8 times as likely as their white peers to receive one or more out-of-school suspensions.

And that's not necessarily because black students are causing more problems, Gregory notes. A variety of studies have found that even after taking achievement, socioeconomic status, self-reported behavior and teacher-reported behavior into account, black students are still punished disproportionately.

IN ONE STUDY, WHEN STUDENTS MISBEHAVED A SECOND TIME, TEACHERS WERE MORE LIKELY TO STEROTYPE THE BLACK STUDENTS AS TROUBLEMAKERS AND RECOMMEND HARSHER DISCIPLINE

Students who are suspended are more likely to drop out of school and have run-ins with the juvenile justice system, a pattern so well documented in the literature that it has earned its own dubious moniker—the "school-to-prison pipeline."

Yet the biases that contribute to the discipline gap can be subtle. Stanford University psychologists Jennifer Eberhardt, PhD, and Jason Okonofua, PhD, explored this in a sample of 57 female teachers of all grade levels from across the country, the majority of whom were white. They asked the teachers how they'd handle certain instances of misbehavior, and found racial stereotypes didn't influence the teachers' decisions after a student's first infraction. But when students misbehaved a second time, teachers were more likely to stereotype the black students as troublemakers and recommend harsher discipline (*Psychological Science*, 2015). Implicit bias might make teachers more likely to assume misconduct is part of a pattern of misbehavior, the authors conclude.

Unfortunately, children can be pegged as troublemakers before they even start kindergarten. The U.S. Department of Education's 2013–14 data reveal that black children represent 19 percent of preschool enrollment, but 47 percent of the out-of-school preschool suspensions. White kids, meanwhile, represent 41 percent of preschool enrollment but just 28 percent of suspensions.

Walter Gilliam, PhD, who directs the Edward Zigler Center in Child Development and Social Policy at Yale University School of Medicine, has spent the last decade documenting preschool expulsions. When it comes to child-related factors, he's found three things make a child more likely to be kicked out of preschool: Being black, being male and looking older than their classmates (*Foundation for Child Development*, 2005). "If you're a big, black boy, the risk is greatest by far," he says.

That squares with a series of field and laboratory studies by Phillip Atiba Goff, PhD, and colleagues, who found that college students of various racial backgrounds overestimated both the age and culpability of black children from toddlers to teens (*Journal of Personality and Social Psychology*, 2014).

RESEARCH POINTS TO WAYS TO START CHIPPING AWAY AT BIAS IN SCHOOLS, MOST OF THOSE METHODS HAVE ONE IMPORTANT THING IN COMMON: MORE SUPPORT FOR TEACHERS.

"In terms of implicit biases, we might see an African-American boy not only as more culpable, but perhaps more dangerous. That imagination might make it more likely they'll be expelled," Gilliam says.

Interventions to Reduce Bias

Research points to ways to start chipping away at bias in schools. Most of those methods have one important thing in common: More support for teachers.

In his work with preschools, Gilliam has found teachers who had regular relationships with a behavioral consultant had the lowest expulsion rates. Ending the practice of expulsion would be good not only for black children, who are disproportionately affected, but for all preschoolers, he says. "There is only one type of child who doesn't benefit from preschool programs, and that's the one who was expelled."

At the high school level, Gregory and her colleagues have developed a program, My Teaching Partner-Secondary, which pairs teachers with coaches for two years. Teachers submit videos of their classroom interactions with kids, and the coaches review the videos and make specific suggestions to help teachers better engage with and motivate students.

In a randomized controlled trial, teachers in the control group asked black high-school students to leave their classrooms for misbehavior at two to three times the rate of non-black students (a group that included white, Latino and Asian-American students). In coaching classrooms, there was no difference in discipline referral rates. Encouragingly, the improvements still held a year after the coaching ended (*School Psychology Review*, 2016).

"The target of our intervention wasn't necessarily classroom management, but on how to create more engaging instruction for the whole class," Gregory says. Yet teachers who created more opportunities for higher-level thinking and problem-solving had more equitable disciplinary patterns. That fits with previous research that shows when students are more engaged, teachers are more likely to avoid misunderstandings and defuse misconduct, she notes.

When it comes to increasing black students' representation in gifted programs, Nicholson-Crotty and his co-authors recommend recruiting more teachers of color to diversify the teaching force. In the meantime, they suggest screening all students for giftedness, and not relying solely on referrals from teachers and parents.

Other research highlights helpful ways for teachers to communicate with students. David Yeager, PhD, at the University of Texas at Austin, and colleagues have developed a strategy known as wise feedback, in which teachers emphasize their high standards and convey their belief that students are capable of meeting their expectations. In one set of studies with junior and senior high school students, wise feedback was shown to improve the quality of students' work and also reduce feelings of mistrust between black students and their teachers (*Journal of Experimental Psychology*, 2014).

But teachers can't do it alone. Harber's research on critical feedback showed that teachers who reported generally strong social support from fellow teachers and administrators were less likely to offer false praise when critiquing the work of black students.

Christopher Liang, PhD, a professor of counseling psychology at Lehigh University, is developing methods to help principals recognize and avoid patterns of racial inequities in their schools. "Principals often report they're aware [of equity issues], but they don't know what to do," he says.

Gregory has seen a growing willingness among educators to confront the touchy topic of racial disparities. "More and more, these dialogues are coming to the surface," she says.

But translating awareness to action will be challenging, especially in the era of standardized testing.

"A lot of the solutions to reduce disparities are focused on social-emotional learning, better relationships and building community, which comes into direct conflict with the accountability movement and focus on test scores," she says.

Still, Gregory sees reasons for optimism in the work teachers are doing every day. "There are wonderful educators and administrators who are showing us, in their daily practice, the way to engage youth and prevent problems," she says. "As researchers we need to ferret out those best practices and figure out how to scale them."

Further Reading
2013–2014 Civil Rights Data Collection: A First Look, *U.S. Department of Education Office of Civil Rights*, 2016

Closing the Racial Discipline Gap in Classrooms by Changing Teacher Practice, Gregory, A., Hafen, C.A., Ruzek, E., Mikami, A.Y., Allen, J.P., & Pianta, R. *School Psychology Review*, 2016

A Lesson in Bias: The Relationship Between Implicit Racial Bias and Performance in Pedagogical Contexts, Jacoby-Senghor, D.S.,

Sinclair, S., & Shelton, J.N. *Journal of Experimental Social Psychology*, 2016

Breaking the Cycle of Mistrust: Wise Interventions to Provide Critical Feedback Across the Racial Divide, Yeager, D.S., Purdie-Vaughns, V., Garcia, J., Apfel, N., Brzustoski, P., Master, A., Hessert, W.T., Williams, M.E., & Cohen, G.L. *Journal of Experimental Psychology*, 2014

Critical Thinking

1. Knowing that African American boys in particular face many biases and disadvantages in schools even as preschoolers, if you were a parent, or wanted to advise a parent of a male African American preschooler, what might you suggest they do to help counteract these often implicit biases?

2. Since many of these biases are more likely to be found among teachers who are often White, what suggestions do you have to better educate and train teachers.

3. What suggestions do you have to help recruit and retain more teachers who are African American?

Internet References

Racial and Ethnic Achievement Gaps

https://cepa.stanford.edu/educational-opportunity-monitoring-project/achievement-gaps/race/

Racial disparities in school discipline are growing, federal data show

https://www.washingtonpost.com/local/education/racial-disparities-in-school-discipline-are-growing-federal-data-shows/2018/04/24/67b5d2b8-47e4-11e8-827e-190efaf1f1ee_story.html?noredirect=on&utm_term=.49b15cde06d6

The Black-White Achievement Gap

https://www.ets.org/Media/Research/pdf/PICBWGAP.pdf

Unequal Opportunity: Race and Education

https://www.brookings.edu/articles/unequal-opportunity-race-and-education/

Prepared by: Chris J. Boyatzis, *Bucknell University* and
Ellen N. Junn, *California State University, Stanislaus*

Article

Nearly Half of Children Have Damaging Childhood Experiences. Here's How to Help Your Child

DESERET NEWS

Learning Outcomes

After reading this article, you will be able to:

- Cite examples of Adverse Childhood Experiences (ACEs) such as significant economic hardship; parents' separation or divorce; parent's death; parent incarceration; seeing or experiencing violence from an adult in one's household; seeing or experiencing violence in one's community; or living with someone who abuses drugs, alcohol, or who has a mental illness.

- Explain differences in the frequency of ACEs experienced by children living in different states in the United States.

- Describe a variety of successful programs and interventions being used with children experiencing traumas and the positive outcomes of these programs.

SALT LAKE CITY—Nearly half of America's children live through adverse childhood experiences that can leave them vulnerable to ongoing and future challenges, sometimes severe, according to a new report that documents not just potential harm, but uneven impact based on race and state.

"The Prevalence of Adverse Childhood Experiences, Nationally, by State, and by Race or Ethnicity," was released by researchers from Child Trends, a Bethesda-based organization that studies American children's lives with an eye toward improving them. The study finds a constellation of events that can add up to "toxic stress" and negatively influence both child development and future adulthood for 45 percent of America's kids.

"This is really a critical public health issue," said Vanessa Sacks, a research scientist who wrote the report with colleague David Murphey, a research fellow.

They studied eight adverse childhood experiences, often called ACEs. Nationwide and across all groups, the most common are economic hardship (defined as "hard to cover basics like food or housing") and parents' separation or divorce. Other adverse experiences studied were a parent's death, parent incarceration, seeing or experiencing violence either from an adult in one's household or outside in one's community, or living with someone who abuses drugs or alcohol or who has a mental illness.

Kids who experience these adverse situations, some traumatic and some more subtle, may have trouble with self-control and struggle to manage emotions, pay attention or maintain personal relationships—"all life skills that are critical for later success in school and for career and interpersonal relationships," said Sacks. "These are really important experiences to recognize and address."

"What we're learning about ACEs reminds us that what happens in childhood—particularly what happens in our families of origin—can shape the trajectory of a child's future well-being," said Institute for Family Studies' Alysse ElHage. "Awareness is key, particularly in communities where these kinds of events—whether we're talking about parental divorce or neighborhood violence—tend to be more commonplace, and where maybe it can be easy to shrug off or overlook ACES as just part of life for some children."

Without mitigation, long-term negative effects are linked to "every major public health issue, from obesity to substance abuse, suicide, depression, smoking, chronic disease and more," Sacks said.

Repeated or prolonged stress may even alter the brain's structure. Besides that, among the "most sobering findings regarding ACEs is preliminary evidence that their negative effects can be transmitted from one generation to the next," including during pregnancy, the report says.

Impact severity hinges not just on the negative experience or degree of a child's resilience, but also on what kind of support system caring adults put in place to help a child overcome what happened. Children and families can be screened and helped.

Racial Differences

The report finds variation in prevalence of negative events among different racial and ethnic groups and also in what they experience. State ACEs rates are different, too.

Nationally, more black (61 percent) and Hispanic children (51 percent) experience at least one adverse experience than white (40 percent) or Asian (23 percent) children. Overall, 11 percent of children have had two adverse experiences, while 10 percent of kids have experienced three or more such events.

No one knows if there's a "tipping point," Sacks said, but experts agree that multiple adverse experiences when one is young raise alarms. Some studies say even one experience creates harm. "The research doesn't show that one experience is worse than another, but a lot of research shows that the more you have, the higher the risk for these negative outcomes," Sacks said.

After poverty and divorce—universal across groups—the most common adverse experience for black children was having an incarcerated parent, while for whites it was living with an adult who has mental illness or abuses drugs or alcohol. For Hispanic kids, the most common experiences after poverty and divorce were living with someone with a substance abuse problem and having a jailed parent. Black children are more likely than others to have had a parent die.

The researchers used 2016 data from the National Survey of Children's Health.

State by State

More children (56 percent) in Arkansas live through an adverse experience than in other states. At least 15 percent of kids in Arizona, New Mexico, Arkansas, Montana and Ohio have experienced three or more adverse experiences, said the report, which was funded by the Annie E. Casey Foundation.

Utah in many ways mirrors the nation when it comes to childhood trauma, with 40 percent experiencing at least one adverse experience. While significant economic hardship and parents splitting up also lead the Beehive State's list of ACEs, the latter is much less common, with just 18 percent of the kids growing up with parental relationships breaking apart,

compared to 25 percent nationally. However, more Utah children live with a parent who has a mental illness, is suicidal or severely depressed, 12 percent compared to 8 percent nationally, Sacks said.

One-third of West Virginia kids experienced significant economic hardship compared on one-fifth in Minnesota, New Hampshire and North Dakota. Similarly, one-third of children in Kentucky and Arkansas have seen their parents separate or divorce, compared to fewer than one-fifth in Illinois, Maryland, Massachusetts and, as noted, Utah.

Even among the rarer adverse experiences there are big differences: Nationally, up to 4 percent of kids have lost a parent or been a victim of or witnessed violence in their neighborhood. But 7 percent of kids have been abused or seen violence in their neighborhoods in Nevada and Hawaii, and 6 percent in Arkansas and Georgia have had a parent or guardian die.

Building Resilience

Showing up for kids is a powerful antidote to adverse experiences.

"One of the most powerful buffers against ACEs is a supportive relationship with a parent/caregiver or other trusted adult," said ElHage. "I think this is so important for us to remember with kids who've faced multiple ACEs: A loving, stable relationship, especially with a child's parents, can make all the difference. For kids who are in unstable families where they don't have a healthy parental relationship, other adults can play a role, such as a grandparent, teachers, coaches or faith leaders."

ElHage has seen it work in her extended family, a story she shares to show there's hope and that even multiple adverse experiences need not define a child's future. One young relative endured parental separation, child abuse and neglect, domestic violence and a parent's drug abuse and incarceration. Despite a diagnosis of PTSD and severe depression, "through the support and stability provided by a loving grandparent, some therapy and especially thanks to the faithful mentorship of a youth pastor in his church, he is now thriving."

Sherese Patton of Detroit is among a group of caring adults who have vowed to show up for the daughter of a close friend who was shot dead in 2011.

"As her father's friends, we have all made a commitment to be there for her and her mother," she said. They want to see that the girl "grows up and is successful as her father intended."

Liz Meredith, of Anchorage, Alaska, is a juvenile probation supervisor and an ACEs instructor. She believes parents must understand what adverse experiences are—and that they're preventable. Children must be allowed to talk about their experience without a parent becoming defensive or "shutting them down" if they played a role in the experience.

Meredith said caring adults can connect affected children to helpful services. "Communities that ensure services to address adverse experiences are accessible for all families through their support for nonprofits, and mental health professionals go far to aid in the healing," she told the Deseret News.

She also suggests treating kids with "universal precautions," which includes giving all kids the benefit of the doubt. A better question than "What is wrong with you?" for a child with behavioral issues is "What happened to you?" said Meredith, author of "Pieces of Me."

Parents also help by taking care of themselves and their own mental and physical health, said Erin C. Parisi, a mental health counselor and addictions specialist in Orlando, Florida. They are role models, even if they don't want to be. "Your kids see what you're doing, so if you're neglecting your own physical or mental health and are unwilling and/or unable to ask for help, you're teaching them to do the same."

She said talking about feelings, interacting, listening, saying "I love you," and working to be "(mostly) happy and healthy with your stuff makes you the best parent and role model possible."

Consistency is a healing tool adults can offer children, promoting a sense of safety and security that helps children cope with stress.

"Kids should not be expected to rise above anything on their own," said Caleb Backe, health and wellness expert for Maple Holistics in Riverdale, New York. "More often than not, they are genuine victims of situations which are beyond their control and sometimes beyond the scope of their understanding. For a child to come out of a difficult situation in a way that will allow them to develop properly down the road, it is imperative that a parent or guardian provides a sense of reliability, guidance,
routine and structure. Children—often adults, too—need those like they need oxygen."

As chaotic circumstances make kids feel adrift, adults should attempt to be a rock to which a child can attach, Backe said.

Critical Thinking

1. Explain why nearly half of the children in America have suffered an Adverse Childhood Experience. What does this imply about our nation and our children?

2. Why do some states have such high rates of ACE, while others are much lower in frequency? What can be done to reduce these traumas to children as a state?

3. Given the definition of ACE, did you, or others you know, live through an Adverse Childhood Experience as a child? How did you cope or how has it affected you (or others) as an adult?

Internet References

ACEs and Toxic Stress: Frequently Asked Questions
https://developingchild.harvard.edu/resources/aces-and-toxic-stress-frequently-asked-questions/
Adverse Childhood Experiences (ACEs)
https://www.cdc.gov/violenceprevention/childabuseandneglect/acestudy/index.html
The association between adverse childhood experience (ACE) and school success in elementary school children
https://www.ncbi.nlm.nih.gov/pubmed/29629790
Got Your ACE Score?
https://acestoohigh.com/got-your-ace-score/
Take the ACE Quiz—And Learn What It Does And Doesn't Mean
https://www.npr.org/sections/health-shots/2015/03/02/387007941/take-the-ace-quiz-and-learn-what-it-does-and-doesnt-mean

Article

Prepared by: Chris J. Boyatzis, *Bucknell University* and
Ellen N. Junn, *California State University, Stanislaus*

Worry Over Kids' Excessive Smartphone Use Is More Justified than Ever Before

JEAN TWENGE

Learning Outcomes

After reading this article, you will be able to:

- Report on the data documenting increases in children's use of smartphones, and the research indicating negative outcomes of this behavior for children.

- Describe how children's smartphone usage is crowding out other their important activities and why this is causing more negative outcomes such as reduced academic achievement, lack of sleep, and increases in depression among children.

- Discuss possible solutions and interventions parents and schools might take to curb this increasing trend in children's smartphone usage.

Parents who fear their kids are spending too much time in front of screens now have more reason for concern.

New research funded by the National Institutes of Health found brain changes among kids using screens more than seven hours a day and lower cognitive skills among those using screens more than two hours a day.

When studies find links between screen time and negative outcomes, some have argued that this is just the latest moral panic over technology.

After all, didn't the parents of baby boomers and Gen Xers worry that their kids were watching too much TV or talking on the phone too much? Those kids turned out OK, right?

So how are portable electronic devices, the chosen technology of today's kids and teens—a generation I call "iGen"—any different?

New research I've conducted on the relationship between portable device use and sleep provides some answers.

Everywhere, All the Time

It almost goes without saying that today's portable devices—including smartphones and tablets—are fundamentally different than the living room television sets and rotary phones of the past.

Since researchers have been tracking TV watching habits, the average U.S. teen has never spent more than two-and-a-half hours a day watching TV. Yet as of 2016, the average teen spent about six hours a day immersed in digital media—more than twice as much time.

This large amount of time spent using digital media is enough to crowd out time once spent on other activities, such as interacting with friends face to face, reading or going out.

And unlike the telephone, digital media apps are designed to hook you. As former Silicon Valley executive Tristan Harris said of smartphone apps, "Your telephone in the 1970s didn't have a thousand engineers . . . updating the way your telephone worked every day to be more and more persuasive."

Second, unlike TV or landline phones, portable devices can be carried everywhere: to school, where teachers say they are a near-constant distraction, and into social situations, where a conversation can instantly be upended by reaching for a buzzing phone. (There's even a word for this: phubbing, a portmanteau of "phone" and "snubbing.")

Sure enough, people have reported enjoying a restaurant dinner with friends less when their phones were available, compared to when they weren't.

The Sleep Factor

Across many studies, kids and teens who spend more time with screens—including both TV and portable devices—also sleep less.

That could be because they spend so much time engaged with their devices that it's coming at the expense of sleep. But there's also a physiological reason: The blue light emitted by electronic screens tricks our brains into thinking it's still daytime, and then we don't produce enough of the sleep hormone melatonin to fall asleep quickly and get high-quality sleep.

Once again, some might argue that TV is just as bad: After all, it also takes up time and emits blue light.

But in a new paper, my co-authors and I decided to parse the two. We studied links between sleep and TV watching as well as links between sleep and portable device use. Then we compared the results.

Drawing from a large survey of parents administered by the U.S. Census Bureau, we found that 2- to 10-year-olds who spent four or more hours a day on portable electronic devices—versus no time—were twice as likely to be significantly sleep deprived. TV time was also connected to less sleep, but not as strongly or consistently.

Among teens ages 14 to 17, those who spent four or more hours a day on portable electronic devices—versus no time—were 44 percent more likely to not sleep enough. However, once portable device time was statistically controlled, watching TV or playing video games on a console had little link to sleep time.

Why would portable devices be more strongly associated with losing sleep?

For one thing, TV is simply not as psychologically stimulating as a portable device like a smartphone, which, unlike a TV, doesn't exist to simply consume media. Smartphones have also become a huge part of social life, whether it's texting with friends or interacting with them on social media.

And unlike TV, smartphones and tablets can be silently carried into the bedroom or even the bed, resulting in some teens using them throughout the night—what some call "vamping."

That might explain why sleep deprivation among teens spiked after 2012—just as smartphone use became common.

The Lesser of Two Evils?

To be clear, we did find that watching many hours of TV was associated with less sleep, especially among elementary-school age children. Watching over three hours a day of TV is also associated with depression—though more weakly than portable device use.

So parents were right to worry about kids watching too much TV in the 1970s and 1980s. But their worries might not have been as justified as today's parents' concerns about smartphones.

So what is a parent—or anyone who wants to sleep well—to do?

First, it's best for smartphones and tablets to stay out of the bedroom after "lights-out" time. Nor is it a great idea to use the devices within an hour of bedtime, as their blue light influences the brain's ability to produce melatonin. Finally, as a general rule, two hours a day or less spent on portable devices is a good guideline. These rules apply to parents, too—not only kids.

Just don't binge-watch TV instead.

Critical Thinking

1. Given the research on possible negative consequences of children's smartphone usage, at what age would you permit your child to have a smartphone? Explain your rationale.

2. Do you think schools should enforce strict rules of not permitting smartphones in the classroom? Why or why not?

3. If you are a parent of a child with a smartphone, explain your rules and rationale for your children in accessing and using their smartphone. How do you discuss this with your children?

Internet References

Banning smartphones for children
https://www.hippocraticpost.com/ageing/banning-smartphones-for-children/

How Do Smartphones Affect Childhood Psychology?
https://psychcentral.com/lib/how-do-smartphones-affect-childhood-psychology/

How Smart Phones Are Causing Kids to Experience 'Altered Childhoods'
https://www.healthline.com/health-news/smart-phones-causing-kids-to-experience-altered-childhoods

How Smartphones Are Affecting the Mind and Body Of Your Children
https://www.lifehack.org/373649/how-smartphones-are-affecting-the-mind-and-body-your-children-2

There's Worrying New Research About Kids' Screen Time and Their Mental Health
http://time.com/5437607/smartphones-teens-mental-health/

Prepared by: Chris J. Boyatzis, *Bucknell University* and
Ellen N. Junn, *California State University, Stanislaus*

Article

Young Trans Children Know Who They Are

A new study shows that gender-nonconforming kids who go on to transition already have a strong sense of their true identity—one that differs from their assigned gender.

ED YONG

Learning Outcomes

After reading this article, you will be able to:

- Describe the newest research on gender identity and gender nonconformity, and the pathways to social transitioning to becoming a transgender individual.

- Understand that gender nonconformity in childhood does not necessarily predict transitioning to a transgender identity.

- Explain that even at very early ages of 3–5 years, children's sense of gender identity is important in helping them make the decision later to socially transition to having a transgender identity.

Since 2013, Kristina Olson, a psychologist at the University of Washington, has been running a large, long-term study to track the health and well-being of transgender children—those who identify as a different gender from the one they were assigned at birth. Since the study's launch, Olson has also heard from the parents of gender-nonconforming kids, who consistently defy gender stereotypes but have not socially transitioned. They might include boys who like wearing dresses or girls who play with trucks, but who have not, for example, changed the pronouns they use. Those parents asked whether their children could participate in the study. Olson agreed.

After a while, she realized that she had inadvertently recruited a sizable group of 85 gender-nonconforming participants, ages 3 to 12. And as she kept in touch with the families over the years, she learned that some of those children eventually transitioned. "Enough of them were doing it that we had this unique opportunity to look back at our data to see whether the kids who went on to transition were different to those who didn't," Olson says.

By studying the 85 gender-nonconforming children she recruited, her team has now shown, in two separate ways, that those who go on to transition do so because they *already* have a strong sense of their identity.

This is a topic for which long-term data are scarce. And as transgender identities have gained more social acceptance, more parents are faced with questions about whether and how to support their young gender-nonconforming children.

"There's a lot of public writing focused on the idea that we have no idea which of these gender-nonconforming kids will or will not eventually identify as trans," says Olson. And if only small proportions do, as some studies have suggested, the argument goes that "they shouldn't be transitioning." She disputes that idea. "Our study suggests that it's not random," she says. "We can't say this kid will be trans and this one won't, but it's not that we have no idea!"

"This study provides further credence to guidance that practitioners and other professionals should affirm—rather than question—a child's assertion of their gender, particularly for those who more strongly identify with their gender," says Russell Toomey from the University of Arizona, who studies LGBTQ youth and is himself transgender.

(A brief note on terms, since there's a lot of confusion about them: Some people think that kids who show any kind of gender nonconformity are transgender, while others equate the term with medical treatments such as hormone blockers or reassignment surgeries. Neither definition is right, and medical interventions aren't even in the cards for young children of the age Olson studied. That's why, in her study, she uses *pronouns* as the centerpiece marker of a social transition. Changing them is a significant statement of identity and is often accompanied by a change in hairstyle, clothing, and even names.)

When the 85 gender-nonconforming children first enrolled in Olson's study, her team administered a series of five tests that asked what toys and clothes they preferred; whether they preferred hanging out with girls or boys; how similar they felt to girls or boys; and which genders they felt they currently were or would be. Together, these markers of identity gave the team a way to quantify each kid's sense of gender.

The team, including James Rae, now at the University of Massachusetts Amherst, found that children who showed stronger gender nonconformity at this point were more likely to socially transition. So, for example, assigned boys who had the most extreme feminine identities were most likely to be living as girls two years later. This link couldn't be explained by other factors, such as how liberal the children's parents were. Instead, the children's gender identity predicted their social transitions. "I think this wouldn't surprise parents of trans kids, and my findings are often 'duh' findings for them," says Olson. "It seems pretty intuitive."

Charlotte Tate, a psychologist from San Francisco State University, says that this quantitative research supports what she and other transgender scholars have long noted through qualitative work: There really is something distinctive and different about the kids who eventually go on to transition. From interviews with trans people, "one of the most consistent themes is that at some early point, sometimes as early as age 3 to 5, there's this feeling that the individual is part of another gender group," Tate says. When told that they're part of their assigned gender, "they'll say, 'No, that's not right. That doesn't fit me.' They have self-knowledge that's private and that they're trying to communicate."

Olson's team also showed that those differences in gender identity are the *cause* of social transitions—and not, as some have suggested, their consequence. After assessing the group of 85 gender-nonconforming children, the team administered the same five tests of gender identity to a different group of 84 transgender children who had already transitioned, and to a third group of 85 cisgender children, who identify with the sex they were assigned to at birth. None of these three groups differed in the average strength of their identities and preferences. In other words, trans girls who are still living as boys identify as girls just as strongly as trans girls who have transitioned to living as girls, *and* as cis girls who have always lived as girls. Put another way: Being treated as a girl doesn't make a trans child feel or act more like a girl, because she might have *always* felt like that.

"Implicit in a lot of people's concerns about social transition is this idea that it changes the kids in some way, and that making this decision is going to necessarily put a kid on a particular path," says Olson. "This suggests otherwise." Children change their gender because of their identities; they don't change their identities because they change their gender.

"The findings of this compelling study provide further evidence that decisions to socially transition are driven by a child's understanding of their own gender," says Toomey. "This is critically important information given that recent public debates and flawed empirical studies erroneously implicate 'pushy' parents, peers, or other sources, like social media, in the rising prevalence of children and adolescents who identify as transgender."

Olson's new findings come on the back of another controversial study, from 2013, in which Thomas Steensma from University Medical Center in Amsterdam studied 127 adolescents who had been referred to a clinic for "gender dysphoria"—a medical term describing the distress when someone's gender identity doesn't match the gender assigned at birth. Only four people in that cohort had socially transitioned in early childhood, and all of them ended up identifying as transgender. By contrast, most of those who had *not* transitioned did not have gender dysphoria later.

"People have taken from that study that a lot of these kids are not going to be trans adults so you shouldn't be socially transitioning them, or that social transitions are changing kids' identities," Olson says. But "we're suggesting that the kids who are socially transitioning seem to be different even before that transition, which shifts the interpretation of that past study." (Steensma did not respond to requests for comment.)

Olson admits that there are weaknesses in her new study. It's relatively small, and all the children came from wealthy, educated, and disproportionately white families. And since it began almost by accident, when parents of gender-nonconforming children approached her, she couldn't preregister her research plans, a growing practice in psychology. (It reduces the temptation to fiddle with one's methods until they yield positive results and instills confidence among other scientists.)

To at least partly address these shortcomings, Olson did a multiverse analysis: She reran her analyses in many different ways to see whether she still got the same result. What if, instead of using all *five* tests of gender identity, she just looked at combinations of four? Or three? Two? The team ran all these what-if scenarios, and in almost all of them, the results were the same. "They went above and beyond the analyses typically conducted and presented in scientific journals," says Toomey. "Their results were robust across these additional tests, suggesting that readers can have a high level of confidence in these findings."

Olson stresses that she has no magic test that can predict exactly which children will transition and which will not. It's a question of probabilities. In her study, based on their answers, all the children got a gender-nonconformity score between 0 and 1. For comparison, those who scored 0.5 had a one-in-three chance of socially transitioning, while those who scored 0.75 had a one-in-two chance.

"How much gender nonconformity is 'enough' to allay the anxieties parents feel around transition is an open question," says Tey Meadow, a sociologist from Columbia University who studies sexuality and gender and has written for *The Atlantic*. Parents are the ultimate arbiters of a child's access to transition, and they make decisions "in a culture that encourages parents to look for every possible alternative to transness," Meadow adds.

"It's not like you can take a blood sample or do an MRI," says Aaron Devor, the University of Victoria's chair of transgender studies, who is himself transgender. "One of the phrases often used is 'consistent, persistent, and insistent.' When you get that constellation, that kid is also a kid who might want to transition. And that's what [Olson's] research is corroborating. It adds some very valuable data."

Devor and others note that Olson's earlier studies suggest that children who *are* supported and affirmed in their transitions are just as mentally healthy as cisgender peers. That reminds him of seminal work by the American psychologist Evelyn Hooker. In the 1950s, when many psychologists saw homosexuality as a mental illness (largely because they had only ever worked with gay people who had records of arrest or mental-health problems), Hooker surveyed a more representative sample and found that gay and straight men don't differ in their mental health. That was instrumental in getting homosexuality removed from a list of mental-health disorders in 1987.

"We're sitting in a similar moment today with transgenderism," says Devor. "The mental-health issues that we see are largely the result of living a life that blocks your expression of your gender. My view is that the work coming out of Olson's group will have an Evelyn Hooker effect."

I am reminded of what Robyn Kanner wrote in *The Atlantic* last year: "Society has done nothing for trans youth for so many years. People have to trust that the youth who sway in the breeze of gender will land on their feet when they're ready. Wherever that is, it'll be beautiful."

Critical Thinking

1. Based on the research in this article, would you advise parents to encourage their nonconforming child to consider becoming transgendered? Why or why not?

2. What would you do if you had a gender nonconforming child who is taking steps in making the social transition to a transgendered identity, and your pediatrician is unfamiliar with transgender issues? What could you do to become more informed?

3. What and how could you help to educate teachers, your relatives, friends, neighbors, and others that transgender children and adults do not differ in their overall mental health as compared to cisgendered children?

Internet References

Explore: Transgender Children & Youth

https://www.hrc.org/explore/topic/transgender-children-youth?utm_source=GS&utm_medium=AD&utm_campaign=BPI-HRC-Grant&utm_content=276042104831&utm_term=what%20is%20a%20trans%20kid&gclid=CjwKCAjwk7rmBRAaEiwAhDGhxPS5sSJJ__xo-IIAqr6QCFejaQ2b_mnVHUz95gJQLYe9Fm47OvBEIBoCnZ8QAvD_BwE

Gender-Diverse & Transgender Children

https://www.healthychildren.org/English/ages-stages/gradeschool/Pages/Gender-Diverse-Transgender-Children.aspx

Growing Up Trans PBS Documentary Series

https://www.pbs.org/wgbh/frontline/film/growing-up-trans/

Mental Health of Transgender Children Who Are Supported in Their Identities

https://pediatrics.aappublications.org/content/137/3/e20153223

This Is My Journey As The Parent Of A Transgender Child

https://www.scarymommy.com/parent-of-transgender-child/

Transgender Kids: Who Knows Best? (2017) Documentary

https://www.imdb.com/title/tt6474208/

Article

Prepared by: Chris J. Boyatzis, *Bucknell University* and
Ellen N. Junn, *California State University, Stanislaus*

When Your Child Is a Psychopath

Barbara Bradley Hagerty

Learning Outcomes

After reading this article, you will be able to:

- Discuss the research showing that even very young children can be diagnosed with conduct disorder and callous and unemotional traits that may be related to impairments in specific brain functioning. Parenting and schooling for these children can be extremely challenging as these children engage in extreme levels of violent or psychopathic behavior, and are unemotional, have an absence of empathy, and fail to recognize distress in others or in themselves.

- Describe the innovative, intense, counseling-based intervention program at Mendota Juvenile Treatment Center for the most mentally ill boys between the ages of 12 and 17 years, and how their program has produced significant improvements and outcomes for their teenagers.

- Understand that horrific and abusive childhood experiences alone may not explain later adult psychopathological behaviors among criminals.

THIS IS A GOOD DAY, Samantha tells me: 10 on a scale of 10. We're sitting in a conference room at the San Marcos Treatment Center, just south of Austin, Texas, a space that has witnessed countless difficult conversations between troubled children, their worried parents, and clinical therapists. But today promises unalloyed joy. Samantha's mother is visiting from Idaho, as she does every six weeks, which means lunch off campus and an excursion to Target. The girl needs supplies: new jeans, yoga pants, nail polish.

At 11, Samantha is just over 5 feet tall and has wavy black hair and a steady gaze. She flashes a smile when I ask about her favorite subject (history), and grimaces when I ask about her least favorite (math). She seems poised and cheerful, a normal preteen. But when we steer into uncomfortable territory—the events that led her to this juvenile-treatment facility nearly

2,000 miles from her family—Samantha hesitates and looks down at her hands. "I wanted the whole world to myself," she says. "So I made a whole entire book about how to hurt people."

Starting at age 6, Samantha began drawing pictures of murder weapons: a knife, a bow and arrow, chemicals for poisoning, a plastic bag for suffocating. She tells me that she pretended to kill her stuffed animals.

"You were practicing on your stuffed animals?," I ask her.

She nods.

"How did you feel when you were doing that to your stuffed animals?"

"Happy."

"Why did it make you feel happy?"

"Because I thought that someday I was going to end up doing it on somebody."

"Did you ever try?"

Silence.

"I choked my little brother."

Samantha's parents, Jen and Danny, adopted Samantha when she was 2. They already had three biological children, but they felt called to add Samantha (not her real name) and her half sister, who is two years older, to their family. They later had two more kids.

From the start, Samantha seemed a willful child, in tyrannical need of attention. But what toddler isn't? Her biological mother had been forced to give her up because she'd lost her job and home and couldn't provide for her four children, but there was no evidence of abuse. According to documentation from the state of Texas, Samantha met all her cognitive, emotional, and physical milestones. She had no learning disabilities, no emotional scars, no signs of ADHD or autism.

But even at a very young age, Samantha had a mean streak. When she was about 20 months old, living with foster parents in Texas, she clashed with a boy in day care. The caretaker soothed them both; problem solved. Later that day Samantha, who was already potty trained, walked over to where the boy was playing, pulled down her pants, and peed on him. "She knew exactly what she was doing," Jen says. "There was an ability to wait until an opportune moment to exact her revenge on someone."

When Samantha got a little older, she would pinch, trip, or push her siblings and smile if they cried. She would break into her sister's piggy bank and rip up all the bills. Once, when Samantha was 5, Jen scolded her for being mean to one of her siblings. Samantha walked upstairs to her parents' bathroom and washed her mother's contact lenses down the drain. "Her behavior wasn't impulsive," Jen says. "It was very thoughtful, premeditated."

"I want to kill all of you," Samantha told her mother.

Jen, a former elementary-school teacher, and Danny, a physician, realized they were out of their depth. They consulted doctors, psychiatrists, and therapists. But Samantha only grew more dangerous. They had her admitted to a psychiatric hospital three times before sending her to a residential treatment program in Montana at age 6. Samantha would grow out of it, one psychologist assured her parents; the problem was merely delayed empathy. Samantha was impulsive, another said, something that medication would fix. Yet another suggested that she had reactive attachment disorder, which could be ameliorated with intensive therapy. More darkly—and typically, in these sorts of cases—another psychologist blamed Jen and Danny, implying that Samantha was reacting to harsh and unloving parenting.

One bitter December day in 2011, Jen was driving the children along a winding road near their home. Samantha had just turned 6. Suddenly Jen heard screaming from the back seat, and when she looked in the mirror, she saw Samantha with her hands around the throat of her 2-year-old sister, who was trapped in her car seat. Jen separated them, and once they were home, she pulled Samantha aside.

"What were you doing?," Jen asked.

"I was trying to choke her," Samantha said.

"You realize that would have killed her? She would not have been able to breathe. *She would have died*."

"I know."

"What about the rest of us?"

"I want to kill all of you."

Samantha later showed Jen her sketches, and Jen watched in horror as her daughter demonstrated how to strangle or suffocate her stuffed animals. "I was so terrified," Jen says. "I felt like I had lost control."

Four months later, Samantha tried to strangle her baby brother, who was just two months old.

Jen and Danny had to admit that nothing seemed to make a difference—not affection, not discipline, not therapy. "I was reading and reading and reading, trying to figure out what diagnosis made sense," Jen tells me. "What fits with the behaviors I'm seeing?" Eventually she found one condition that did

seem to fit—but it was a diagnosis that all the mental-health professionals had dismissed, because it's considered both rare and untreatable. In July 2013, Jen took Samantha to see a psychiatrist in New York City, who confirmed her suspicion.

"In the children's mental-health world, it's pretty much a terminal diagnosis, except your child's not going to die," Jen says. "It's just that there's no help." She recalls walking out of the psychiatrist's office on that warm afternoon and standing on a street corner in Manhattan as pedestrians pushed past her in a blur. A feeling flooded over her, singular, unexpected. Hope. Someone had finally acknowledged her family's plight. Perhaps she and Danny could, against the odds, find a way to help their daughter.

Samantha was diagnosed with conduct disorder with callous and unemotional traits. She had all the characteristics of a budding psychopath.

PSYCHOPATHS HAVE ALWAYS been with us. Indeed, certain psychopathic traits have survived because they're useful in small doses: the cool dispassion of a surgeon, the tunnel vision of an Olympic athlete, the ambitious narcissism of many a politician. But when these attributes exist in the wrong combination or in extreme forms, they can produce a dangerously antisocial individual, or even a cold-blooded killer. Only in the past quarter century have researchers zeroed in on the early signs that indicate a child could be the next Ted Bundy.

Researchers shy away from calling children psychopaths; the term carries too much stigma, and too much determinism. They prefer to describe children like Samantha as having "callous and unemotional traits," shorthand for a cluster of characteristics and behaviors, including a lack of empathy, remorse, or guilt; shallow emotions; aggression and even cruelty; and a seeming indifference to punishment. Callous and unemotional children have no trouble hurting others to get what they want. If they do seem caring or empathetic, they're probably trying to manipulate you.

Researchers believe that nearly 1 percent of children exhibit these traits, about as many as have autism or bipolar disorder. Until recently, the condition was seldom mentioned. Only in 2013 did the American Psychiatric Association include callous and unemotional traits in its diagnostic manual, *DSM-5*. The condition can go unnoticed because many children with these traits—who can be charming and smart enough to mimic social cues—are able to mask them.

More than 50 studies have found that kids with callous and unemotional traits are more likely than other kids (three times more likely, in one study) to become criminals or display aggressive, psychopathic traits later in life. And while adult psychopaths constitute only a tiny fraction of the general population, studies suggest that they commit half of all violent crimes. Ignore the problem, says Adrian Raine, a psychologist at the University of Pennsylvania, "and it could be argued we have blood on our hands."

Researchers believe that two paths can lead to psychopathy: one dominated by nature, the other by nurture. For some children, their environment—growing up in poverty, living with abusive parents, fending for themselves in dangerous neighborhoods—can turn them violent and coldhearted. These kids aren't born callous and unemotional; many experts suggest that if they're given a reprieve from their environment, they can be pulled back from psychopathy's edge.

"I don't know what you call this emotion," one psychopathic prisoner said, looking at a photo of a fearful face, "but it's what people look like just before you stab them."

But other children display callous and unemotional traits even though they are raised by loving parents in safe neighborhoods. Large studies in the United Kingdom and elsewhere have found that this early-onset condition is highly hereditary, hardwired in the brain—and especially difficult to treat. "We'd like to think a mother and father's love can turn everything around," Raine says. "But there are times where parents are doing the very best they can, but the kid—even from the get-go—is just a bad kid."

Still, researchers stress that a callous child—even one who was born that way—is not automatically destined for psychopathy. By some estimates, four out of five children with these traits do not grow up to be psychopaths. The mystery—the one everyone is trying to solve—is why some of these children develop into normal adults while others end up on death row.

A TRAINED EYE CAN SPOT a callous and unemotional child by age 3 or 4. Whereas normally developing children at that age grow agitated when they see other children cry—and either try to comfort them or bolt the scene—these kids show a chilly detachment. In fact, psychologists may even be able to trace these traits back to infancy. Researchers at King's College London tested more than 200 five-week-old babies, tracking whether they preferred looking at a person's face or at a red ball. Those who favored the ball displayed more callous traits two and a half years later.

As a child gets older, more-obvious warning signs appear. Kent Kiehl, a psychologist at the University of New Mexico and the author of *The Psychopath Whisperer*, says that one scary harbinger occurs when a kid who is 8, 9, or 10 years old commits a transgression or a crime while alone, without the pressure of peers. This reflects an interior impulse toward harm. Criminal versatility—committing different types of crimes in different settings—can also hint at future psychopathy.

But the biggest red flag is early violence. "Most of the psychopaths I meet in prison had been in fights with teachers in elementary school or junior high," Kiehl says. "When I'd interview them, I'd say, 'What's the worst thing you did in school?'

And they'd say, 'I beat the teacher unconscious.' You're like, *That really happened?* It turns out that's very common."

We have a fairly good idea of what an adult psychopathic brain looks like, thanks in part to Kiehl's work. He has scanned the brains of hundreds of inmates at maximum-security prisons and chronicled the neural differences between average violent convicts and psychopaths. Broadly speaking, Kiehl and others believe that the psychopathic brain has at least two neural abnormalities—and that these same differences likely also occur in the brains of callous children.

The first abnormality appears in the limbic system, the set of brain structures involved in, among other things, processing emotions. In a psychopath's brain, this area contains less gray matter. "It's like a weaker muscle," Kiehl says. A psychopath may understand, intellectually, that what he is doing is wrong, but he doesn't *feel* it. "Psychopaths know the words but not the music" is how Kiehl describes it. "They just don't have the same circuitry."

In particular, experts point to the amygdala—a part of the limbic system—as a physiological culprit for coldhearted or violent behavior. Someone with an undersize or underactive amygdala may not be able to feel empathy or refrain from violence. For example, many psychopathic adults and callous children do not recognize fear or distress in other people's faces. Essi Viding, a professor of developmental psychopathology at University College London recalls showing one psychopathic prisoner a series of faces with different expressions. When the prisoner came to a fearful face, he said, "I don't know what you call this emotion, but it's what people look like just before you stab them."

Why does this neural quirk matter? Abigail Marsh, a researcher at Georgetown University who has studied the brains of callous and unemotional children, says that distress cues, such as fearful or sad expressions, signal submission and conciliation. "They're designed to prevent attacks by raising the white flag. And so if you're not sensitive to these cues, you're much more likely to attack somebody whom other people would refrain from attacking."

Psychopaths not only fail to recognize distress in others, they may not feel it themselves. The best physiological indicator of which young people will become violent criminals as adults is a low resting heart rate, says Adrian Raine of the University of Pennsylvania. Longitudinal studies that followed thousands of men in Sweden, the U.K., and Brazil all point to this biological anomaly. "We think that low heart rate reflects a lack of fear, and a lack of fear could predispose someone to committing fearless criminal-violence acts," Raine says. Or perhaps there is an "optimal level of physiological arousal," and psychopathic people seek out stimulation to increase their heart rate to normal. "For some kids, one way of getting this arousal jag in life is by shoplifting, or joining a gang, or robbing a store, or getting into a fight." Indeed, when Daniel Waschbusch, a clinical psychologist at Penn State Hershey Medical Center, gave the most severely callous and unemotional children he worked with a stimulative medication, their behavior improved.

The second hallmark of a psychopathic brain is an overactive reward system especially primed for drugs, sex, or anything else that delivers a ping of excitement. In one study, children played a computer gambling game programmed to allow them to win early on and then slowly begin to lose. Most people will cut their losses at some point, Kent Kiehl notes, "whereas the psychopathic, callous unemotional kids keep going until they lose everything." Their brakes don't work, he says.

Faulty brakes may help explain why psychopaths commit brutal crimes: Their brains ignore cues about danger or punishment. "There are all these decisions we make based on threat, or the fear that something bad can happen," says Dustin Pardini, a clinical psychologist and an associate professor of criminology at Arizona State University. "If you have less concern about the negative consequences of your actions, then you'll be more likely to continue engaging in these behaviors. And when you get caught, you'll be less likely to learn from your mistakes."

Researchers see this insensitivity to punishment even in some toddlers. "These are the kids that are completely unperturbed by the fact that they've been put in time-out," says Eva Kimonis, who works with callous children and their families at the University of New South Wales, in Australia. "So it's not surprising that they keep going to time-out, because it's not effective for them. Whereas reward—they're very motivated by that."

This insight is driving a new wave of treatment. What's a clinician to do if the emotional, empathetic part of a child's brain is broken but the reward part of the brain is humming along? "You co-opt the system," Kiehl says. "You work with what's left."

WITH EACH PASSING YEAR, both nature and nurture conspire to steer a callous child toward psychopathy and block his exits to a normal life. His brain becomes a little less malleable; his environment grows less forgiving as his exhausted parents reach their limits, and as teachers, social workers, and judges begin to turn away. By his teenage years, he may not be a lost cause, since the rational part of his brain is still under construction. But he can be one scary dude.

Like the guy standing 20 feet away from me in the North Hall of Mendota Juvenile Treatment Center, in Madison, Wisconsin. The tall, lanky teenager has just emerged from his cell. Two staff members cuff his wrists, shackle his feet, and begin to lead him away. Suddenly he swivels to face me and laughs—a menacing laugh that gives me chills. As young men yell expletives, banging on the metal doors of their cells, and others stare silently through their narrow plexiglass windows, I think, *This is as close as I get to* Lord of the Flies.

The psychologists Michael Caldwell and Greg Van Rybroek thought much the same thing when they opened the Mendota facility in 1995, in response to a nationwide epidemic of youth violence in the early '90s. Instead of placing young offenders in a juvenile prison until they were released to commit more—and more violent—crimes as adults, the Wisconsin legislature set up a new treatment center to try to break the cycle of pathology. Mendota would operate within the Department of Health Services, not the Department of Corrections. It would be run by psychologists and psychiatric-care technicians, not wardens and guards. It would employ one staff member for every three kids—quadruple the ratio at other juvenile-corrections facilities.

Caldwell and Van Rybroek tell me that the state's high-security juvenile-corrections facility was supposed to send over its most mentally ill boys between the ages of 12 and 17. It did, but what Caldwell and Van Rybroek didn't anticipate was that the boys the facility transferred were also its most menacing and recalcitrant. They recall their first few assessments. "The kid would walk out and we would turn to each other and say, 'That's the most dangerous person I've ever seen in my life,'" Caldwell says. Each one seemed more threatening than the last. "We're looking at each other and saying, 'Oh, no. What have we done?,'" Van Rybroek adds.

What they have done, by trial and error, is achieve something most people thought impossible: If they haven't *cured* psychopathy, they've at least tamed it.

Many of the teenagers at Mendota grew up on the streets, without parents, and were beaten up or sexually abused. Violence became a defense mechanism. Caldwell and Van Rybroek recall a group-therapy session a few years ago in which one boy described being strung up by his wrists and hung from the ceiling as his father cut him with a knife and rubbed pepper in the wounds. "Hey," several other kids said, "that's like what happened to me." They called themselves the "piñata club."

But not everyone at Mendota was "born in hell," as Van Rybroek puts it. Some of the boys were raised in middle-class homes with parents whose major sin was not abuse but paralysis in the face of their terrifying child. No matter the history, one secret to diverting them from adult psychopathy is to wage an unrelenting war of presence. At Mendota, the staff calls this "decompression." The idea is to allow a young man who has been living in a state of chaos to slowly rise to the surface and acclimate to the world without resorting to violence.

Caldwell mentions that, two weeks ago, one patient became furious over some perceived slight or injustice; every time the techs checked on him, he would squirt urine or feces through the door. (This is a popular pastime at Mendota.) The techs would dodge it and return 20 minutes later, and he would do it again. "This went on for several days," Caldwell says. "But part of the concept of decompression is that the kid's going to get tired at some point. And one of those times you're going to come there and he's going to be tired, or he's just not going to have any urine left to throw at you. And you're going to have a little moment where you're going to have a positive connection there."

Cindy Ebsen, the operations director, who is also a registered nurse, gives me a tour of Mendota's North Hall. As we pass the metal doors with their narrow windows, the boys peer out and the yelling subsides into entreaties. "Cindy, Cindy, can you get me some candy?" "I'm your favorite, aren't I, Cindy?" "Cindy, why don't you visit me anymore?"

She pauses to banter with each of them. The young men who pass through these halls have murdered and maimed, carjacked and robbed at gunpoint. "But they're still kids. I love working with them, because I see the most success in this population," as opposed to older offenders, Ebsen says. For many, friendship with her or another staff member is the first safe connection they've known.

Forming attachments with callous kids is important, but it's not Mendota's singular insight. The center's real breakthrough involves deploying the anomalies of the psychopathic brain to one's advantage—specifically, downplaying punishment and dangling rewards. These boys have been expelled from school, placed in group homes, arrested, and jailed. If punishment were going to rein them in, it would have by now. But their brains do respond, enthusiastically, to rewards. At Mendota, the boys can accumulate points to join ever more prestigious "clubs" (Club 19, Club 23, the VIP Club). As they ascend in status, they earn privileges and treats—candy bars, baseball cards, pizza on Saturdays, the chance to play Xbox or stay up late. Hitting someone, throwing urine, or cussing out the staff costs a boy points—but not for long, since callous and unemotional kids aren't generally deterred by punishment.

I am, frankly, skeptical—will a kid who knocked down an elderly lady and stole her Social Security check (as one Mendota resident did) really be motivated by the promise of Pokémon cards? But then I walk down the South Hall with Ebsen. She stops and turns toward a door on our left. "Hey," she calls, "do I hear internet radio?"

"Yeah, yeah, I'm in the VIP Club," a voice says. "Can I show you my basketball cards?"

Ebsen unlocks the door to reveal a skinny 17-year-old boy with a nascent mustache. He fans out his collection. "This is, like, 50 basketball cards," he says, and I can almost see his reward centers glowing. "I have the most and best basketball cards here." Later, he sketches out his history for me: His stepmother had routinely beat him and his stepbrother had used him for sex. When he was still a preteen, he began molesting the younger girl and boy next door. The abuse continued for a few years, until the boy told his mother. "I knew it was wrong, but I didn't care," he says. "I just wanted the pleasure."

At Mendota, he has begun to see that short-term pleasure could land him in prison as a sex offender, while deferred

gratification can confer more-lasting dividends: a family, a job, and most of all, freedom. Unlikely as it sounds, this revelation sprang from his ardent pursuit of basketball cards.

After he details the center's point system (a higher math that I cannot follow), the boy tells me that a similar approach should translate into success in the outside world—as if the world, too, operates on a point system. Just as consistent good behavior confers basketball cards and Internet radio inside these walls, so—he believes—will it bring promotions at work. "Say you're a cook; you can [become] a waitress if you're doing really good," he says. "That's the way I look at it."

He peers at me, as if searching for confirmation. I nod, hoping that the world will work this way for him. Even more, I hope his insight will endure.

IN FACT, THE PROGRAM at Mendota has changed the trajectory for many young men, at least in the short term. Caldwell and Van Rybroek have tracked the public records of 248 juvenile delinquents after their release. One hundred forty-seven of them had been in a juvenile-corrections facility, and 101 of them—the harder, more psychopathic cases—had received treatment at Mendota. In the four and a half years since their release, the Mendota boys have been far less likely to reoffend (64 percent versus 97 percent), and far less likely to commit a violent crime (36 percent versus 60 percent). Most striking, the ordinary delinquents have killed 16 people since their release. The boys from Mendota? Not one.

"We thought that as soon as they walked out the door, they'd last maybe a week or two and they'd have another felony on their record," Caldwell says. "And when the data first came back that showed that that wasn't happening, we figured there was something wrong with the data." For two years, they tried to find mistakes or alternative explanations, but eventually they concluded that the results were real.

The question they are trying to answer now is this: Can Mendota's treatment program not only change the behavior of these teens, but measurably reshape their brains as well? Researchers are optimistic, in part because the decision-making part of the brain continues to evolve into one's mid-20s. The program is like neural weight lifting, Kent Kiehl, at the University of New Mexico, says. "If you exercise this limbic-related circuitry, it's going to get better."

To test this hypothesis, Kiehl and the staff at Mendota are now asking some 300 young men to slide into a mobile brain scanner. The scanner records the shape and size of key areas of the boys' brains, as well as how their brains react to tests of decision-making ability, impulsivity, and other qualities that go to the core of psychopathy. Each boy's brain will be scanned before, during, and at the end of their time in the program, offering researchers insights into whether his improved behavior reflects better functioning inside his brain.

No one believes that Mendota graduates will develop true empathy or a heartfelt moral conscience. "They may not go from the Joker in *The Dark Knight* to Mister Rogers," Caldwell tells me, laughing. But they can develop a *cognitive* moral conscience, an intellectual awareness that life will be more rewarding if they play by the rules. "We're just happy if they stay on this side of the law," Van Rybroek says. "In our world, that's huge."

How many can stay the course for a lifetime? Caldwell and Van Rybroek have no idea. They're barred from contacting former patients—a policy meant to ensure that the staff and former patients maintain appropriate boundaries. But sometimes graduates write or call to share their progress, and among these correspondents, Carl, now 37, stands out.

Carl (not his real name) emailed a thankful note to Van Rybroek in 2013. Aside from one assault conviction after he left Mendota, he had stayed out of trouble for a decade and opened his own business—a funeral home near Los Angeles. His success was especially significant because he was one of the harder cases, a boy from a good home who seemed wired for violence.

"I remember when I bit my mom really hard, and she was bleeding and crying," Carl says. "I remember feeling so happy, so overjoyed."

Carl was born in a small town in Wisconsin. The middle child of a computer programmer and a special-education teacher, "he came out angry," his father recalls during a phone conversation. His acts of violence started small—hitting a classmate in kindergarten—but quickly escalated: ripping the head off his favorite teddy bear, slashing the tires on the family car, starting fires, killing his sister's hamster.

His sister remembers Carl, when he was about 8, swinging their cat in circles by its tail, faster and faster, and then letting go. "And you hear her hit the wall." Carl just laughed.

Looking back, even Carl is puzzled by the rage that coursed through him as a child. "I remember when I bit my mom really hard, and she was bleeding and crying. I remember feeling so happy, so overjoyed—completely fulfilled and satisfied," he tells me on the phone. "It wasn't like someone kicked me in the face and I was trying to get him back. It was more like a weird, hard-to-explain feeling of hatred."

His behavior confused and eventually terrified his parents. "It just got worse and worse as he got bigger," his father tells me. "Later, when he was a teenager and occasionally incarcerated, I was happy about it. We knew where he was and that he'd be safe, and that took a load off the mind."

By the time Carl arrived at Mendota Juvenile Treatment Center in November 1995, at age 15, he had been placed in a psychiatric hospital, a group home, foster care, or a juvenile-corrections center about a dozen times. His police record listed 18 charges, including armed burglary and three "crimes against persons," one of which sent the victim to the hospital. Lincoln Hills, a high-security juvenile-corrections facility, foisted him on Mendota after he accumulated more

than 100 serious infractions in less than four months. On an assessment called the Youth Psychopathy Checklist, he scored 38 out of a possible 40—five points higher than the average for Mendota boys, who were among the most dangerous young men in Wisconsin.

Carl had a rocky start at Mendota: weeks of abusing staff, smearing feces around his cell, yelling all night, refusing to shower, and spending much of the time locked in his room, not allowed to mix with the other kids. Slowly, though, his psychology began to shift. The staff's unruffled constancy chipped away at his defenses. "These people were like zombies," Carl recalls, laughing. "You could punch them in the face and they wouldn't do anything."

He started talking in therapy and in class. He quit mouthing off and settled down. He developed the first real bonds in his young life. "The teachers, the nurses, the staff, they all seemed to have this idea that they could make a difference in us," he says. "Like, *Huh! Something good could come of us. We were believed to have potential.*"

Carl wasn't exactly in the clear. After two stints at Mendota, he was released just before his 18th birthday, got married, and at age 20 was arrested for beating up a police officer. In prison, he wrote a suicide note, fashioned a makeshift noose, and was put on suicide watch in solitary confinement. While there, he began reading the Bible and fasting, and one day, he says, "something very powerful shifted." He began to believe in God. Carl acknowledges that his lifestyle falls far short of the Christian ideal. But he still attends church every week, and he credits Mendota with paving the way for his conversion. By the time he was released, in 2003, his marriage had dissolved, and he moved away from Wisconsin, eventually settling in California, where he opened his funeral home.

Carl cheerfully admits that the death business appeals to him. As a child, he says, "I had a deep fascination with knives and cutting and killing, so it's a harmless way to express some level of what you might call morbid curiosity. And I think that morbid curiosity taken to its extreme—that's the home of the serial killers, okay? So it's that same energy. But everything in moderation."

Of course, his profession also requires empathy. Carl says that he had to train himself to show empathy for his grieving clients, but that it now comes naturally. His sister agrees that he's been able to make this emotional leap. "I've seen him interact with the families, and he's phenomenal," she tells me. "He is amazing at providing empathy and providing that shoulder for them. And it does not fit with my view of him at all. I get confused. *Is that true? Does he genuinely feel for them? Is he faking the whole thing? Does he even know at this point?*"

After talking with Carl, I begin to see him as a remarkable success story. "Without [Mendota] and Jesus," he tells me, "I would have been a Manson-, Bundy-, Dahmer-, or Berkowitz-type of criminal." Sure, his fascination with the morbid is a little creepy. Yet here he is, now remarried, the father of a 1-year-old son he adores, with a flourishing business. After our phone interview, I decide to meet him in person. I want to witness his redemption for myself.

THE NIGHT BEFORE I'm scheduled to fly to Los Angeles, I receive a frantic email from Carl's wife. Carl is in police custody. His wife tells me that Carl considers himself polyamorous, and had invited one of his girlfriends over to their apartment. (This woman denies ever being romantically involved with Carl.)* They were playing with the baby when his wife returned. She was furious, and grabbed their son. Carl responded by pulling her hair, snatching the baby out of her arms, and taking her phone to prevent her from calling the police. She called from a neighbor's house instead. (Carl says he grabbed the baby to protect him.) Three misdemeanor charges—spousal battery, abandonment and neglect of a child, and intimidation of a witness—and the psychopath who made good is now in jail.

I go to Los Angeles anyway, in the naive hope that Carl will be released on bail at his hearing the next day. A few minutes before 8:30 a.m., his wife and I meet at the courthouse and begin the long wait. She is 12 years Carl's junior, a compact woman with long black hair and a weariness that ebbs only when she gazes at her son. She met Carl on OkCupid two years ago while visiting L.A. and—after a romance of just a few months—moved to California to marry him. Now she sits outside the courtroom, one eye on her son, fielding calls from clients of the funeral home and wondering whether she can make bail.

"I'm so sick of the drama," she says, as the phone rings again.

Carl is a tough man to be married to. His wife says he's funny and charming and a good listener, but he sometimes loses interest in the funeral business, leaving most of the work to her. He brings other women home for sex, even when she's there. And while he's never seriously beaten her up, he has slapped her.

"He would say sorry, but I don't know if he was upset or not," she tells me.

"So you wondered if he felt genuine remorse?"

"Honestly, I'm at a point where I don't really care anymore. I just want my son and myself to be safe."

Finally, at 3:15 p.m., Carl shuffles into the courtroom, handcuffed, wearing an orange L.A. County jumpsuit. He gives us a two-handed wave and flashes a carefree smile, which fades when he learns that he will not be released on bail today, despite pleading guilty to assault and battery. He will remain in jail for another three weeks.

Carl calls me the day after his release. "I really shouldn't have a girlfriend and a wife," he says, in what seems an uncharacteristic display of remorse. He insists that he wants to keep his family together, and says that he thinks the domestic-violence classes the court has mandated will help him. He seems sincere.

When I describe the latest twist in Carl's story to Michael Caldwell and Greg Van Rybroek, they laugh knowingly. "This counts as a good outcome for a Mendota guy," Caldwell says. "He's not going to have a fully healthy adjustment to life, but he's been able to stay mostly within the law. Even this misdemeanor—he's not committing armed robberies or shooting people."

His sister sees her brother's outcome in a similar light. "This guy got dealt a shittier hand of cards than anybody I've ever met," she tells me. "Who deserves to have started out life that way? And the fact that he's not a raving lunatic, locked up for the rest of his life, or dead is *insane.*"

I ask Carl whether it's difficult to play by the rules, to simply be *normal.* "On a scale of 1 to 10, how hard is it?" he says. "I would say an 8. Because 8's difficult, very difficult."

I've grown to like Carl: He has a lively intellect, a willingness to admit his flaws, and a desire to be good. Is he being sincere or manipulating me? Is Carl proof that psychopathy can be tamed—or proof that the traits are so deeply embedded that they can never be dislodged? I honestly don't know.

AT THE SAN MARCOS Treatment Center, Samantha is wearing her new yoga pants from Target, but they bring her little joy. In a few hours, her mother will leave for the airport and fly back to Idaho. Samantha munches on a slice of pizza and suggests movies to watch on Jen's laptop. She seems sad, but less about Jen's departure than about the resumption of the center's tedious routine. Samantha snuggles with her mom while they watch *The BFG,* this 11-year-old girl who can stab a teacher's hand with a pencil at the slightest provocation.

Watching them in the darkened room, I contemplate for the hundredth time the arbitrary nature of good and evil. If Samantha's brain is wired for callousness, if she fails to experience empathy or remorse because she lacks the neural equipment, can we say she is evil? "These kids can't help it," Adrian Raine says. "Kids don't grow up wanting to be psychopaths or serial killers. They grow up wanting to become baseball players or great football stars. It's not a choice."

Samantha knows that her thoughts about hurting people are wrong, and she tries to suppress them. But the cognitive training cannot always compete.

Yet, Raine says, even if we don't label them evil, we must try to head off their evil acts. It's a daily struggle, planting the seeds of emotions that usually come so naturally—empathy, caring, remorse—in the rocky soil of a callous brain. Samantha has lived for more than two years at San Marcos, where the staff has tried to shape her behavior with regular therapy and a program that, like Mendota's, dispenses quick but limited punishment for bad behavior and offers prizes and privileges—candy, Pokémon cards, late nights on weekends—for good behavior.

Jen and Danny have spotted green shoots of empathy. Samantha has made a friend, and recently comforted the girl after her social worker quit. They've detected traces of self-awareness and even remorse: Samantha knows that her thoughts about hurting people are wrong, and she tries to suppress them. But the cognitive training cannot always compete with the urge to strangle an annoying classmate, which she tried to do just the other day. "It builds up, and then I have to do it," Samantha explains. "I can't keep it away."

It all feels exhausting, for Samantha and for everyone in her orbit. Later, I ask Jen whether Samantha has lovable qualities that make all this worthwhile. "It can't be all nightmare, can it?," I ask. She hesitates. "Or can it?"

"It is not all nightmare," Jen responds, eventually. "She's cute, and she can be fun, and she can be enjoyable." She's great at board games, she has a wonderful imagination, and now, having been apart for two years, her siblings say they miss her. But Samantha's mood and behavior can quickly turn. "The challenge with her is that her extreme is so extreme. You're always waiting for the other shoe to drop."

Danny says they're praying for the triumph of self-interest over impulse. "Our hope is that she is able to have a cognitive understanding that 'Even though my thinking is different, my behavior needs to walk down this path so that I can enjoy the good things that I want.'" Because she was diagnosed relatively early, they hope that Samantha's young, still-developing brain can be rewired for some measure of cognitive morality. And having parents like Jen and Danny could make a difference; research suggests that warm and responsive parenting can help children become less callous as they get older.

On the flip side, the New York psychiatrist told them, the fact that her symptoms appeared so early, and so dramatically, may indicate that her callousness is so deeply ingrained that little can be done to ameliorate it.

Samantha's parents try not to second-guess their decision to adopt her. But even Samantha has wondered whether they have regrets. "She said, 'Why did you even want me?,'" Jen recalls. "The real answer to that is: We didn't know the depth of her challenges. We had no idea. I don't know if this would be a different story if we were looking at this now. But what we tell her is: 'You were ours.'"

Jen and Danny are planning to bring Samantha home this summer, a prospect the family views with some trepidation. They're taking precautions, such as using alarms on Samantha's bedroom door. The older children are larger and tougher than Samantha, but the family will have to keep vigil over the 5-year-old and the 7-year-old. Still, they believe she's ready, or,

more accurately, that she's progressed as far as she can at San Marcos. They want to bring her home, to give it another try.

Of course, even if Samantha can slip easily back into home life at 11, what of the future? "Do I want that child to have a driver's license?," Jen asks. To go on dates? She's smart enough for college—but will she be able to negotiate that complex society without becoming a threat? Can she have a stable romantic relationship, much less fall in love and marry? She and Danny have had to redefine success for Samantha: simply keeping her out of prison.

And yet, they love Samantha. "She's ours, and we want to raise our children together," Jen says. Samantha has been in residential treatment programs for most of the past five years, nearly half her life. They can't institutionalize her forever. She needs to learn to function in the world, sooner rather than later. "I do feel there's hope," Jen says. "The hard part is, it's never going to go away. It's high-stakes parenting. If it fails, it's going to fail big."

Critical Thinking

1. Imagine you are a parent or educator, what specific signs or behaviors might you look for if you are worried about a child who might have conduct disorder with callous and unemotional traits? What would you do to help such a child?

2. Based on the data from the Mendota Juvenile Treatment Center, do you think that children with this disorder can be cured? Explain why or why not.

3. Imagine that you are a teacher, how would you try to protect other children from being harmed by a child in the classroom with extreme conduct disorder?

Internet References

Can We Identify Psychopathy in a Young Child?
https://www.psychologytoday.com/us/blog/fulfillment-any-age/201611/can-we-identify-psychopathy-in-young-child

Can You Call a 9-Year-Old a Psychopath?
https://www.nytimes.com/2012/05/13/magazine/can-you-call-a-9-year-old-a-psychopath.html

Conduct disorders and psychopathy in children and adolescents: aetiology, clinical presentation and treatment strategies of callous-unemotional traits
https://www.ncbi.nlm.nih.gov/pmc/articles/PMC5607565/

Is My Child a Psychopath?
https://www.verywellfamily.com/is-my-child-a-psychopath-4175470

Article

Prepared by: Chris J. Boyatzis, *Bucknell University* and
Ellen N. Junn, *California State University, Stanislaus*

A Court Put a 9-Year-Old in Shackles for Stealing Chewing Gum—an Outrage That Happens Every Single Day

Research shows that shackling is bad for kids and unnecessary for courtroom safety. So why do judges keep doing it?

BRYAN SCHATZ

Learning Outcomes

After reading this article, you will be able to:

- Define juvenile shackling and understand the legal implications.

- Cite the pros and cons for the use of juvenile shackling.

- Be familiar with whether juvenile shackling is used extensively throughout the United States and whether the trend is increasing or decreasing in recent years.

The nine-year-old stole [1] a 14-stick pack of Trident "Layers" chewing gum, Orchard Peach and Ripe Mango flavor, worth $1.48. He'd lingered by the beverage isle of the Super 1 Foods in Post Falls, Idaho, for a while before bailing out the front door. The theft led to a missed court appearance, which led to an arrest and a night spent in a juvenile jail. The next day, the third-grader appeared in court, chained and shackled.

At least 100,000 children are shackled in the US every year, according to estimates by David Shapiro, a campaign manager at the Campaign Against Indiscriminate Juvenile Shackling. (Formal data on numbers of shackled kids does not exist.) As juvenile justice practices have grown more punitive over the past several decades, shackling has become far more common. This month, the American Bar Association (ABA) passed a resolution calling for an end to this practice because it is harmful to juveniles, largely unnecessary for courtroom safety—and contradicts existing law. "We're not just talking handcuffs here. These kids are virtually hog-tied," says John D. Elliott, a South Carolina defense attorney who worked on the resolution. "The only difference is their hands are in front."

The restraints—which include handcuffs, belly chains, and leg irons—are used on kids of all ages and often don't fit the severity of their crime: The majority of kids are in court for non-violent offenses, like shoplifting or truancy.

The ABA says that this practice is contrary to law because it undermines the accused's right to be presumed innocent. In adult criminal court, if the defendant is seen by the jury in any sort of restraint, that's almost always considered a mistrial, explains Judge Jay Blitzman from Massachusetts, who worked on the ABA's resolution and helped pass anti-shackling policy for juveniles in his state. "You're sending a message, and it's not subliminal. It's: 'This guy is dangerous.'" The ABA argues that these anti-shackling principles observed in adult court should apply with equal, if not greater, force for children.

"We're not just talking handcuffs here. These kids are virtually hog-tied."

There's plenty of behavioral science establishing that harsh treatment of young offenders is counterproductive. Even one day of unnecessary detention can have profoundly negative impacts on children's mental and physical health. And shackling, the ABA argues, goes against the therapeutic goals of the juvenile justice system because it humiliates kids: Child psychologists have testified that publicly shackling children can be so damaging to their developing personal identity that it can lead to further criminal behavior in the future.

Indeed, the mother of the nine-year-old alluded to this in an interview with Idaho's *Coeur d'Alene Press:* "He feels already like he's the outcast of the family, like he's not as good as everybody else," she said, adding that he fears becoming like his father, who has served time in jail.

The rise in juvenile shackling began in the 1980s, when states started passing tough-on-crime laws in response to a perceived rise in youth crime. Influential criminologists predicted a coming wave of "superpredator" juvenile criminals, including "elementary school youngsters who pack guns instead of lunches." The prediction didn't come true, but it spurred a rush toward harsher punishment for kids, including life without parole, mandatory minimums, and automatic transfer to adult court for certain offenses. This hardened approach extended to courthouse security after multiple fatal shootings in courts across the country, most notably a 2005 incident in an Atlanta courthouse that left two people dead. As Elliott puts it, the courts became "virtually unyielding" after that.

> **Massachusetts implemented an anti-shackling rule in 2010 and since then "there really have never been issues with its implementation."**

To this day, many judges, prosecutors, and law enforcement officers argue that juvenile shackling preserves courtroom safety and order. But there's little evidence to support that claim, argues the ABA, especially given that several states have curtailed the practice with little to no ill effects. Since Florida's Miami-Dade County outlawed shackling kids in 2006, not one of the more than 20,000 children who have appeared in court

unbound has escaped or harmed anyone, according to 2011 data. Florida eliminated indiscriminate shackling statewide in 2009, and in the two years following the ruling, officials reported only one disruptive incident. Massachusetts implemented an anti-shackling rule in 2010 and since then "there really have never been issues with its implementation," says Blitzman.

Several states are currently considering legislation or court orders to limit the use of shackling, including Nebraska, Indiana, Connecticut, Minnesota, Utah, and Tennessee.

Colorado is also debating an anti-shackling bill. Ann Roan, the state training director for the Colorado Office of the State Public Defender, says she is optimistic that it will pass during this year's legislative session. She explains why: "It's just hard to come up with any research at all that says shackling doesn't harm children."

Critical Thinking

1. What is your opinion about whether juveniles should be shackled or not? What evidence would you cite for your views?

2. Do you think shackling of alleged juvenile defendants serves a deterrent purpose? Given the cognitive development of juveniles, why or why not?

3. How would you feel if you were shackled as a juvenile? What might be the future psychological consequences of being shackled? How can you balance the needs of the juvenile versus the victim?

Internet References

American Bar Association, ABAjournal.com
http://www.abajournal.com/news/article/should_juveniles_be_shackled_in_court_or_sentenced_to_life_without_parole_a

Juvenile Justice Information Exchange, JJIE.org
http://jjie.org/aclu-wants-supreme-court-to-review-shackling-of-juveniles/

National Conference of State Legislators, NCSL.org
http://www.ncsl.org/research/civil-and-criminal-justice/states-that-limit-or-prohibit-juvenile-shackling-and-solitary-confinement635572628.aspx

National Association for Public Defense.us
http://www.publicdefenders.us/?q=node/450

National Juvenile Defender Center, njdc.info
http://njdc.info/campaign-against-indiscriminate-juvenile-shackling/
http://njdc.info/wp-content/uploads/2014/01/Shackling-Inno-Brief-2013.pdf

Article

Prepared by: Chris J. Boyatzis, *Bucknell University* and
Ellen N. Junn, *California State University, Stanislaus*

85 Million Children Work in Dangerous Conditions: Are Governments Fulfilling Their Promise to Prevent This?

JODY HEYMANN, ALETA SPRAGUE, AND NICOLAS DE GUZMAN CHORNY

Learning Outcomes

After reading this article, you will be able to:

- Describe the use of child labor around the world and its immediate and long-term impact on children.

- Describe the Convention on the Rights of the Child and how nations have respected, or not, its protections for children.

- Understand different types of labor that children conduct in different parts of the world.

Mining is a notoriously dangerous job. Tunnels can collapse, explosions and falling rocks are common, and the air is often filled with dust or even toxic gases. While the world breathed a collective sigh of relief when the 33 Chilean miners were rescued in 2010, around 12,000 people die in similar accidents each year.

So why do we let so many children do it—in 2014?

Mining falls squarely within the definition of "hazardous work," as defined by the International Labour Organization (ILO). According to the ILO, there are 168 million child laborers worldwide, including 85 million in jobs that directly endanger their health and safety. In countries around the world, kids work in gold mines, salt mines, and stone quarries—while millions more toil in fields, factories, or construction sites.

As noted in the first post in our series last week, November 20th marks the 25th anniversary of the Convention on the Rights of the Child (CRC), a landmark U.N. agreement that laid the foundation for strengthening children's rights around the world. Among other fundamental rights, the CRC recognizes "the right of the child to be protected ... from performing any work that is likely to be hazardous" and explicitly calls on ratifying countries to take legislative measures to ensure implementation of these rights. Yet a quarter century later, how much progress has the world really made toward ending child labor and shielding children from dangerous work conditions?

As it turns out, while a majority of CRC States parties have passed legislation to prevent hazardous child labor, only 53 percent legally protect children from hazardous work in all circumstances. In nearly a quarter of States parties, the minimum age for hazardous work is under 18, while 2 percent haven't established a minimum age whatsoever. In an additional 21 percent of States parties, although the minimum age is 18, legal exceptions allow younger children to do hazardous work in certain circumstances.

And while the problem is particularly severe in lower-income countries, child labor remains a global phenomenon—especially in the agricultural sector. In the U.S. (one of only three countries that are not parties to the CRC), federal regulations include exceptions that allow children to perform agricultural work at *any* age, subject to some limitations on work during school hours. Even when not technically classified as "hazardous," agricultural work often involves direct contact with poisonous pesticides, strenuous work, and long hours under the sun.

Earlier this year, in a survey of child workers in U.S. tobacco fields aged seven to 17, Human Rights Watch found that most children worked 50–60 hours per week, while 66 percent reported symptoms consistent with acute nicotine poisoning. According to the Bureau of Labor Statistics, the rate of fatalities for children aged 15–17 engaged in agricultural work is

4.4 times higher compared to children working in other jobs. Yet despite these risks, legal loopholes mean millions of children labor in fields around the world.

The consequences of child labor last a lifetime. Whether the work is hazardous or not, evidence shows that child laborers tend to have poorer health and complete less education than children who do not work. A study conducted in Guatemala, for example, showed that having worked between the ages of six and 14 increased the probability of health problems as an adult by over 40 percent. Another study conducted in Vietnam showed that the highest grade attained by working children was three grades lower than for children who did not work, even after controlling for family and regional characteristics.

Enacting laws that protect all children from performing hazardous work is a first step toward improving children's health and access to education. Yet full accountability for ending child labor and upholding children's other fundamental rights will also require participation from citizens to ensure adequate protections are both legislated and implemented. Citizens all over the world should have access to simple tools to monitor their countries' progress and pitfalls.

That's why in commemoration of the CRC's 25th anniversary, the WORLD Policy Analysis Center is releasing a series of maps, factsheets, and infographics that show where countries currently stand and what they could achieve. With this information, we hope to empower citizens all over the world to make change happen. Only when policymakers can identify viable solutions to eliminating child labor while supporting adequate family income, and citizens can access tools to hold their leaders accountable for commitments made, will child labor truly become a relic of the past.

Critical Thinking

1. Why is child labor still used in many countries? What are some political and economic reasons child labor still exists in some places?

2. What is your personal or moral position on child labor? Do you feel there are important distinctions in the acceptability between different types of labor and in different circumstances? Is running a lemonade stand in one's neighborhood "child labor"? Why or why not? In what ways does a 10-year-old mowing the family's lawn differ from a 10-year-old working for many hours a day collecting tobacco leaves on a tobacco farm?

3. If human-rights organizations learn that some nations are making children engage in exploitive and dangerous child labor, what can the rest of the world do? Should other countries intervene?

Internet References

The Atlantic
http://www.theatlantic.com/business/archive/2014/12/how-common-is-chid-labor-in-the-us/383687/

Bureau of Labor Statistics
http://www.bls.gov/opub/rylf/pdf/chapter2.pdf

Child Labor Public Education Project (University of Iowa)
https://www.continuetolearn.uiowa.edu/laborctr/child_labor/about/us_laws.html

https://www.continuetolearn.uiowa.edu/laborctr/child_labor/about/us_history.html

U.S. Department of Labor
http://www.dol.gov/dol/topic/youthlabor/

http://www.dol.gov/whd/childlabor.htm

Heymann, Jody; Sprague, Aleta; de Guzman Chorny, Nicolas. "85 Million Children Work in Dangerous Conditions: Are Governments Fulfilling Their Promise to Prevent This?," *Huffington Post*, November 2014. Copyright ©2014 by Dr. Jody Heymann. Reprinted by permission.

Article

Prepared by: Chris J. Boyatzis, *Bucknell University* and
Ellen N. Junn, *California State University, Stanislaus*

Unlocking Emily's World

*Cracking the code of silence in children
with autism who barely speak*

CHRIS BERDIK

Learning Outcomes

After reading this article, you will be able to:

- Describe and define what autism is and how the diagnosis
  is made.

- Understand some of the prevailing theories about the causes
  of autism.

- Be aware of what treatments exist for autism and describe
  the research supporting the various treatments.

Emily Browne is laughing, and nobody really knows why. The 14-year-old with a broad face and a mop of curly brown hair has autism. She drifts through her backyard in Boston's Dorchester neighborhood, either staring into the distance or eyeballing a visitor chatting with her dad, Brendan, and her 15-year-old sister, Jennifer, on the nearby patio. That's where the laughter started—a conversational chuckle from somebody on the patio that Emily answered with a rollicking, high-pitched guffaw. Then another, and another, and another.

Emily is growing up, her father says. She is learning new words in her classroom at Joseph Lee School in Dorchester.

Emily can't join the conversation. She is among the 30 percent of children with autism who never learn to speak more than a few words—those considered "nonverbal" or "minimally verbal." Emily was diagnosed with autism at two, but Brendan and his wife, Jeannie, knew something was wrong well before then.

"There was no babbling. She didn't play with anything. You could be standing beside her and call her name, and she wouldn't look at you," says her dad. "Emily was in her own little world."

"We were worried about Emily from pretty much her 12-month checkup … and we had talked with the doctor about the fact that she didn't make any sounds. She didn't really pay attention to anybody, which seemed a little unusual."

But why? What is it about the brains of "minimally verbal" kids like Emily that short circuits the connections between them and everyone else? And can it be overcome? That's the research mission of Boston University's new Center for Autism Research Excellence, where Emily is a study subject.

Partly because of the expanding parameters of what is considered autism, the number of American children diagnosed with autism spectrum disorder has shot up in recent years, from one in 155 children in 1992 to one in 68 in 2014, according to the Centers for Disease Control and Prevention. And Helen Tager-Flusberg, a BU College of Arts & Sciences professor of psychology who has studied language acquisition and autism for three decades and heads the Autism Center, says minimally verbal children are among the most "seriously understudied" of that growing population.

Backed by a five-year, $10 million grant from the National Institutes of Health awarded in late 2012, her team includes researchers and clinicians from Massachusetts General Hospital, Harvard Medical School, Beth Israel Deaconess Medical Center, Northeastern University, and Albert Einstein College of Medicine in New York City. The researchers are focusing on the areas of the brain used for understanding speech, the motor areas activated to produce speech, and the connections between the two. They'll combine functional magnetic resonance imaging (fMRI), electroencephalography (EEG), and neural models of how brains understand and make speech. The models were developed at BU by Barbara Shinn-Cunningham, a professor of biomedical engineering in the College of Engineering, and Frank Guenther, a professor of speech, language, and hearing sciences at BU's Sargent College of Health & Rehabilitation Sciences. They'll also run the first clinical trials of a novel therapy using music and drumming to help minimally verbal children acquire spoken language.

Ultimately, Tager-Flusberg and her colleagues hope to crack the code of silence in the brains of minimally verbal children and give them back their own voices. Getting these kids to utter complete sentences and fully participate in conversation is years away. For now, the goal is to teach words and phrases in a way that can rewire the brain for speech and allow more traditional speech therapy to take hold.

"Imagine if you were stuck in a place where you could not express anything and people were not understanding you," says Tager-Flusberg, who is also a professor of anatomy and neurobiology and of pediatrics on Boston University's Medical Campus. "Can you imagine how distressing and frustrating that would be?"

On a hot, muggy morning in late August, Emily's dad escorts her into the Autism Center on Cummington Mall for a couple hours of tests. It's part of a sound-processing study comparing minimally verbal adolescents with high-functioning autistic adolescents who can speak, as well as normal adolescents and adults.

The investigation is painstaking, because every study must be adapted for subjects who not only don't speak but may also be prone to easy distraction, extreme anxiety, aggressive outbursts, and even running away. "[Minimally verbal children] do tend to understand more than they can speak," says Tager-Flusberg. "But they won't necessarily demonstrate in any situation that they are following what you are saying."

"The study at BU especially was interesting to us because it focused on the kind of autism that Emily has … I know autistic children can behave a certain way—they can be antisocial and so forth—but no one seemed to be addressing the fact that some of these kids can't communicate."

That's obvious in Emily's first task, a vocabulary test. Seated before a computer, she watches as pictures of everyday items pop up on the screen, such as a toothbrush, a shirt, a car, and a shoe. When a computer-generated voice names one of these objects, Emily's job is to tap the correct picture. Emily's earlier pilot testing of this study showed that she understands more than 100 words. But today, she's just not interested. Between short flurries of correct answers, Emily weaves her head, slumps in her chair, or flaps her elbows as the computer voice drones on—car … car … car and then umbrella … umbrella …

umbrella. When one of the researchers tries to get Emily back on task, she simply taps the same spot on the screen over and over. Finally, she gives the screen a hard smack.

The next session is smoother. Emily is given a kind of IQ test in which she quickly and (mostly) correctly matches shapes and colors, identifies patterns, and points out single items within increasingly complicated pictures of animals playing in the park, kids at a picnic, or cluttered yard sales.

Emily's First Words

Emily is minimally verbal, not nonverbal. "Words do come out of her," her dad explains. She'll say "car" when she wants to go for a ride or "home" when she's out somewhere and has had enough. Sometimes she communicates with a combination of sounds and signs or gestures, because she has trouble saying words with multiple syllables. For instance, when she needs a "bathroom," her version sounds like, "ba ba um," but she combines it with a closed hand tilting 90 degrees—pantomiming a toilet flush.

"That's a handy one," her dad says. "She uses it to get out of things. When she's someplace she doesn't want to be, she'll ask to go to the bathroom five or six times."

The first word Emily ever said was "apple" when she was four years old. "We were going through the supermarket, and she grabbed an apple. Said it, and ate it. It was amazing to me," her dad recalls.

The final item on the morning agenda is an EEG study, in which Emily must wear a net of moist electrodes fitted over her head while she listens to a series of beeps in a small, soundproof booth. The researchers have tried EEG with Emily twice before in pilot testing. The first time, she tolerated the electrode net. The second time, she refused. This time, with her dad to comfort her and a rewarding snack of gummi bears, Emily dons the neural net without protest.

The point of this study is to see how well Emily's brain distinguishes differences in sound—a key to understanding speech. For instance, normally developing children learn very early, well before they can speak, to separate out somebody talking from the birds chirping outside the window or an airplane overhead. They also learn to pay attention to deviations in speech that matter—the word "cat" versus "cap"—and to ignore those that don't—cat is cat whether mommy or daddy says it.

"The brain filters out what's important based on what it learns," says Shinn-Cunningham. Some of this sound filtering is automatic, what brain researchers call "subcortical." The rest is more complicated, a top-down process of organizing sounds and focusing the brain's limited attention and processing power on what's important.

EEG measures electrical fields generated by neuron activity in different parts of the brain. "Novel sounds should elicit a larger-than-normal brain response, and that should register on the EEG signal," Shinn-Cunningham explains. There are 128 tiny EEG sensors surrounding Emily's head and upper neck. Each sensor is represented as a line jogging along on the computer monitor outside the darkened booth where Emily sits with her dad holding her hand, watching a silent version of her favorite movie, *Shrek.*

Today's experiment is focused on the automatic end of sound-processing. A constant stream of beeps in one pitch is occasionally interrupted by a higher-pitched beep. How will Emily's brain respond? Most of the time, the 128 EEG lines are tightly packed as they move across the screen. However, muscle movements generate large, visible peaks and troughs in the signals when Emily blinks or lolls her head from side to side. Once, just after a gummi bear break, several large, concentrated spikes show her chewing.

Shifts in attention are much more subtle, and the raw data will have to be processed before anything definitive can be said about Emily's brain. The readout is time-coded with every beep, and the researchers will be particularly interested in the signals from the auditory areas in the brain's temporal cortex, located behind the temples.

The beep test has six five-minute trials. But, after about twenty minutes, Emily is getting restless. It's been a long morning. She starts scratching at the net of sensors in her hair. She's frustrated that *Shrek* is silent. The EEG signals start to swing wildly. From inside the booth, stomping and moans of protest can be heard. When the booth's door is opened at the end of the fourth trial, Emily's eyes are red. She's crying. Her father and the researchers try to cajole her into continuing.

"Just two more, Emmy," her dad says. "Can you do two more for daddy?" And Emily answers with a word she can speak, quite loudly. "Noooo!" They call it a day. Emily will return to the center as the experiments move from beeps to words, and they can finish the last two trials then. All in all, it's been a successful morning. "She did great," says Tager-Flusberg.

In one room at the Autism Center, the researchers have rigged up a mock MRI, using a padded roller board that can slide into a cloth tunnel supported by those foam "noodles" kids use in swimming pools. It's for helping the children in these studies learn what to expect in the real brain scanners operated by Massachusetts General Hospital.

"We've been finishing up our pilot projects for the scanning protocols and trimming them down to a time the kids will tolerate," says Tager-Flusberg. "At first, the imaging folks at MGH

said we need 40 to 50 minutes in the scanner for each subject. I said, 'well that's not happening. These kids won't last that long.'"

The brain scans will be done with the adolescents as well as a group of younger minimally verbal kids, aged six to ten. The younger kids will also participate in an intervention study of a new therapy called Auditory-Motor Mapping Training (AMMT). The therapy was developed by Gottfried Schlaug, a neurologist who runs the Music and Neuroimaging Lab at Beth Israel Deaconess Medical Center. In AMMT, a therapist guides a child through a series of words and phrases, sung in two pitches, while tapping on electronic, tonal drum pads.

"The idea, from a neuroscience perspective," says Schlaug, is that, "maybe in autistic children's brains one of the problems is that the regions that have to do with hearing don't communicate with the regions that control oral motor activity."

> **"The first time she ever actually said a word to me that I understood, we were in Stop & Shop ... She reached into the bin and she picked up an apple and said 'apple.'"**

Many of the same brain areas activated when we move our hands and gesture are also activated when we speak. So, combining the word practice with drumming could help reconnect what Schlaug calls the "hearing and doing" regions of the brain. The initial results, from pilot work on a handful of children in 2009 and 2010, were promising. After five weeks of AMMT, kids who had never spoken before were able to say things like, "more please" and "coat on." That's when Schlaug sought out Tager-Flusberg.

Being Involved in Research

"I was aware of her importance in the field of autism research, and we wanted to discuss these findings with somebody who was an expert to ask if what we were seeing was believable," says Schlaug, who is one of the principal investigators for the Autism Center. For the intervention study, the researchers aim to recruit about 80 minimally verbal children who will be randomized to either 25 sessions of AMMT or a similar therapy that differs in a few vital respects. (The control group subjects will have the option of getting AMMT after the study is complete.)

All the children will get brain scans before and after the therapy to see if improvements in vocal ability correspond with changes in the brain. "I would consider it a great success if we could turn on the brain's ability to say words in an appropriate context," says Schlaug. After that, he says, maybe AMMT could be scaled up to teach longer words and more complex phrases, or just get kids to a point where more traditional speech therapy could be effective.

Of course, as Tager-Flusberg stresses, the children classified as minimally verbal are, "an enormously variable population," both in their facility with words and the other behavioral measures of the autism spectrum. The standards of improvement, and the hopes of the families joining in the center's research, are no doubt just as varied.

Emily, for instance, goes to a public grade school in Boston. She's in a special program for students with autism, and she has done well there. "She's a relatively happy child," her dad says. "She can count to 20. She knows her ABCs." She can even spell a few words. Cat. Dog. Love.

Learning about Emily

Emily takes music classes at the local Boys & Girls Club, as well as dance and movement classes on Saturdays. Plus, the Brownes are a tight family. Brendan is an insurance underwriter, Jeannie teaches kindergarten part time, and Jennifer is a sophomore at the Boston Latin School. They've learned the fuller meanings of Emily's limited vocabulary. When Emily says "pink," for instance, she means yogurt, because her first yogurt was pink, strawberry, and delicious. When she says "orange," that means quesadilla (her favorite food) because of the orange cheese they used at her school when she learned to make them.

Back on the patio in the Browne's backyard, Emily's dad explains how she used to run away a lot. She'd take off on him in the grocery store and flee across the parking lot, oblivious to traffic. Once caught, she'd be perfectly calm, even laughing. She also used to hit people for no particular reason. Both behaviors abated after Emily started taking the antipsychotic drug risperidone. Still, transitions are tough for her, and she's entering her final year at the school she's attended since she was three. Her parents are searching for the right high school.

"We still treat her like a child, but she's a teenager now," her dad says. "I don't know what it's going to be like when she's 23. Will she be able to live independently? And this communication piece is really key to that, which is why we jumped at the research."

"They gave me a list of 100 words ... quite a few of them I realized not only could she understand but she could say them ... So I learned a lot more about Emily. We're used to Emily the way she is, but Emily is growing and growing up."

It's nearing lunch time. Emily is making noises, slamming the lid of the grill and vocalizing a kind of "aaaahheeeeahhh," drawing attention to herself.

"Emmy, you want some lunch? Are you hungry?" her dad asks.

"Orange?" Emily says. They go inside and get out the tortillas, salsa, and cheese. It's time for the visitor to head home. "Goodbye, Emily," he calls from the front door. "Bye," she answers with a half wave.

"Very good!" her dad exclaims. "See, that was spontaneous!"

Critical Thinking

1. How would you counsel parents of a newly diagnosed autistic child? What advice or suggestions would you give to the parents?

2. Design an educational program to help autistic children and parents stick to their treatment programs.

3. Based on the existing research about autistic children's outcomes, what areas of additional research do you think need to be developed further? Give a research-based justification for your answer.

Internet References

AutismResearchInstitute.com
http://www.autism.com/

AutismSociety.org
http://www.autism-society.org/

AutismSpeaks.org
https://www.autismspeaks.org/what-autism

Centers for Disease Control and Prevention, CDC.gov
http://www.cdc.gov/ncbddd/autism/index.html

National Institute of Neurological Disorders and Stroke, NIH.gov
http://www.ninds.nih.gov/disorders/Autism/detail_Autism.htm

WebMD.com
http://www.webmd.com/brain/autism/